CW00673930

IRELAND'S
ADVENTURE
BUCKET LIST
GREAT OUTDOOR EXPERIENCES

Helen Fairbairn is a full-time outdoor writer and has written numerous walking guidebooks, exploring destinations as diverse as America's Rocky Mountains, the European Alps and Scotland's highlands and islands. At home in Ireland, she has spent the last 20 years researching and writing about the country's top walks. Her previous walking guides for The Collins Press include *Ireland's Best Walks*, *Ireland's Wild Atlantic Way*, *Dublin & Wicklow*, and *Northern Ireland*. In her spare time Helen enjoys a wide range of adventure activities, including whitewater and sea kayaking, surfing, rock climbing and mountain biking.

Unless otherwise credited, all the photographs in this book are the work of Irish landscape photographer **Gareth McCormack**. For more information or to license Gareth's images, see www.GarethMcCormack.com.

Many of the activities in this book are risk sports. The author and The Collins Press accept no responsibility for any injury, loss or inconvenience sustained by anyone using this guidebook.

Advice to Readers

Every effort is made by authors to ensure the accuracy of our guidebooks. However, changes can occur after a book has been printed. Prices rise, services providers alter their business models, and access routes to outdoor destinations are sometimes adjusted. If you notice discrepancies between this guidebook and the facts on the ground, please let us know, either by email to enquiries@collinspress.ie or by post to The Collins Press, West Link Park, Doughcloyne, Wilton, Cork, T12 N5EF, Ireland.

Acknowledgements

Good company is a vital part of every enjoyable adventure, and there are many people I've shared these wonderful experiences with. Valli Schafer, Hannah Birt and Michael Gallagher are prime partners in crime. Gareth, Erin and Geordan: we have countless happy outdoor memories already and there'll be many more to come. Big thanks too to Neil Gallagher for sharing your canoe, and Eoghan Mullan for your caving expertise.

IRELAND'S
ADVENTURE
BUCKET LIST
GREAT OUTDOOR EXPERIENCES

Helen Fairbairn

The Collins Press

To Erin and Geordan:
I wish you many years of happy adventures.

First published in 2018 by
The Collins Press
West Link Park
Doughcloyne
Wilton
Cork
T12 N5EF
Ireland

Reprinted 2020, 2021

A CIP record for this book is available from the British Library.

Paperback ISBN: 978-1-84889-343-6

Design and typesetting by Bright Idea
Typeset in Frutiger and Oswald
Printed in Poland by Białostockie Zakłady Graficzne SA

CONTENTS

Adventure Location Map – Activity List

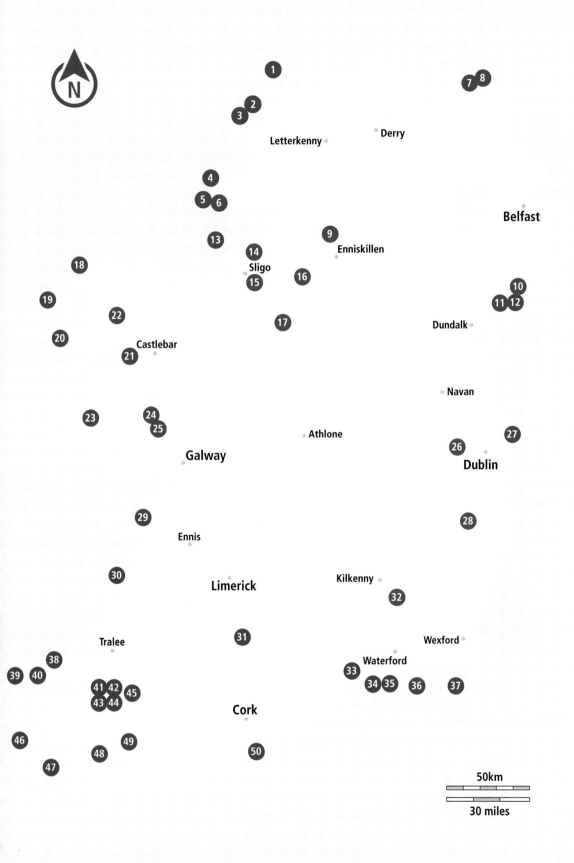

INTRODUCTION

DO THE WORDS 'ADVENTURE', 'exploration' and 'wilderness' mean anything to you? They do to me. I can't read them without my pulse quickening slightly and my mind starting to ponder the prospect of exciting new journeys and experiences. I'm intrigued by wild natural landscapes, and love getting in amongst them, feeling their atmosphere and wondering at the forces that created them. If exploring them means engaging in an outdoor activity, I know the rewards will be even greater.

Adventures don't have to be long or exotic to be worthwhile. Yes, we'd all jump at the opportunity to spend a month trekking through Patagonia or navigating the mighty peaks and rivers of the Himalaya. But major expeditions are not the only way to enjoy the outdoors, and there are countless exciting landscapes and activities waiting to be discovered right here in Ireland.

Though it's a relatively small country on a global scale, what Ireland lacks in size it easily counters with accessibility and scenic variety. Our long history, open mountains and incredible Atlantic coastline offer such an assortment of landscapes, you can stand on a lofty summit one day, then kayak through sea arches the next. Forget complicated arrangements; it's quite possible to complete most Irish adventures in a single day. Of course, if you want to prolong the experience and really get in tune with nature, nothing beats staying away for several nights, but this will be through choice rather than logistical necessity.

The diversity of Ireland's landscapes means an array of different skills are required to explore them. You may consider yourself a hillwalker and be familiar with upland environments, but have you ever tried caving or snorkelling to discover the world underground or beneath the waves? It's only when you expand your horizons and try a whole range of activities that you appreciate the full extent of the country's natural riches.

Each new activity requires a different set of skills and equipment. I have included introductions for each activity discussed, giving an overview of the sport and suggesting how you might get involved. How far you choose to take it is up to you. You could pick the adventures that attract you, contact the recommended guides and pay them to bring you out. You'll be assured of some unforgettable experiences and can leave it at that. On the other hand, you might be inspired to use these outings as a springboard to a whole new pursuit, developing the skills to enjoy many similar adventures in the future. If you're keen, it doesn't take long to gain the knowledge and proficiency required to start heading off on your own. Personally, I love learning from the expertise of professionals, but find independent adventures more rewarding. Doing your own trip planning increases your understanding of your chosen environment, and reliance on your personal skills brings a wonderful sense of satisfaction, confidence and freedom.

Just one request: these outings are memorable largely because they take you to unspoilt places endowed with charismatic scenery. And it's up to all outdoor users to ensure they stay that way. Please be considerate to both the environment and the people who live in it, following the principles of Leave No Trace to ensure the landscape remains as attractive for those who come after you. See www.leavenotraceireland.org /seven-principles for full details of what's involved.

At the end of the day, adventure is an attitude. It's about wanting to get off the beaten track and use your outdoor skills to explore the natural wonders around you. What I have done here is to compile a list of what I consider the best experiences of that kind in Ireland. I've enjoyed every trip in the book, and I hope you do too.

MOUNTAIN HIKING

IRELAND is a fantastic country for mountain walking. Wild locations, rocky ridges and long-distance views all form part of a typical day out. Just a couple of hours of exertion can bring you deep into the heart of nature, to dramatic and hidden places that few people have ever visited. The sense of fulfilment that comes from standing atop a lofty summit, with incredible scenery stretching away in all directions, is simple unbeatable.

Ireland's peaks may not be considered high on a global scale, but they do offer a perfect playground for one-day excursions. Most Irish hillwalks start close to sea level and involve 600m to 1,000m of vertical ascent. The mountains are high enough to offer a challenging day out, yet it's quite possible to scale several peaks and still be down in time for dinner.

There are other factors too that make Irish hillwalking unique. The lack of trees is one

Did you know?

Ireland's mountains owe much of their present form to the last ice age. The U-shaped valleys, deep-sided corries and sharp arêtes that characterise many of the country's peaks were all chiselled by gouging ice flows, which ended some 10,000 years ago.

consideration; most upland terrain is bereft of vegetation more than ankle high, allowing continuous and far-reaching views. All the highest ranges are located around edge of the country, which means most summits give fabulous coastal as well as inland panoramas.

This bucket list goes straight for the jugular and describes routes up the highest peak in each

Above: In the west of Ireland you're likely to have the hills to yourself. Above Lough Fee, Connemara.
Previous page: Connemara's Maumturk Mountains in are amongst the most rugged ranges in Ireland.

Views encompass both mountain and coastline from many of the country's finest ranges. Benbrack, in the Twelve Bens.

province. Each of these hikes is a classic in its own right, and if you complete them all you'll get a very good impression of the country's mountains. Yet this is just a small sample of what's available. With at least 80 other genuinely high-quality mountain walks located all round Ireland, there are enough trips and excursions to keep you busy for years to come.

Ireland's Mountains at a Glance

Ireland has a total of 14 mountains over 900m high, and another 268 hills between 600m and 900m high. The country is relatively flat in the centre, with all the major mountain groups scattered around the coast.

The Mourne Mountains and Wicklow Mountains are the most notable ranges in the east, while the west coast boasts the Derryveagh Mountains, the Twelve Bens and the MacGillycuddy's Reeks. As a general guide, counties Down, Donegal, Mayo, Galway, Kerry and Wicklow contain the most rugged and extensive uplands in the country.

The experience of hiking in the Irish hills varies significantly depending on the route's location and popularity. Proximity to large cities makes ranges like the Wicklow and Mourne Mountains particularly popular, and informal paths have formed across many of these peaks. Once you venture further west, the number of people you meet reduces significantly, and the sense of isolation can be powerful. In more remote regions there is little or no sign of previous footfall, and walkers must be entirely self-reliant.

The Basics

There are very few signposts on Irish hills, so you must depend on your own navigational skills to complete each route safely. Even where informal paths have formed underfoot, these should not be relied on for navigational guidance. You'll need to carry a map and compass to orientate yourself around all routes, and know how to use them.

Besides navigation, the other main consideration is the weather. Check the forecast carefully before heading out, and try to wait for a clear, calm day. Remember that conditions on the tops are often very different from those in the valley, with wind speeds significantly higher and the air much colder. Temperatures drop around 1°C for every 100m of altitude gained, with wind-chill making it feel colder again.

The weather can also deteriorate very quickly on mountains. The main message is to carry warm and waterproof clothing on even apparently sunny days, and be prepared to turn back if conditions change. Low cloud can be particularly problematic, as you'll have to navigate by compass with no visible landscape markers to help you. High winds are dangerous near steep cliffs, while wet grass and rocks become slippery underfoot.

The lack of paths and rugged nature of some Irish mountains means you'll need to be aware of hazards like concealed holes or soft bog. If the terrain is tricky, slow down and take care with your foot placement. Be particularly vigilant during the descent, because most accidents happen on the way down. Avoid walking alone unless you're experienced and confident, and make sure to have a designated backup person who knows your plans and when you should return.

Essential Equipment

Hillwalking is not an expensive pastime. The most important piece of kit is a pair of well-fitting hiking boots, followed by warm underlayers and a good waterproof jacket. In your backpack, be sure to carry a map and compass, food and water, and a mobile phone in case of emergencies. Should the need arise, call 999 or 112 and ask for Mountain Rescue.

In terms of mapping, the long-established, standard reference for Irish walkers in is the Ordnance Survey of Ireland (OSi) 1:50,000 *Discovery* series. These maps are of a high standard and cover the entire country, with some sheets available with a waterproof covering.

Getting Started

If you have little or no previous hillwalking experience, the best way to get started is to join a local club. Most clubs organise regular excursions, and offer routes with a choice of difficulty level. These outings are led by experienced walkers, and let you visit local peaks as part of a larger group. To find your local club, go to www.mountaineering.ie/localclub.

Many clubs also hold an annual walking festival, and these can be a great way of exploring different parts of the country in the company of local walkers. Search online to find up-to-date details for forthcoming events.

Extending your Skills

To progress your knowledge of mountain safety and navigation, consider taking a Mountain Skills training course. These are run by qualified practitioners all round Ireland, and teach participants how to travel safely and competently around mountain environments. Other courses focus on mountain leadership or winter snow skills. To see a calendar of upcoming courses, check www.mountaineering.ie.

Irish mountain walking is great fun in winter too. The Mourne Mountains under heavy snow.

Finding Out More

Books: *Ireland's Best Walks: A Walking Guide* by Helen Fairbairn describes 65 of the top walking routes from around the country, many of which are hillwalks. There is also a wide range of regional walking guides, each concentrating on different parts of the country.

Online: www.mountainviews.ie provides practical details about scaling all Ireland's mountains, with walkers' comments detailing different routes up each peak.

www.mountaineering.ie is the website for Mountaineering Ireland, and contains a wealth of practical information for hillwalkers, climbers and mountaineers.

SLIEVE DONARD

The highest peak in Ulster is a hillwalker's classic, offering fabulous views across the heart of the Mourne Mountains.

Great for

- Standing atop a lofty summit set between mountain and sea
- Hiking beside the famous Mourne Wall on both the ascent and descent

Conditions

- A dry, clear day in any season

Trip Details

- Distance: 9km (5½ miles)
- Time: 4–5 hours
- Ascent: 850m (2,800ft)
- Maps: OSNI 1:50,000 sheet 29, or OSNI 1:25,000 Activity Map *The Mournes*

Access

- **To the start:** The walk starts at the Bloody Bridge car park, 3km south of Newcastle, along the A2 to Kilkeel.
- Grid Ref: J 388 271
- GPS: 54.174225, -5.873941

- **To the finish:** The route finishes at the large parking area for Donard Park, at the southern end of Newcastle town.
- Grid Ref: J 375 305
- GPS: 54.205969, -5.894050

Enjoying a well-earned break beside the Mourne Wall at the summit of Slieve Donard.

At 850m high, Slieve Donard is the highest peak in the province of Ulster. Towering over the town of Newcastle, its wonderful coastal and mountain views exert a magnetic attraction that draws hillwalkers from near and far.

Many walkers climb Donard from Newcastle, ascending along the Glen River Track and retracing their steps on the descent. This is a rather more interesting, almost-circular variation, which approaches the mountain along the equally lovely Bloody Bridge River.

Route finding is relatively simple throughout, thanks to a series of maintained footpaths and the guidance of the Mourne Wall. However, the start and finish points are separated by 3.5km of road – a road that carries a lot of fast-moving traffic and does not make for pleasant walking. Unless you have two vehicles at your disposal, it is best to leave your car at Donard Park and arrange alternate transport to the start; consider using a bike, a local taxi, or either the Mourne Rambler or No. 37 Ulsterbus service.

A Smugglers' Trail

The Bloody Bridge Path, at the start of this route, was a notorious smuggling trail during the 18th and 19th centuries. Illicit goods such as spirits, tobacco and silk were landed in isolated coves under the cover of night, then transferred to the backs of ponies and carried through the mountains for distribution inland. The village of Hilltown was a favourite destination; thriving trade and enthusiastic public support meant that by 1835 almost half of its buildings were pubs.

From top: During the summer the Bloody Bridge path passes through swathes of blooming gorse; Enjoying a well-earned break beside the Mourne Wall at the summit of Slieve Donard; Waterfall along the Glen River, in Donard Wood near the end of the route.

The Hike

The Bloody Bridge footpath begins just across the road from the southern end of the car park. Pass through a narrow entrance gate and join the well-constructed stone path. **Bloody Bridge River**, or the Mid-Pace River as it was once known, rushes over a series of rock slabs beside the path. The original Bloody Bridge was named after gruesome events in 1641, when nine local Protestants and their minister were massacred at the bridge.

The path climbs along the right bank, becoming rougher as it progresses. After 1km you may want to cross the river and join a rough quarry track that lies just out of sight, up to the left. Alternatively, you can continue to pick your way along the river, crossing the stream where necessary. Both options involve 2km of steady ascent before you reach an old quarry.

Leave the quarry via a grassy track on the right and climb to a broad col. Here the view suddenly opens out westwards across the wider Mournes, with the Annalong Valley immediately beneath you.

The col also marks your rendezvous with the **Mourne Wall**, which acts as your guide for the central part of the route. Turn right in front of the wall and follow the granite blocks directly up the slopes of Slieve Donard. The ascent is now steep and sustained; some 300m of altitude is gained in less than a kilometre. Fortunately, short grass underfoot makes for fairly easy progress.

The **summit** itself is marked by a stone tower and trig point, with a large summit cairn and a smaller one about 100m north that dates from early Christian times. On a clear day the views are magnificent; you can survey the entire Mourne range, with Lough Neagh and the Sperrin Mountains visible to the north-west, and the Isle of Man lying across the Irish Sea.

The Mourne Wall turns sharply west at the summit, marking your line of descent. Drop steeply down to the col beneath Slieve Commedagh, where you leave the wall behind. Turn right onto a path that descends down the centre of the valley to the north-east. The path is partially paved with stone slabs and while the first section is steep, the gradient soon eases. As you descend, the Glen River gathers force beside you, which you follow all the way to the end of the route.

Shortly before leaving the mountains you will notice a conspicuous beehive structure on the opposite side of the river. This is an old ice house, used by the Slieve Donard Hotel before the advent of refrigeration. Now pass through a gate and enter Donard Wood, where you are immediately surrounded by a mixture of pine and deciduous trees.

Continue to follow the path as it descends along the tumbling falls of the Glen River, keeping to the left bank at the first bridge and crossing the river at two subsequent bridges. Finish by passing the grassy expanse of Donard Park to reach the parking area.

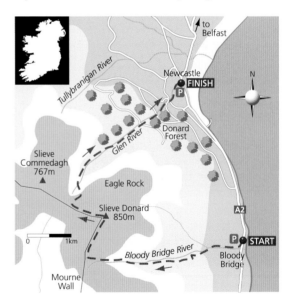

MWEELREA

This challenging but impressive circuit over Connacht's highest mountain features two airy ridges and fabulous coastal views.

Great for

- Enjoying a surge of exhilaration while traversing a high rock arête
- Appreciating fabulous views across the wilderness of Connemara and Mayo

Conditions

- A clear day with calm winds

Trip Details

- Distance: 15km (9½ miles)
- Time: 6–7 hours
- Ascent: 1,070m (3,510ft)
- Map: OSi 1:50,000 sheet 37

Access

- The route starts and finishes at Delphi Mountain Resort, 5km south of Doo Lough along the R335. Note that Delphi is a private hotel and not a public car park. Large groups should use the lay-bys around Doo Lough and shuttle walkers to Delphi from there.
- Grid Ref: L 840 652
- GPS: 53.621863, -9.753995

Exhilarating walking along the ridge to Ben Lugmore.

There are fine views across Mweelrea's east face from point 495m.

This horseshoe circuit on Mweelrea (814m) ranks right up there amongst the best hillwalks in the country. As well as being Connacht's highest summit, Mweelrea is an engaging and complex mountain with so many ridges and subsidiary peaks that it offers almost endless possibilities for exploration.

There are several quality routes up the mountain, including a precipitous ascent from the northern shore of Doo Lough through atmospheric Coum Dubh. However, the scenic variety and topographic purity of this horseshoe makes it probably the most satisfying route of all.

Remember that there are no easy routes on Mweelrea; this is a big mountain surrounded by a great deal of difficult and dangerous ground. Save the trip for clear conditions, and make sure to leave enough time to get down in daylight.

The Hike

From Delphi car park, look for a gravel track that passes around the right-hand side of the hotel. Follow this onto another track, which veers right into the forest and then begins to run along the southern side of the Owennaglogh River. Keep right at several track junctions and stay beside the river as you cross a large clearing.

Just before you enter the next band of trees, turn left at a track junction, then keep left again at the following junction. This trail leads to the southern boundary of the forest, then swings right and begins to descend along the western edge of the trees.

At this point the track disappears into the bog and you have a choice to make. In wet conditions it

Delphi Death March

From a historic perspective, the Delphi valley is most renowned for the infamous death march of 30–31 March 1849. In the depth of the Great Famine, hundreds of starving locals were sent 16km on foot from Louisburg poorhouse to Delphi Lodge, on the shore of Lough Finn. After being refused assistance, the group was forced to retrace their steps. The combination of hunger and blizzard conditions meant some 400 people perished. Visit the Famine Museum in Louisburg to learn the full story.

is best to traverse across the rough hillside, heading directly towards the unnamed summit at 495m. In dry conditions it is easier to trace the banks of the Owennaglogh and Sruhaunbunatrench rivers to reach the col just north of point 495m.

Whichever route you choose, it is worth climbing to the top of **point 495m** to appreciate the fine views across Mweelrea's magnificent east face. Now descend north-west to the col and begin the climb up the shoulder. As you gain height the terrain becomes easier underfoot, though the gradient is steep at times. There is a brief respite near the 700m contour, where a great cleft cuts into the shoulder.

Above the cleft the ridge swings north, and the slopes converge in an **airy arête** that feels almost alpine in nature. Follow the apex of the ridge and make the final, steep climb to the top. The **summit** itself is curiously flat, adorned with a modest cairn perched on the very edge of the east face. Along with impressive coastal views, the sensational vista includes the Twelve Bens and the Maumturks to the south.

Descend north-east to a col, then climb to the summit of Ben Bury, which is steeply cut on its northern side. Now descend south-east to reach a cairn

in the gap between Ben Bury and the Ben Lugmore ridge. This cairn marks the top of The Ramp, which plunges east down into Coum Dubh.

Continue south-east along the crest of the ridge, now passing along the most entertaining and exhilarating terrain on the mountain. A faint path means progress is surprisingly straightforward, despite the rocks and occasional exposure. **Ben Lugmore** (803m) is the penultimate summit on the ridge. From here you drop down into a grassy gap and then climb a short distance to an unnamed top. Now turn north-east and enjoy more excellent, easy walking along a broader ridge to point 760m.

At the end of the ridge, turn south-east and follow an easy shoulder down towards Delphi Mountain Resort. A straightforward descent deposits you on some rough and boggy ground in the Owennaglogh Valley. Follow an old boundary wall towards Delphi. Just before the buildings you must ford the Owennaglogh River, a simple task in normal water levels, but probably impossible in flood. If you are stuck there are two iron girders carrying a water pipe that will suffice as a makeshift bridge. All that remains is to cross a fence and follow a forestry track the short distance back to Delphi.

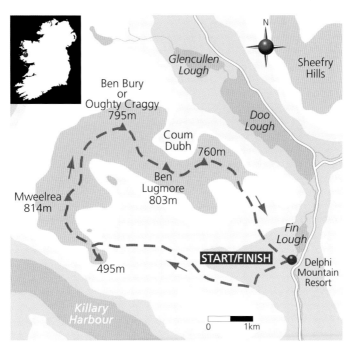

LUGNAQUILLA

Fraughan Rock Glen and Art's Lough are memorable highlights of this route up Leinster's highest peak.

👍 Great for

- Peering into precipitous twin corries on either side of the summit
- Discovering Art's Lough tucked away on high mountain slopes

☁ Conditions

- A dry day with good visibility

🗺 Trip Details

- Distance: 13km (8 miles)
- Time: 5–6 hours
- Ascent: 800m (2,620ft)
- Maps: OSi 1:50,000 sheet 56, EastWest Mapping 1:30,000 *Lugnaquilla & Glendalough*, or Harvey Superwalker 1:30,000 *Wicklow Mountains*.

🚧 Access

- The circuit starts and finishes at a large car park at Baravore, at the head of Glenmalure. Glenmalure is generally reached via the Military Road from Laragh.
- Grid Ref: T 066 942
- GPS: 52.988005, -6.413050

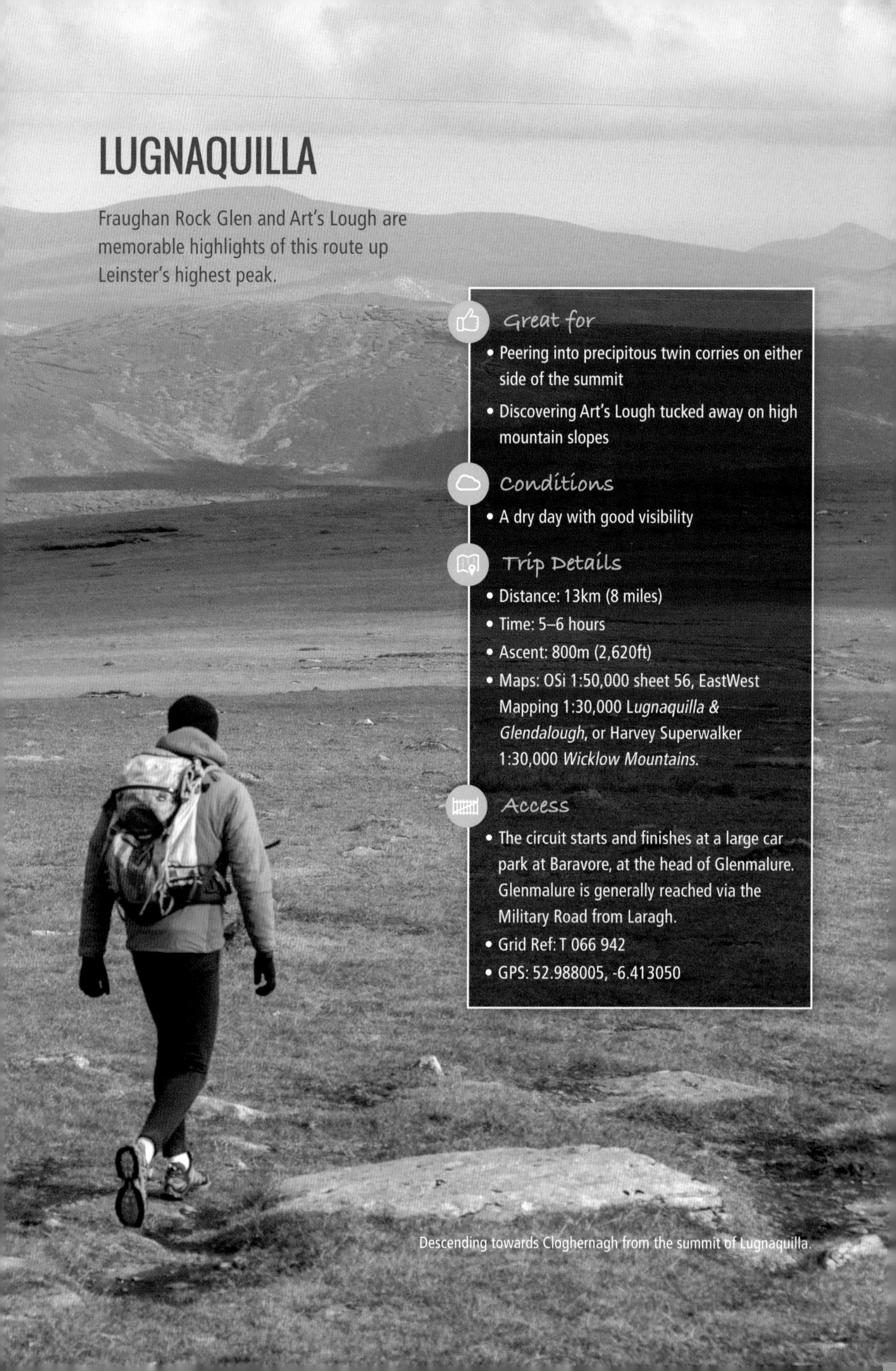

Descending towards Cloghernagh from the summit of Lugnaquilla.

At 925m high, Lugnaquilla is the highest mountain in Leinster, and the thirteenth highest peak in Ireland. It is also a fabulous viewpoint. On a clear day, the summit panorama includes much of Wicklow, south Leinster and even Wales.

This circuit begins at the head of Glenmalure, and is the most popular way to climb the mountain. The scenery is varied throughout, with an approach through the dramatic, cliff-fringed valley of Fraughan Rock Glen, and a descent past secluded Art's Lough, a high, wild lake that is surely one of Wicklow's most beautiful sights.

One word of warning: Lugnaquilla is notorious for bad weather, and is covered by cloud five days out of seven. The summit plateau is bordered by steep cliffs binding the twin corries of the North Prison and South Prison, and navigation can also be tricky on the descent. The paths here are most accurately displayed on the EastWest Mapping sheet, but enough hazards remain that the walk is best avoided in poor visibility.

The Hike

At the north-western corner of the car park, there is a road ford across the Avonbeg River. Turn right in front of the ford and follow a footpath upstream for 100m, then cross the river via a footbridge. On the opposite bank, turn right onto a vehicle track. Continue past the rustic Glenmalure Youth Hostel, then turn left at a track junction.

The track climbs steadily through the forest, then emerges at **Fraughan Rock Glen**. The scenery here is immediately impressive, with the Benleagh cliffs towering overhead on the right. On the southern (left) side of the valley is a forestry plantation; you will descend along the western edge of these trees at the end of the circuit.

For now, follow the track to the base of a waterfall, then climb steeply up the right-hand side of the falls. Pass over the lip of the headwall into the rugged, hanging valley above. Keep following the bank of the main stream to the top of another rise, then

The Benleagh cliffs tower above the track in Fraughan Rock Glen.

cross a boggy hollow and climb straight up the slope ahead. You can choose your line of ascent depending on how steep you want the climb to be – the slope is steepest to the south and tapers off to the north.

Salvation awaits at the ridgeline, where the rough ground is replaced by a gentle slope of close-cropped grass – a perfect walking surface that extends right across the summit plateau. Head left along the ridge, and the prominent **summit cairn** will soon come into view to the south. Walk diagonally across the plateau to reach it. Lugnaquilla's trig point sits atop a massive circular plinth and offers fabulous 360-degree views, with a nearby orientation plaque to help you identify the landmarks.

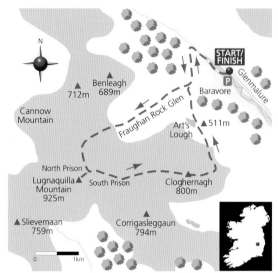

Leinster's highest point: the 925m summit of Lugnaquilla.

Your next goal is Cloghernagh. Sweep north-east around the rim of the South Prison, then follow a wide path east along the top of a broad ridge. Cloghernagh's 800m-high summit is distinguished by a small cairn, and expansive views to the east.

Take care now to locate the correct descent route to Art's Lough, which is hidden from view below. From Cloghernagh, follow a faint path that descends east for 200m, then veers north-east to reach a clifftop on the northern edge of the shoulder. At the western corner of the cliffs, turn left onto another narrow path that is marked by occasional cairns of white stone.

This path traverses north along the top of the cliff, then descends along a grassy ramp. A short distance later, **Art's Lough** comes into view below. The ramp carries you almost all the way to the lake, which makes a natural place for a break.

When you're ready, look for a wire fence that runs parallel to the lake, just above its eastern shore. Follow the fence north to a corner, then turn right, following a boggy path along the left side of the fence. Descend steeply beside a forestry plantation, heading back towards Fraughan Rock Glen.

Towards the bottom of the slope, veer left and pass through a gate around 150m west of the forest. Cross the river and then climb the opposite bank to join the main track through the glen. Turn right here and retrace your initial steps back to the start.

CARRAUNTOOHIL

This challenging route visits the three highest peaks in Ireland, and is perhaps the finest mountain horseshoe in the country.

 Great for

- Bagging the country's three highest summits in one day
- Challenging yourself across a notoriously exposed ridgeline

Conditions

- A dry, calm and clear day, without snow or ice on the summits.

Trip Details

- Distance: 13.5km (8½ miles)
- Time: 6–7 hours
- Ascent: 1,200m (3,940ft)
- Maps: OSi 1:50,000 sheet 78, OSi 1:25,000 *MacGillycuddy's Reeks*, or Harvey Superwalker 1:30,000 *MacGillycuddy's Reeks*.

Access

- The route starts and finishes at a large car park at the base of the Hydro Road. This is located along the Killorglin–Glencar road, around 1.5km north of Lough Acoose. If this car park is full, there's also a large lay-by around 1km south along the road towards Lough Acoose.
- Grid Ref: V 772 871
- GPS: 52.023277, -9.7896547

Approaching Carrauntoohil from the Beenkeragh Ridge, with Coomloughra Lough below.

Caher, Ireland's third highest mountain, seen from Carrauntoohil.

Carrauntoohil stands head and shoulders above any other mountain in Ireland. Its summit is the highest point in the country at 1,039m, but it is also heavily fortified, with precipitous slopes and fearsome crags protecting it on all sides. There are several routes to the top, but none of them are easy, and all require solid route finding and confidence over steep ground. For details of an alternate approach, see page 139.

This route follows the classic Coomloughra Horseshoe, which offers 5km of incredible ridgetop walking above 800m high. The circuit includes the summits of Beenkeragh (1,010m), Carrauntoohil and Caher (1,001m), Ireland's second, first and third highest summits respectively.

The crux of the route comes at a sharp, exposed arête that links Beenkeragh to Carrauntoohil. This ridge is notorious amongst Irish hillwalkers – it's actually a Grade 1: *Easy* scramble – so you'll need a cool head and favourable weather to cross it in safety. The rocks become treacherous in wet or windy conditions. Also note that snow and ice can linger

up here as late as Easter. Always be prepared to turn back if conditions are not on your side once you get to the ridge.

The Hike

Begin by crossing a stile at the back of the car park, beside a Mountain Rescue board. Turn right onto a concrete track known as the Hydro Road, which climbs steadily for 2km to reach the dam at the western end of **Lough Eighter**. There is now an impressive perspective of the ring of mighty peaks you are about to tackle.

Cross the lough's outlet stream and follow a path that climbs north-east towards Skregmore. The lower slopes are covered by heather, but this gives way to boulders and shattered slabs of rock as the slopes converge in a spiky crest. Follow the ridge over point 747m to reach the summit of Skregmore (848m). The already expansive views include Brandon Mountain at the tip of the Dingle Peninsula.

Head south-east along the ridge, crossing another unnamed summit at 851m. This brings you to the foot

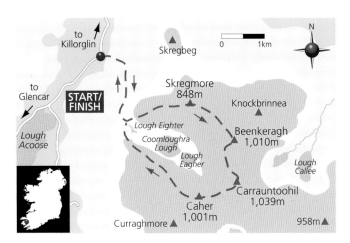

of a wide, rocky ridge beneath Beenkeragh. Follow a path up through the boulders and outcrops, perhaps using your hands for support in places. **Beenkeragh** – Ireland's second highest summit – is marked by a small cairn. More dramatic is the sudden, breathtaking view into the abyss of Hag's Glen, and across a dizzying void to the cliffs on the north face of Carrauntoohil.

Amid all this exposure, it is no surprise that most walkers are slightly intimidated by the sight of the next obstacle: the Beenkeragh Ridge, which links this mountain to Carrauntoohil. This **rock arête** is just under 1km long, and has precipitous drops on both sides. If you proceed slowly and carefully, you'll find there is really only one 30m section that is particularly exposed.

Begin by following a path that descends steeply just beneath the western crest of the shoulder. This brings you to the start of the ridge itself. Keep to the top of the arête until a sheer drop rears up on the left, and the trail moves to the right side of the ridge to avoid it. About halfway along you confront the rise known as The Bones at 959m. Follow the path back to the steeper, left-hand side to bypass this exposed rib, before returning to the right again.

As the ridge merges with broader slopes, a short, steep climb brings you to the top of **Carrauntoohil**. The summit is distinguished by a large metal cross and a circular stone shelter, and probably by several other walkers who have ascended by different routes. New views also extend east along the serrated ridge of the MacGillycuddy's Reeks, and south across the Black Valley.

Descend south-west from Carrauntoohil to a col, where the ridge narrows once more for the short, steep climb to the small cairn that marks the top of **Caher**. From here, continue west across a slightly lower summit at 975m, then begin the long descent home. After an initial rocky stretch the ground turns to peat, and a pleasant path leads down Caher's north-western spur. Head for the western tip of Lough Eighter, where you can reverse your outward journey back to the start.

A large metal cross marks Ireland's highest point.

SCRAMBLING

CHILDREN are born loving to scramble. There's an innate human instinct to explore vertical obstacles, though spoilsport parents do their best to curb it. For some people the advice sinks deep, the desire to clamber around rocks curtailed for good. In others the urge is merely suppressed for a while, until they discover a legitimate outlet for their impulse to climb. Scrambling is one of the truest adult expressions of this childhood instinct. The same could be claimed for rock climbing, but the more extreme technical difficulty of that sport demands stop-start progress. Scrambling, at its best, involves near constant movement, making quick decisions about the route you want to take over easier-angled rocks.

The physical challenge is there and yes, a background element of danger. Yet the idea is to keep within your natural abilities, bypassing obstacles that are truly hazardous to flow smoothly up rock that offers just the right amount of difficulty for you. You're aware of the exposure all around you – high on a mountain ridge, how could you not be? – yet the moves should feel exhilarating without too much

Scrambling Grades Explained

Grade 1: *Easy* The use of hands is required for occasional progress, but holds are generally large and the exposure not too daunting. These routes are achievable by most fit and experienced hillwalkers.

Grade 2: *Moderate* Hands are required more often to negotiate sustained sections of rock. You may encounter significant exposure or tricky route finding. Difficulties are harder to avoid and retreat can be awkward. Previous scrambling experience is recommended, and a rope may be appreciated for confidence.

Grade 3: *Difficult* These are effectively Moderate rock climbs. They require moves on steep rock in very exposed locations. All but the most confident rock climbers will welcome a rope in some places. A good head for heights, the ability to abseil and previous scrambling experience are all essential.

Above: There are more limited scrambling opportunities outside Munster. The Corranbinna Ridge in Mayo's Nephin Beg Mountains.
Opposite: The Beenkeragh Ridge near Carrauntoohil is a Grade 1 scramble, and must be the most popular route in the country.

fear attached. The sense of achievement you feel after a kilometre or more of this engrossing progress is something that will stay with you forever.

Irish Scrambling at a Glance

Despite its large number of mountains, Ireland is not renowned for its scrambling. The main reason for this is the country's geology. The last mountain-building period took place here around 300 million years ago. Since then the slopes have been eroded by the weather and chiselled away by successive ice ages, leaving often rounded stumps just a fraction of their original size. Over the last 7,000 years many of the remaining hills have also been covered by a thick layer of peat, often enveloping the rock entirely.

None of this is good news for scramblers, who need significant sections of exposed rock for their outings. While rocky outcrops can be found in many of Ireland's highest ranges, long ridges of firmly bedded stone are relatively rare. Various gullies and ridges attract scramblers in places like Donegal's Derryveagh Mountains and Connemara's Twelve Bens, but there's no doubt the best routes lie further south in the province of Munster.

The four routes described here – one from County Sligo, two from County Kerry and one from County Cork – are generally accepted amongst the best-quality scrambles in the country. They all follow the crest of long, rocky ridges and bring you to the top of some of the most interesting and dramatic mountains in Ireland. They're graded at the easier end of the scale, so if you're a confident outdoor enthusiast you should find something here to suit you even if you've never scrambled before.

The Basics

Scrambling usually takes place in high mountain environments, and occupies the middle ground between hillwalking and rock climbing. By definition it means using your hands as well as your feet to gain

From top: Crossing the Beenkeragh Ridge in winter is a whole new challenge; Even short sections of rock can be fun. Exposed pinnacles above Coumshingaun, in the Comeragh Mountains; The Cummeenapeasta Ridge in the MacGillycuddy's Reeks is Ireland's highest and most continuous ridgeline.

height, yet the terrain should not be severe enough to require the continuous use of ropes.

All documented scrambles are given a grade, so you know what sort of difficulties to expect. Note, however, that grades refer to dry conditions; routes become considerably trickier after rain. Steep patches of wet grass are particularly treacherous. Under snow and ice all scramble grades should be discounted, and outings considered only if you have winter mountaineering skills.

Even in fine weather, it is always advisable to scramble with a partner. One of the main hazards is loose rock, both in terms of holds coming off in your hands and debris being dislodged onto people below. Gullies are especially hazardous because they act as funnels for falling stone. Even on larger crags you need to take care, because the freeze-thaw of Irish winters can cause apparently solid rocks to crack away from their foundations.

Route finding is another challenge. Even though your route may be graded easy, many scrambles depend on your own decision-making in terms of exactly which line you take, and it's easy to stray off course. This can be dangerous if there are precipitous drops nearby, or steeper crags that require rock-climbing skills. As a general rule, err on the side of caution, and don't climb anything you can't reverse. Educate yourself beforehand about any escape routes, and be prepared to backtrack if necessary to return to easier ground. Leave yourself plenty of time when setting out, so you can deal with any issues before it gets dark.

Essential Equipment

The amount of equipment you need depends on the technical difficulties of the route. Grade 1 scrambles require nothing more than hillwalking gear: good boots, a backpack, warm and waterproof clothing, food, mobile phone, map and compass. A rope is not generally required at this level.

At Grade 2 a rope is considered optional, but unless your entire party is confident and experienced, it's best to carry one just in case. Ropes are standard at Grade 3, though you can choose when to employ them. If you need to retreat at this level, it is often safest to abseil, which is only possible with the correct equipment.

Only use proper climbing rope, around 9mm thick. There is some debate about the best length to carry for scrambling purposes. Some people believe a lighter half rope (30m long) is sufficient because scrambling steps are usually short. Others point out that a rope is doubled for abseiling and recommend the standard 50m. As you become more experienced you can make your own decision.

If you're carrying a rope you'll also need a harnesses, belay device, selection of slings and a small rack of climbing gear. Generally, people start to wear helmets when a rope is in use, though helmets are never a bad idea at any level, especially if there's a risk of loose rock.

In case of emergencies, call 999 or 112 and ask for Mountain Rescue.

Getting Started

The first stage of becoming a scrambler is to be a confident and experienced hillwalker. If you're a complete beginner, your local walking club is a great place to start. Find your closest club at: www.mountaineering.ie/localclub

As you progress onto harder routes, you'll need to add the skills of a rock climber. Again, rope-work, abseiling and general competency moving across rock can all be developed through your local climbing club. Go to the 'Start Climbing' section of www.mountaineering.ie to see a list of climbing groups around Ireland.

As with most other aspects of mountaineering, there are also professional instructors who can teach you the necessary skills. **Simply Mountains** (tel: 087 677 7503; www.simplymountains.com) and **Kerry Climbing** (tel: 087 744 0523; www.kerryclimbing.ie) both offer scrambling-specific courses, as do several other operators around the country.

Finding Out More

Books: The only scrambling-specific guide currently published in Ireland is *Scrambles in Ulster and Connacht* by Alan Tees. It provides maps and descriptions for 24 scrambles and easy rock climbs.

Online: www.mountaineering.ie is the website for Mountaineering Ireland, though it contains limited information specific to scramblers.

KINGS MOUNTAIN – Annach Re Mhor

Abseiling into this 100m-high canyon high on Kings Mountain is an experience you'll never forget.

👍 Great for

- Feeling the trepidation as you descend into the bowels of the earth
- Enjoying fabulous coastal views from the airy prow of Benbulbin

☁ Conditions

- A dry day with good visibility

🗺 Trip Details

- Grade of Scramble: 3: *Difficult*
- Distance: 5km (3 miles)
- Time: 2–2½ hours
- Ascent: 400m (1310ft)
- Map: OSi 1:50,000 sheet 16

A steep descent leads to a large pinnacle, where you exit Annach Re Mhor on the right.

⛩ Access

- The route begins outside a community house on the southern side of Kings Mountain. Begin by heading to the village of Rathcormack, around 5km north of Sligo town along the N15. Turn right here onto a minor road signed for Glencar Lake. After another 2km, turn right at a T-junction. Around 800m later you reach a yellow house with shutters, on the left side of the road, situated just before one signpost indicating a right-hand bend and another marked 'Cul de Sac'. Park outside this house as considerately as possible – large groups should leave most of their vehicles elsewhere.
- Grid Ref: G 703 426
- GPS: 54.331417 -8.457776

Above: Abseiling through the cave-like hole into the deeper recesses of Annach Re Mhor.

The trip through the canyon is relatively short, but there are good options for extending it if you fancy a longer excursion. The approach through Kings Gully is also one of the classic access routes to Benbulbin. At 526m high, this iconic mountain is the defining landmark of County Sligo. While it can't compare to the drama of the gorge, Benbulbin is flanked by vertical escarpments over 100m high, and standing at the tip of its lofty prow is another exhilarating experience. The route is described here as an optional side trip, which adds another 8.5km, 320m of ascent and 2–3 hours to your day. Ideally, you would visit Benbulbin first and save Annach Re Mhor as the grand finale on the way down.

Guided Excursions

If you have no experience of abseiling but still want to complete this route, contact **Carraig Climbing** (tel: 087 6647 285; www.carraigclimbing.com). You will be taught how to abseil at an easier venue in the morning, before testing your new skills in the canyon in the afternoon. Expect to pay around €150 for up to four people.

This is an unusual scrambling route because it is essentially a hillwalk with just one technical difficulty: a 15m abseil. Yet the terrain that lies at the bottom of the rope is nothing short of spectacular. This is Annach Re Mhor, a striking rock canyon that must be surely one of the most dramatic natural features on any Irish mountain. The great gash it cuts in the side of Kings Mountain is visible from miles away, forming a massive triangular wedge that threatens to calve off at any moment.

The canyon itself is around 5m wide and up to 100m deep, with sheer walls rising threateningly on both sides. The atmosphere inside is primordial; in a land where tectonic movements have long since ceased, this is geology at its most insistent. The gorge provides sanctuary to rare species of plant, but at times seems far from sheltered. As well as all your abseiling gear you should carry extra clothing in case the wind is howling, though, and also bring a helmet to protect against stone fall.

Right: At its deepest, the chasm of Annach Re Mhor is around 5m wide and 100m high.

The Scramble

From the community house, walk 30m east along the road towards the lane marked as a cul de sac. Turn left here and follow the lane past three houses to a metal gate. Pass through the gate into a grassy field, then turn left and head north-east, across the field towards the base of Kings Mountain.Cross a wire fence at the upper left side of the field to reach open hillside. An old, grassy track can now be seen zigzagging up the steep slope ahead. Follow this up the hillside, enjoying increasing expansive views across Glencar and Sligo town below.

The trail soon swings north into the deep valley of **Kings Gully**. Around 200m after entering the gully, the path crosses the channel of a shallow stream coming down the slope from the right. The side trip to Benbulbin continues straight ahead here, but to reach the canyon don't cross the channel, instead turning right and looking uphill. You should see a length of wire fencing with wooden posts located around 100m above, to the right of the stream. This fence marks the entrance to Annach Re Mhor.

Climb the hillside to reach the fence at grid ref: G 70833 43682. Cross the fence, and you'll see two rock walls beginning to form in front of you. Descend between the ramparts, now following a faint path underfoot. The rock rises on both sides for 200m until you reach what appears to be a dead end. Continue ahead and examine the bottom right corner of the headwall, where a **cave-like hole** tunnels through the rock and allows access deeper into the ravine.

Three abseil anchors are attached to the rock beside the hole. Fix your rope here, then abseil down the chimney below. The passage is not vertical, but involves several steep steps and large blocks of rock. Make sure you're wearing a helmet, and keep it on until you exit the chasm, as loose rocks can be dislodged at any time. Standing below the abseil as others descend is particularly perilous, so keep tucked out of harm's way.

You are now right in the bowels of the canyon, dwarfed between **towering walls**, one of which has a luxuriant cloak of moss. Make your way along the scree-scattered base, passing over a rise and then climbing again to a slight corner. The ravine now drops away beneath you, with Glencar visible ahead.

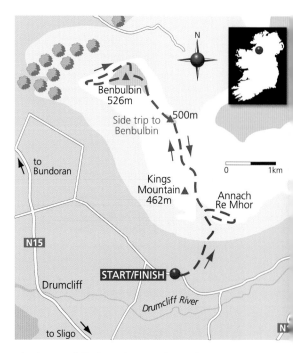

Clamber carefully down the steep, loose slope to the bottom of a **large pinnacle**. Here you should turn right and climb a short grass slope that brings you out of the chasm.

Having exited the ravine, turn right and climb diagonally across a shallow gully. You must now traverse a steep grass slope on a narrow ledge. This slope is very exposed, and care is needed; avoid it altogether in wet weather. Gradually the angle relents, and you arrive back at the fence at the start of Annach Re Mhor. Now simply retrace your outward journey down the slope to your car.

Side trip to Benbulbin

If you want to add the extension to Benbulbin, continue straight ahead along the path through Kings Gully. The upper part of the gully is steep, and you'll have to traverse carefully across the slope. It's not long before you reach the top on the right side of a stream. The trail fades amid a cluster of peat hags, but you should cross a fence and continue north beside the stream.

As the slope becomes more rounded, cross the stream and climb north-west to reach point 459m. The flat terrain means you should now be able to see the trig pillar at the summit of Benbulbin, some 2km further north-west. The easiest way to get there is to head north across rougher ground to an unnamed rise at 500m. Here you reach the top of Benbulbin's northern cliffs, and can enjoy a sudden view into the abyss below, as well as a long-range panorama towards Donegal.

Follow the cliffs north-west, then climb to the **summit trig point**. The real climax of the route is still to come, though. Head west towards the mountain's sharp prow, passing a several peculiar bog pools on the way. The sides of the plateau taper inexorably inwards until the ground disappears entirely. The exposure and views at the very **apex** of the mountain are nothing short of sensational, but please don't get too close to the edge.

Head east now and walk along the top of the northern cliffs to return to the summit of Benbulbin. Follow a broad ridge back to the rise at 500m, then reverse your outward journey through Kings Gully.

Enjoy the view along Benbulbin's precipitous northern cliffs as part of an optional side trip.

BRANDON MOUNTAIN – Faha Ridge

This suberb route leads across a dramatic ridgeline to finish at one of Ireland's best-loved peaks.

 Great for

- Controlling your heart rate along a fantastically exposed rock arête
- Contrasting the outward ridgeline with a return in the depths of the corrie

 Conditions

- A dry day with good visibility and little wind

Trip Details

- Grade of Scramble: 1: *Easy*
- Distance: 9km (5½ miles)
- Time: 5½–6½ hours
- Ascent: 900m (2,950ft)
- Maps: OSi 1:50,000 sheet 70, or OSi 1:25,000 *Brandon Mountain*

 Access

- The route starts and finishes at a car park in Faha, just north-west of the village of Cloghane. From Cloghane, head 2km north along the R585 to a crossroads, the turn left onto a road signed for *Cnoc Bhréanainn*, the Irish name for Brandon Mountain. Follow the lane for 2.5km to reach the car park at the end of the road, where there is space for 8–10 vehicles.
- Grid Ref: Q 494 120
- GPS: 52.239325, -10.205650

Brandon's summit has magnificent 360-degree views, including over the coastline of west Dingle.

Faha Ridge: the route follows the skyline as closely as you dare. (Tom O'Sullivan)

Faha Ridge is one of most spectacular mountain routes in Ireland. It follows a sharp arête between two plunging glacial corries, and ends at Brandon Mountain, one of the country's most charismatic summits. The views are breathtaking throughout, and the descent through the dark battlements of Coumaknock, past a series of paternoster lakes, ensures the drama continues right to the end. Little wonder it's considered a classic of Irish scrambling!

There are two ways to tackle the ridge. The first is by sticking religiously to the crest, in which case it deserves a rating of Grade 3: *Difficult*. You'll need to carry a rope and slings, and be prepared for two 15m abseils. Most people follow a path that winds around the most serious obstacles, which reduces the technical difficulty to Grade 1: *Easy*. Be aware that whichever route you choose, there's no avoiding the exposure, which is impressive for over a kilometre. There are no escape routes either, other than reversing the ridge. Vertigo sufferers need not apply!

The rock is firm and friction is good in dry conditions. The trickiest sections come at a couple of down-climbs through short chimneys, where some might appreciate the reassurance of a rope. On the final ascent to the plateau the route climbs a grassy slope that is both steep and exposed, and becomes treacherous in the wet. One final word of warning: Brandon's coastal location means it often generates its own cap of cloud. Watch the forecast carefully before heading out, both because of the dangers of confronting precipitous terrain in poor visibility and because it would be a shame to miss out on the views.

If you like this...

If Faha Ridge has whetted your appetite, why not try the other main scramble on the massif, the East Ridge of Brandon Peak? Ranked at Grade 2: *Moderate*, this route starts from a lay-by at grid ref: Q 491 084. The ridge itself is a tale of two halves: a steep start and a gentler upper crest. Most of the scrambling comes low down on buttresses of rough sandstone, which can be tackled head-on or avoided at will. The highlight is a thrilling 15m *Moderate* pitch up an immaculate cracked slab. Finish by looping south across Gearhane and following the mountain's south-east ridge back to the road.

Guided Excursions

If you would like a professional mountain guide to lead you safely over Faha Ridge, contact **Simply Mountains** (tel: 087 677 7503; www.simplymountains. com) or **Kerry Climbing** (tel: 087 744 0523; www.kerryclimbing.ie).

The Scramble

Start by joining a grassy track that heads off from the top right corner of the car park. Follow the signs through a gate and out onto open mountainside, where the stony path is marked by a series of white poles. The trail leads to a well-tended grotto, then climbs diagonally along the hillside ahead. You will return along this path at the end of the route.

For now, play close attention to your surroundings from the grotto onwards. Continue along the path until you pass the second of two tumbledown walls. Turn right here, climbing north across open ground to reach the ridge above. Once at the apex of the ridge, turn left beside another old wall. From a navigational perspective the route is now straightforward: simply follow the crest of the ridge as closely as you can all the way to the Brandon plateau.

A grassy hillwalk brings you to the 822m summit of **Benagh**. Pause here to appreciate the incredible views into the deep corries that flank the rest of the ridge. Your route traverses the sharp arête that separates these two glacial craters. The scrambling starts on the descent from Benagh, with the ridge narrowing perceptibly and the ground becoming rockier underfoot. The trail is clearer now; it follows the crest of the undulating ridge, weaving past outcrops and pinnacles and bypassing most of the steep sections.

Eventually you arrive at the ridge's most famous feature, an exposed, **knife-edge slab** that tilts to the left. You can choose to cross this or not. The crossing is not hard but it is airy, and you will need to have a head for heights. It ends in a sheer 15m cliff, which can be descended only by abseil. However, you will find a rock chimney on the right-hand side of the cliff, which you can clamber down using Grade 2: *Moderate* moves. If this all seems too intimidating, don't cross the slab, but drop down a shorter and easier chimney on the right just before it. Then continue along the foot of the slab, where the two routes converge again.

A few more scrambling moves bring you to a deep col. Ahead the ridge rears precipitously upward, passing unambiguously into rock-climbing territory. Avoid these difficulties by following the path onto the slope to the right. The ground here is still very steep and exposed, but a series of rough, grassy steps weaves up through the outcrops to reach Brandon North Peak at 891m. It is an absorbing climb, and a shock to crest the ridge and suddenly see the coastline of the Dingle Peninsula laid out in all its glory below.

Turn left now and enjoy an easy walk south along

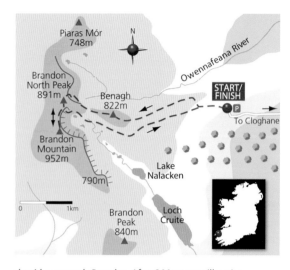

the ridge towards Brandon. After 300m you will notice a signpost marking a well-trodden path that drops left into Coumaknock. This is your descent route. For now, continue past the signpost and climb for another 500m to reach the top of the mountain. At 952m, this is the country's ninth highest peak, and the highest outside the MacGillycuddy's Reeks. The **summit** is decorated by a trig point, a large metal cross and a stone oratory dedicated to St Brendan. There are also magnificent 360-degree views stretching from the tip of Dingle all the way to the Iveragh Peninsula.

Having appreciated the panorama, turn around and reverse your ascent as far as the signpost. Turn right here and drop into **Coumaknock**, an imposing corrie with a line of paternoster lakes stretching along the basin floor. The descent down the headwall negotiates a series of steep zigzags, where hands are called on for support in places.

The trail along the corrie floor is atmospheric, and marked by splashes of yellow paint. Follow it through a maze of rock outcrops, crossing streams and passing several loughs and pools along the way. Eventually the path leaves the corrie and bears left, climbing a small rise on the southern slope of Benagh. The trip finishes with a long, easy descent, past the grotto and back to the car park.

Opposite: The exposed knife-edge slab that forms the crux of Faha Ridge. Cross it carefully or avoid it by dropping right just before it. (www.kerryclimbing.ie)

MACGILLYCUDDY'S REEKS – Cummeenapeasta Ridge

Possibly the best scramble in Ireland, this tremendous route takes you along an exposed ridgeline more than 900m high.

Tackling the knife-edge ridge beneath Knocknapeasta, with Cruach Mhór and Big Gun visible behind. (www.kerryclimbing.ie)

👍 Great for

- Testing your nerve as you scramble above a vertical abyss some 200m high
- Pulling over rocks with all of Ireland's tallest peaks ranged across the skyline ahead

☁ Conditions

- Dry ground, good visibility and light wind

🗺 Trip Details

- Grade of Scramble: 2 – *Moderate*
- Distance: 12km (7½ miles)
- Time: 6–7 hours
- Ascent: 1,100m (3,610ft)
- Maps: OSi 1:50,000 sheet 78, OSi 1:25,000 *MacGillycuddy's Reeks*, or Harvey Superwalker 1:30,000 *MacGillycuddy's Reeks*.

🚪 Access

- The route starts and finishes at Cronin's Yard, at the end of the road in Hag's Glen. There is a €2 charge for using the car park here, while facilities include a tearoom, camping, showers and toilets (see croninsyard.com).
- Grid Ref: V 836 873
- GPS: 52.026536, -9.695809

30

The Cummeenapeasta Ridge arcs high above its namesake lough, and is renowned amongst Irish scramblers for its bold moves, fearsome exposure and incredible views. Several sections of the rocky arête are truly knife-edge, with almost a kilometre of blocks, slabs and pinnacles aligned at an altitude of over 900m.

The main difficulties lie between the summits of Cruach Mhór and Knocknapeasta, where steady nerves and a good head for heights are essential. Some of the obstacles can be bypassed with the help of narrow paths, but in other places there is no avoiding a confident move across the rock. In international terms the ridge lies somewhere between Crib Goch in Wales and Aonach Eagach in Scotland, requiring more scrambling moves than the former but being less technical than the latter. Some groups choose to carry a short walking rope for extra security, which can be employed should the need arise. In terms of navigation the OSi 1:25,000 map provides the most detail, though once you're on the ridge the way ahead is obvious. Given the amount of exposure it is best to avoid the route entirely in poor visibility, or in wet and windy weather. Full mountaineering equipment is required to complete it in winter conditions.

Guided Excursions

If you'd prefer to complete the ridge with the security of a professional mentor, local guides include **Kerry Climbing** (tel: 087 744 0523; www.kerry climbing.ie), **Simply Mountains** (tel: 087 677 7503; www.simplymountains.com) and **Hidden Ireland Tours** (tel: 087 221 4002; www.hiddenireland tours.com).

The Scramble

Begin by passing through a metal gate at the top of Cronin's Yard. Follow a wide track along a field and past two more gates, then begin to climb gently above the Gaddagh River. After roughly 1km you arrive at a tributary stream, with a green metal bridge spanning the water ahead. Don't cross the bridge, but head upstream along eastern bank. Cross a metal stile after 200m, then climb south-east up the increasingly steep and sometimes boggy slope. Aim for the northern shore of Lough Cummeenapeasta,

The Serpent's Lair

Knocknapeasta translates from Irish as 'Hill of the Serpent'; the snake itself is said to inhabit the depths of Lough Cummeenapeasta. As you're passing this lake, look into its waters. You may not spot the great reptile, but you should be able to see a length of rope descending into the lough directly below Knocknapeasta summit. This is attached to the submerged wing of a US army aircraft, which crashed into the mountain on 17 December 1943, killing all five crewmen on board.

which offers good views west to Carrauntoohil and makes a natural spot for a rest. When you're ready, head east from the lake and climb over large, steep rocks to reach the top of **Cruach Mhór** (932m). The summit is marked by a stone grotto, and provides your first views south across the Iveragh Peninsula. Your main focus will be drawn closer to hand, however, to the imposing, **saw-toothed ridge** that now heads south towards Big Gun.

Progress along the top of the ridge is complicated at first by some huge chunks of rock, and the best solution is to follow an intermittent path just right of the crest. Return to the arête at a notch, then scramble carefully along the apex to reach the small cairn that marks Big Gun (939m).

The ridge swings south-west now, and you should descend along the crest to a grassy col. As you begin the ascent to Knocknapeasta (988m) the shoulder narrows to a **rocky knife-edge** once again, though the main difficulties can be bypassed using a path on the left. Rejoin the ridgeline just before the summit of the fourth highest mountain in Ireland. This is one of the most incredible viewpoints in the country, encompassing all of Ireland's mightiest peaks as well as the fearsome-looking ridge you have just traversed. High levels of adrenaline help to enhance your appreciation further.

The difficult terrain is now behind you, and you can stride south along a wide, stony ridge. Arc south-west as you descend to a grassy col, then make a short ascent to the 973m summit of **Maolán Buí**. From here you can shorten the route home by 2km if you descend north-west along the shoulder known as The Bone. The steep descent over rock and grass can be tricky, however, and you can enjoy the views further by continuing west.

Head across an intermediary rise to reach Cnoc an Chuillin (958m), the final peak on the ridge. Now descend to a col and climb Cnoc na Toinne, a grassy rise with a long, flat top. About a third of the way along this plateau, at grid reference: V 814 835, look out on the right for a small cairn that marks the top of the path known as The Zig Zags. This descends through steep switchbacks on the northern side of the ridge, and deposits you near the base of the Devil's Ladder. Turn right here onto a well-worn path, which takes you past the north-western shore of Lough Callee. Continue along the base of Hag's Glen, watching out for a fork in the path around 1.5km beyond the lake. Turn right here and complete the final kilometre back to Cronin's Yard.

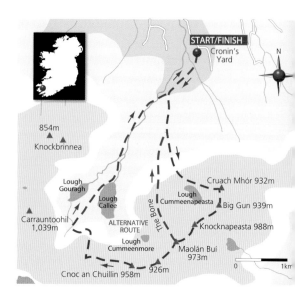

Carry full mountaineering equipment to complete the ridge in winter conditions.

HUNGRY HILL – South-west Ridge

The highest peak on the Beara Peninsula offers an easy but scenic ridgetop scramble all the way from base to summit.

👍 Great for

- Picking your line up grassy gullies and rocky steps
- Lifting your head from the engrossing terrain to enjoy fabulous coastal views

☁ Conditions

- A dry day with good visibility

🗺 Trip Details

- Grade of Scramble: 1 – *Easy*
- Distance: 11.5km (7 miles)
- Time: 5–6 hours
- Ascent: 660m (2170ft)
- Map: OSi 1:50,000 sheet 84

🎟 Access

- The route starts and finishes at Park Lough, at the foot of the south-west ridge. Access the area via the R572 Glengarriff–Castletownbere road. Turn north onto a minor road near Rossmackowen Bridge, around 6km east of Castletownbere; use your OS map to locate the correct turning. There are a couple of informal parking spaces beside the lough itself – continue to the end of the minor road, pass through a gate onto a rough track, then park beside a track junction just before the lough. Alternatively, park along the verge at the bottom of the minor road, near the junction with the R572, then walk the extra kilometre to the lake.
- Grid Ref: V 748 484
- GPS: 51.673774, -9.808889

Climbing one of the sandstone blocks that thrust skyward from the top of the ridge.

The south summit of Hungry Hill provides great views across the mountains of Beara.

Hungry Hill, the highest point on the Beara Peninsula at 685m, is one of the most rugged mountains in Ireland. Its slopes are guarded by great blocks of sandstone that burst through the grass and thrust skyward. The endless crags present a formidable picture, and indeed the eastern side of the mountain is so steep – cut by a pair of dramatic, lake-filled corries – that progress here is reserved for rock climbers.

For most scramblers, the 1.5km south-west ridge offers a far more manageable proposition. While it still looks imposing from below, the crags here are steep only in places, with easier-angled lines of weakness and grassy gullies never far away. You can choose your line of ascent to cross as many outcrops as you like or to avoid them all together. The large number of variations means the scramble merits a rating of Grade 1: *Easy*, though there are plenty of options for short *Moderate* or *Hard* sections if you want to take them on.

From the summit, two alternative descent routes are described. The longer, more interesting option follows Hungry Hill's north-west ridge, though a direct alternative is also available, saving you some 5.5km on the day's total distance.

The Scramble

From Park Lough, the south-west ridge lies directly ahead of you, its endless rock slabs quickening the heart with excitement or fear, depending on your perspective. A grassy ramp can be seen making a diagonal ascent up the southern slopes to a notch in the middle of the ridge, which some people use to access the second part of the shoulder. This would mean missing half the fun, however, so unless you're short of time, continue north-west along the track.

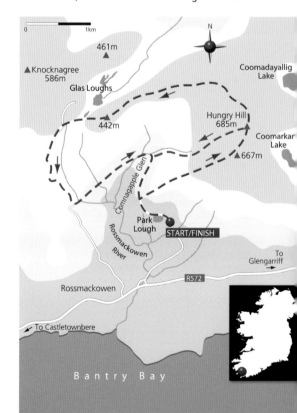

The track forms part of the Beara Way, and will also be used at the end of the circuit. For now, follow it for 350m to the western tip of the ridge. The crags here descend right down to track level, and with the rocky crest stretching away behind, the ridge looks more difficult than it actually is. Turn right, pick your first line of weakness between the slabs, and begin making your way uphill.

There's no defined route to follow: it's simply a matter of weaving your way around and over the succession of small crags. Pick whichever route suits your party's abilities, staying generally close to the apex of the ridge. As a rule, the easiest ground lies to the left, so if you are faced with an obstacle that seems too tricky, head left to bypass it on that side.

The angle of ascent is relentless, with a mixture of **grass gullies and rock steps** bringing you to the midway point, in the notch at the top the grassy ramp. This is a good place to take a break, and appreciate the fine views over Bantry Bay with your back to a tall, vertical cliff.

The second part of the ridge is much the same as the first, with extensive rock outcrops and lines of weakness on the left. The terrain is consuming, and it comes as something of a surprise to ease over the top of the shoulder and see a swathe of boggy moorland stretching ahead. This is Hungry Hill's summit plateau, and there is barely a rock in sight.

Head east for 300m to the large cairn that marks the south summit (667m). The views are even better from official summit, so continue north for another 450m to reach the **trig pillar**. Here the marvellous coastal views to the south are joined by an extensive panorama across the mountains of Bearagh and Iveragh to the west.

You now have a choice of descent routes. The quickest option lies directly west from the trig point, descending the valley just north of the south-west ridge into Comnagapple Glen. Keep just left of a small stream for the easiest progress, which can still be steep and picky in places. At the bottom of the valley, turn left onto the Beara Way track to return to Park Lough.

A longer circuit can be made by following the mountain's **north-west ridge**, over point 442m. From the trig point, begin by walking north for 300m,

Geology in your Hands

As you pull yourself over the outcrops of Hungry Hill's south-west ridge, spare a thought for the history beneath your hands. The mountain's distinctive geology is typical of the south Kerry and west Cork region. A great swathe of sandstone over 5km thick was laid here some 400 million years ago, then folded and contorted into successive mountain ranges. In the millennia since then the rock has been sculpted by glaciers and weathered by the elements, leaving the unique scramblers' playground we enjoy today.

then descend north-west onto the ridge. This shoulder sees a return to rugged rock outcrops, so progress is not quick. While not necessitating any scrambling manoeuvres, you'll need to weave across a labyrinth of exposed ribs and crags. A series of red and yellow paint splashes help guide you to point 442m, though navigation can be tricky in poor visibility. From point 442m, descend west to a small lough in a broad col, then continue south-west for another 300m to join a bog track. Turn left here and follow this track downhill for 1.5km. Now turn left again onto a path marked as the Beara Way. This leads around the lowers slopes of Comnagapple Glen, and joins the same track you used at the start of the day. Simply follow this back to the start at Park Lough.

Hungry Hill's south-west ridge. The route scrambles along the skyline.

ROCK CLIMBING

YOU'RE PERCHED on a narrow ledge high on a mountain ridge. The view is incredible, the rock almost sheer as it drops away on both sides. You have reached this point by searching out tiny weaknesses in the otherwise blank rock – a finger edge here, a crack there – pitting your strength and agility against an age-old formation. To fall would be fatal, but you have a safety rope and the skill to use it, and feel in control. Only at the top will you allow the euphoria to take over, and revel in the glory – yes, tinged with relief – at the fantastic positions you have just worked through.

Does this description intrigue you or terrify you? If your response is terror then you're not alone; many people instinctively know that rock climbing is not for them. But if vertigo doesn't kick in at the mere thought of a cliff, and you like physical challenges in remote locations, perhaps climbing is worth a try.

This section begins with a Quick Crag Guide to Ireland – a brief summary of the best climbing venues around the country. There is then a selection of three full-day adventures, each featuring a classic rock route that offers a thrilling climbing experience.

The routes are all graded at the easier end of the scale, though you would need to be confident leading up to *Severe* grade to complete the trips independently. Yet all three routes are accessible to novices too, if you engage the services of a local instructor to guide you through the day. Depending on the route and your previous experience, the instructor may recommend a day's training before heading out. Alternatively, you may be taught everything you need to know during the trip itself. Either way, there's little to stop you experiencing the challenge, excitement and occasional spasm of terror that is rock climbing in Ireland.

Irish Rock Climbing at a Glance

Climbing is an exciting pursuit anywhere in the world, but Irish rock climbing has a character all its own. Not only is the country endowed with a fabulous array of crags, both around the coast and in mountain settings, but the sport here has remained true to its traditional roots.

Generally speaking, international climbing falls into two categories. First comes 'sport' climbing, where

Jargon Buster

To become a real rock climber, you'll have to start talking its language. Here are a few pointers to get you started:

Gear – metal safety devices that attach the rope to the rock

Rack – your collection of gear

Abseil – to lower yourself down a cliff using a rope

Belay – to secure the end of the rope holding your partner

Crux – the hardest move on a route

Pitch – one rope-length of climbing; short routes are single pitch, longer routes are multi-pitch

metal bolts are drilled into the cliff face to provide regular, safe anchor points for climbers to attach their ropes to. Then there's 'traditional' climbing, where the rock is left in its natural state, and each climber must insert – then remove – their own anchors by carefully placing metal wedges or camming devices into cracks in the rock.

Irish climbing falls very definitely within the traditional camp. This makes routes tougher, and means climbers need to develop a skill set that is more akin to mountaineering than indoor climbing. Each individual is 100 per cent responsible for securing his or her own route, and must be confident in a wide range of gear-placement techniques.

All climbing routes are given a grade, giving you an idea of the technical difficulties you'll encounter during the ascent. You need to begin by understanding the Irish grading system, which is the same as the British system, but different from scales used elsewhere. Most people start on routes graded *VD* (short for 'Very Difficult'). There are then several increasing levels of difficulty before the *Extreme* grades kick in, which range from *E1* up to *E11*, the grade of the current hardest traditional climb in the world.

As well as familiarising yourself with grades and placing your own safety gear, another factor that makes Irish climbing rather wilder than elsewhere is the climate. In countries like Spain and Australia climbing has a broad appeal – what's not to like about hanging around on warm rock in T-shirt and shorts? To climb here requires a somewhat hardier disposition. The rock may warm up for a few months each summer, but most Irish climbers have as many tales of numb fingers and shivering belay stances as they do of sun cream and heat. The weather is just one more variable you'll learn to cope with as your climbing career progresses.

Essential Equipment

Most novice rock climbers start life as a 'seconder', which means you'll be supporting a more experienced leader, and following up the crag in second place. This is good news, because seconders need rather less gear than leaders; a pair of rock shoes, a helmet, a harness and belay device will suffice to get going. Your footwear is the most important thing to get right, as snug, well-fitting climbing shoes are essential for optimum grip on the rock.

When you start to lead routes, you will need to make a more significant financial outlay. A 50m climbing rope and a full rack of gear will cost at least €1,500. This is largely a once-off expense, however – the rope will need to be replaced if it becomes frayed after heavy use or you take a significant fall, but the rack will last for years.

In addition to your climbing equipment, you will need to carry all the food and clothing necessary to keep yourself safe in an outdoor environment. If you're attempting a mountain route, expect to cart a heavy backpack of gear! Also make sure to carry a mobile phone. In case of emergencies, call 999 or 112 and ask for mountain rescue or coastguard as appropriate.

Getting Started

There are three main ways to begin rock climbing. First you should find out where your closest indoor climbing wall is (see www.mountaineering.ie for a list of Irish venues). Most walls offer coaching sessions, including introductory lessons for novices. This is a warm, safe environment in which to master the basics, and find out if you're mentally and physically suited to the challenges of the sport.

To get a taste of outdoor climbing, a good option is to contact a qualified guide or adventure centre specialising in rock skills. You will be brought to a crag and shown how to approach a route safely. In the longer term, nothing beats joining a local club or otherwise hooking up with a more experienced partner. A partner you know and trust is both essential and invaluable. Most clubs have a core of experienced members who are pleased to share their knowledge with others. To find clubs focused on rock climbing, go to the 'Start Climbing' section of www.mountaineering.ie.

Extending Your Skills

A fun way to extend your skills is to head to one of the climbing festivals that take place around the country each year. The best one for beginners is the annual Colmcille Climbers Climbfest, in County Donegal, which usually takes place over the May bank holiday weekend.

You can also attend a formal training course. Many outdoor centres and instructors run courses aimed at improving your skills and developing your capacity to lead. Other courses focus on winter mountaineering. For details of upcoming courses, check with individual providers or see www.mountaineering.ie.

Finding Out More

Books: *Rock Climbing in Ireland* by David Flanagan describes over 400 climbing routes, spread across 22 crags all around Ireland. There's also a range of six regional guidebooks, providing more details on routes in The Mournes, Fair Head, Donegal, The Burren, Wicklow and Dalkey.

Online: www.mountaineering.ie is the first port of call for Irish climbing information online. It lists local climbing clubs and events, and offers advice to beginners on how to get started in the sport.

www.climbing.ie maintains the Irish Climbing Route Database, which lists most routes in Ireland, organised by county and then by crag. Accompanying maps and photos make this an invaluable online resource. The forum here – along with the **Irish Climbers Facebook Group** – is also a good way to connect with other climbing enthusiasts.

QUICK CRAG GUIDE TO IRELAND

Malin Head

Fair Head

Donegal
Sea stacks

Derryveagh
Mts

Bluestack Mts

Muckross Head

Slieve Donard

Slieve Binnian

Mweelrea

The Twelve Bens

Dalkey
Quarry

Luggala

Ailladie   Ail na Cronain

Wicklow Mts

The Burren

Lugnaquilla

Dunshean
Head

Carrauntoohil

MacGillycuddy's
Reeks

Climber on *Electra* (*E1 5b*), on the summit tor of Slieve Binnian in the Mourne Mountains.

The Mourne Mountains

The Mournes offer over 1,000 climbing routes, spread across at least 25 different crags. Almost all the rock is high-friction granite, set amid wild mountain scenery. Perhaps the most distinctive venues lie on the summits themselves. Peaks like **Slieve Binnian** and **Hen Mountain** are crowned by an array of summit tors, rounded and fissured crags that thrust through the peat just as they once rose above the ice sheets of the last ice age. A calm day is required to climb these locations, but the views are simply fantastic.

The **Annalong Valley** boasts the widest selection of routes in the region, ranging from single-pitch, entry-level routes at Lower Cove, to Buzzard's Roost, a conspicuous and overhanging bastion of rock on the lower north slopes of Slieve Binnian. This crag is home to *Divided Years*, one of the hardest rock routes in Ireland, which has been graded between *E8* and *E10* by the handful of people who have climbed it since it was established in 1994.

Also in the Annalong Valley is the renowned entry-level route FM. This five-pitch outing is a classic of the area, described on page 47.

Fair Head

Lying just metres from the sea on the north Antrim coast, Fair Head is renowned as the toughest natural climbing arena in Ireland. It's no coincidence that when the world's most famous climber, Alex Honnold, first visited the country in 2016, this was his chosen destination. Alex quickly proceeded up the local classic *The Complete Scream*, which is graded at a demanding *E7*. True to form he completed it solo, without using a safety rope.

While most mere mortals wouldn't dream of such an undertaking, there are routes to challenge a wide array of climbers. This is not a beginner's crag – you need to be confident climbing at least to *VS* level before coming here. The dolerite rock is unremittingly steep and shares its volcanic origins with the nearby Giant's Causeway. Imagine the hexagonal columns of the causeway, then extend them upwards for 50m. Many of the routes involve jamming your fingers, hands and feet into the fissures between these vertical columns. It is a unique and thrilling venue, but mentally intimidating and physically tiring, with skinned knuckles coming as standard.

Donegal

With over 3,000 routes spread across the length and breadth of the county, Donegal has a wealth of documented rock lines, and many more still waiting to be discovered. There are multi-pitch mountain epics in places like the **Derryveagh Mountains** and **Bluestack Mountains**, but most routes lie around periphery of the county.

Amongst countless high-quality coastal locations, **Malin Head** and **Muckross Head** stand out as favourites. Muckross is a short, accessible cliff separated from the waves by a single ledge, and is one of the steepest crags in Ireland. Yet it has positive holds, and you find yourself pulling moves here you wouldn't dream of attempting elsewhere. Ankle hooks, thigh squeezes, you name it – every part of your body comes into play at Muckross.

Climbing in Donegal doesn't stop at the mainland – numerous cliff-fringed islands offer yet further possibilities. Some of the most adventurous outings lie on offshore **sea stacks**, and routes here do not have to be technically demanding to provide a memorable day out. Beginners can enjoy these trips as much as veterans; see page 43 for one such outing.

The Burren

In a region renowned for swathes of exposed limestone, it comes as little surprise that the Burren offers a range of climbing options. Inland areas are covered with short limestone cliffs, liberally decorated with all the cracks, fissures and pockmarks associated with this type of rock. This makes for easy climbing, and there are countless options here for beginners. If you're just starting out one of the best spots is **Ail na Cronain**, beside Ailwee Cave. This cliff has over 70 short and accessible routes, all ranging from *Diff* to *HVS*.

Clare is most renowned for its coastal climbing, however. There are sea cliffs throughout the county – even the 320m precipice beneath the Cliffs of Moher Visitor Centre has been climbed, though the length of the nine-pitch epic means it's rarely repeated.

The most popular coastal crag is **Ailladie**, located between Doolin and Fanore. This atmospheric place has a non-tidal platform for belaying, and is something of a suntrap on summer afternoons. There are plenty of harder routes here (*HVS* and above), but few easy options. If you're new to climbing, head across the road to the **Ballyryan** crag, where various short, fun routes are used by local outdoor centres to introduce beginners to the sport.

Left: A typically acrobatic move on *Cois Farraige* (*VS 4b*), at Muckross Head, Donegal.
Right: Ireland has a fantastic variety of climbing routes, along the coast as well as on inland mountain crags.

Climbing *Classical Revival* (*HVS 4c, 5a, 4c*) high above Lough Belshade, in the Bluestack Mountains of Donegal.

Kerry

For a county as large and mountainous as Kerry, there's less climbing here than you might imagine. The classic easy route is *Howling Ridge*, a long, multi-pitch journey that finishes at the summit of **Carrauntoohil**. For full details of this trip, see page 51.

In terms of mountain crags, the **Gap of Dunloe** offers the most options. With over 300 routes spread around the valley, there are lines here to suit most people. Kerry also has a number of coastal crags, especially around the Dingle Peninsula. The impressive sandstone cliffs at **Dunshean Head**, near Dingle town, make this one of the most popular choices, with routes ranging from *VD* to *E4*.

Dublin & Wicklow

For new climbers based in Dublin, it won't be long before you're introduced to **Dalkey Quarry**. Located within the southern suburbs of the city, this quarry may be the result of human rather than natural endeavour, but it provides a pretty convenient training venue. Most routes are single-pitch, and there are challenges for beginners and experts alike.

Further south in Wicklow the mountains could never be described as rugged, but there are several decent crags where the rock thrusts through its boggy blanket. The imposing granite cliffs of **Luggala** are once such location, occupying a superbly scenic spot on the shore of Lough Tay. More popular and equally as scenic, the upper valley at **Glendalough** is another option. There are high-quality lines here of all grades and lengths, with several routes of such character they're considered national classics.

DONEGAL SEA STACKS

Choose from two offshore venues to sample the adventure of stack climbing, with swirling waves and isolation just some of the factors involved.

👍 *Great for*
- Combining the challenge of navigating both sea and rock
- Feeling astounded at having reached such an unlikely outpost

☁ *Conditions*
- A calm sea and dry rock

Perfect conditions for *Heavens Hexes (HS 4a)* on Tor na Dumhcha.

Donegal has so much fabulous offshore climbing, it's hard to pick out a single route. There are high-quality climbs on an almost endless array of stacks and islands, and choosing the right one for you depends on two main variables.

First of these is your climbing ability. There is great stack climbing across a whole range of grades, starting at *VD* or lower. Yet with this sort of route, the actual rock moves are only part of a much bigger adventure. The logistics of the sea crossing, the isolation of the location, the yawning exposure to a surging ocean and the final abseil off the top are all factors that don't exist on most inland climbs. All this extra 'atmosphere' means sea stacks are not a good place to push your technical limits. Unless you have nerves of steel, pick a route well within your abilities – you're guaranteed a fabulous day out regardless of the grade of the ascent.

A Seaworthy Craft?

Reaching your chosen sea stack is at least half the battle, and your selection of watercraft will be determined by the rock's location and the size of your group. Inflatable dingies, sea kayaks and chartered RIBs are just some of the choices available. Remember your mooring ropes, too – you'll need to tether the boat to the base of the stack while you make your climb.

The other variable affecting route selection is the condition of the sea. All stacks involve open-water crossings to get yourself and your gear to the start of the route. Some crossings are short and sheltered, while others involve a kilometre or more of open ocean. Once at your location, the swell must be small

A Tyrolean traverse is a spectacular way to access Tor na Dumhcha.

enough to let you land on an often precarious ledge. You will need to develop the skills of a sea kayaker to judge when conditions are safe, and it's no surprise that sheltered, inshore stacks are climbed far more regularly than remote outliers.

Many of the offshore routes in Donegal have been pioneered by Iain Millar, a climbing guide based locally (see Guided Excursions below). Iain documents each ascent and his website includes a free, downloadable route guide to Donegal's sea stacks, as well as guides to all the main climbing islands.

Guided Excursions

If you don't feel confident heading offshore on your own, contact **Iain Millar** (tel: 087 758 4810; www. uniqueascent.ie) or **Bren Whelan** (tel: 087 665 7790; donegalclimbing.ie), who will happily guide you up a route. This option is open even to complete beginners with no previous experience of climbing. Expect to pay around €200 for a full day for two people.

The Climb – Tor na Dumhcha

This small stack lies at grid reference: B 802 303. It features 12 different routes, mostly under 20m high and ranging in grade from *Diff* to *HVS*. The rock is excellent quality, with high-friction granite giving you extra confidence in your moves. The routes themselves follow **well-defined cracks and corners** and have several stars to denote their quality. You should be able to climb several routes in a day, as with a single-pitch crag inland.

What makes this venue stand out is its accessibility. Yes, it is technically a sea stack, cut off from the mainland, with the ocean surging all around, yet it is tucked into the edge of a bay, and the channel separating it from the shore is just 10m wide. The crossing is as narrow and sheltered as it's possible to get, and a blow-up dingy or a paddleboard is quite sufficient to ferry you across. You can still climb here on days when more exposed stacks become inaccessible.

In fact, Tor na Dumhcha lies so close to the shore, it offers the opportunity for another fun, climbing-related challenge: a **Tyrolean traverse**. This is a sort of horizontal zip line, formed by pulling a rope tight between two high points. Climbers dangle beneath

Trip Details – Tor na Dumhcha

- Grade of climbs: 12 routes ranging from *Diff* to *HVS*
- Length of climbs: around 17m
- Map: OSi 1:50,000 sheet 1

Access – Tor na Dumhcha

- Begin by heading along the R257 to Gweedore. North of the village, look out for the hotel Teac Jack. Just north of the hotel, turn west along the L5293. Turn left after 300m, then continue to the end of the road and park above a beach. Now walk north along the coastal path for 800m, to a headland overlooking the stack. Scramble down the rocks to the channel, then cross to a relatively easy landing ledge on the eastern side of the stack.
- Grid Ref: B 799 295
- GPS : 55.112255, -8.315673

the rope in their harnesses and use their arms to pull themselves across the gap. It is a thrilling and spectacular way to cross a chasm, if fairly strenuous on the arms. The rope takes a while to rig and must be anchored safely, so only contemplate this access method if you know what you're doing. If you do set one up, the crossing is an experience you won't forget.

The Climb – An Bhuideal

Rising from the sea at grid reference: G 549 902, An Bhuideal is an iconic stack renowned for its unique profile. The experience of reaching and climbing it provides a truly adventurous day out. And the good news is that it's not overly demanding; providing you can get calm sea conditions, you only need to climb to *Severe* standard to complete this unforgettable route.

The stack is split into two adjacent towers. The easiest climbing lies on the conical, 45m-high **Main Stack**, which is breached by a superb two-pitch *Severe*. Begin by landing at the base of the stack's

Approaching the distinctive offshore stack of An Bhuideal, home to an incredible two-pitch *Severe*.

eastern face, just left of the North Tower. The route ascends the huge **skyline arête** at the southern end of this face.

The first pitch is 25m long. Start on a secure, non-tidal ledge in the centre of the east face. From here, climb up and diagonally left to reach a small and exposed ledge on the apex of the ridge. Set up your belay here. For the second pitch, simply follow the crest of the ridge all the way to the summit. The exposure is significant, but every hold is large and secure. The final few metres to the top crosses a knife edge and is particularly memorable.

The view from the tiny, airy summit will take your breath away, with the North Tower beside you and an array of stacks and cliffs all around. There are plenty of good gear placements to secure an abseil (using medium to large hexes), and you may be able to reuse anchor points that have already been rigged. It is then a relatively simple abseil down the east face back to your start point.

If you prefer a tougher challenge, the **North Tower** also offers a three-pitch route graded at *VS*. This slender stack is reminiscent of the Old Man of Hoy, but is not for the fainthearted. The guide describes it as 'one of the most exposed and scary climbs in Ireland... the summit feels like it sways slightly as you sit on it.' You have been warned.

 Trip Details – An Bhuideal

- Grade of climb: *Severe* 4a
- Length of climb: 50m/2 pitches
- Map: OSi 1:50,000 sheet 10

 Access – An Bhuideal

- The stack of An Bhuideal is located 100m from the coast, around 1.5km north of Port. In very calm conditions, the best option is to sea kayak from the slipway at Port. Alternatively you can reduce the sea crossing to 300m by walking over the western slopes of Port Hill, then scrambling down a promontory to a south-facing storm beach, and launching a portable dingy from there. Take the utmost care with sea conditions; this coastline is exposed to most Atlantic swells and calm conditions are hard to find.
- Grid Ref: G 548 891
- GPS: 54.747612, -8.702366

SLIEVE LAMAGAN – FM

This excellent multi-pitch climb is not overly difficult, and carries you to a scenic summit right in the heart of the Mourne Mountains.

Great for

- Enjoying lofty belay perches high above the Annalong Valley
- Trusting the friction of granite to smear up 50° slabs

Conditions

- Dry rock and as nice a day as possible

Trip Details

- Grade of climb: *VD* with optional *Severe* finish
- Length of climb: 6 pitches
- Whole trip distance: 11.5km (7 miles)
- Whole trip time: 6–7 hours
- Whole trip ascent: 560m (1,840ft)
- Maps: OSNI 1:25,000 Activity Map *The Mournes*, OSNI 1:50,000 sheet 29

Access

- Start and finish at Carrick Little car park, some 4km west of Annalong village. From the A2 road in Annalong, turn north-west beside a church, then turn right 1.5km later. The free public car park is located 2.5km further along, on the opposite side of a T-junction. Alternatively, two private car parks can be found a short distance along the Carrick Little track, where you will benefit from extra security in exchange for a small fee.
- Grid Ref: J 345 219
- GPS: 54.128634, -5.943228

At the top of the route, with Blue Lough and Slieve Binnian behind. (Daniel Sercombe, iclimbedamountain.wordpress.com)

Slieve Lamagan (704m) is a pyramid-shaped peak that lies right at the heart of the Mourne Mountains. Its central location gives it some of the best views in the range, yet as a destination it is better known to climbers than walkers. This is thanks to the great slabs of exposed granite that guard its southern face – slabs that are breached by a classic, entry-level rock climb known as *FM*.

This is one of the longest rock routes in the Mournes, with over 160m of technical climbing. Split into six pitches, the overall feeling is one of mountaineering – scaling an entire peak with rope and gear. Yet while the slabs appear fearsome from the approach, the majority of the route is angled at a relatively benign 45–55°. The rock is clean and solid, and protection is generally good, though there would be a couple of unpleasant run-outs if the leader took an uncontrolled slide down the slabs.

Most of the route is graded *VD* (*Very Difficult* – almost as easy as rock climbing gets). There is a choice of routes for the final pitch and you can opt either to continue the *VD* grade or slip up a notch to *Severe* for the final short pitch. If you have the requisite experience, the severe option is recommended as a thrilling culmination to the route.

Guided Excursions

Though it lies at the easier end of the scale for rock climbing, this route still requires previous experience of multi-pitch lead climbing. If you don't have the necessary skills yourself, consider hiring the services of a local guide. Try **Jonny Parr** (tel: 077 7319 6943; www.jonnyparrclimbing.com) or **Paul Swail** (tel: 077 9345 3278; www.paulswailguiding.com), with an average day out costing around £200 for two people.

The Walk In

Begin by heading along the track immediately east of Carrick Little car park. The track climbs steadily north and brings you to the Mourne Wall after 1km. Cross the stile and continue straight ahead, skirting the boundary of Annalong Wood and continuing to a stream crossing. Around 200m beyond the stream, veer right at a fork in the path.

Slieve Lamagan now lies directly ahead. Follow the path for another 500m, then strike left, scrambling

A Fitting Ascent

If you approach Slieve Lamagan by way of a rock climb, you'll be doing true justice to its name. The peak translates from Irish as 'The Mountain of Crawling', apparently because both hands and feet are needed to reach the top. While there are approaches that can be completed with feet alone, you'll certainly be calling all limbs into play to breach the massive rock slabs of the south face.

up a steep slope of heather and grass. Aim for the clean apex of slabs at the south-eastern corner of the mountain, handily marked as 'Lamagan Slabs' on some maps. The route starts at the base of this, below a distinctive white streak in the rock.

Looking upwards from the start, two steeper bands of cliff are visible above, one at mid height and the other at the top. These rock steps form the third and final pitches respectively, and are interspersed with easier-angled slab climbing.

The Climb

Pitch 1: 35m
Climb the cracks just left of a steep corner to reach a good ledge. Then head up more easy cracks to a wide, sloping belay ledge above.

Pitch 2: 45m
Choose from several options to climb the slab above, heading towards a dark corner in the steep wall higher up. Belay at the base of this wall.

Pitch 3: 15m
Step out left, then make a committing high step. This is the crux of the route, and a hidden handhold up on the left is key if you can find it. Follow a corner above, climbing just left of a white streak on the rock. Belay as soon as possible to avoid rope drag.

Pitch 4: 15m
Follow easy grooves to a ledge beneath the upper slabs, keeping to the right side of a patch of grass. From here there are two options for completing the route.

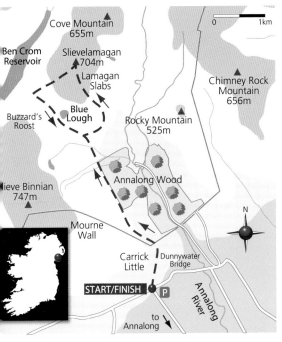

Pitches 5 & 6, Direct Finish: 20m, 15m

The direct finish is more enjoyable and satisfying, but warrants the harder grade of *Severe*. Climb the blank slabs diagonally left from the grass patch, heading towards a prominent steep corner in the headwall. Belay at the base of this corner. For the final pitch, climb directly up the corner. The rock here is vertical – it's the steepest part of the entire route – but there are plenty of large holds to ease your progress. The grand finale is an exposed and thrilling pull over the final block.

Pitches 5 & 6, Traditional Finish: 15m, 20m

If the direct route seems too intimidating, you can stay within the original grade of *VD* by sticking to the traditional finish line. From the top of pitch 4, traverse to the right, crossing the slabs to a corner of broken rock. Belay here, then finish up the broken ground above.

Slieve Lamagan from the approach path. The route climbs the prow of slabs on the right. (Daniel Sercombe, iclimbedamountain.wordpress.com)

col, and descend more gently towards Blue Lough. The conspicuous prow of rock to your right is Buzzard's Roost, home to one of the hardest rock climbs in Ireland.

Around 500m below Blue Lough you reach the trail junction passed on your outward journey. Continue straight ahead here, then retrace your initial steps back to the car park.

The Walk Out

If you can't get enough of a good thing, there is an opportunity for even more climbing from the top of the route. Traverse a good distance right to reach the base of another giant slab. This is the start of *Upper FM*, which adds an extra 100m of climbing at grade *VD*.

Most people are happy to call it a day at the top of *FM*. Pack up your gear, then scramble across terraces of heather and rock to reach the small cairn at the summit of Slieve Lamagan. The view from here encompasses all the main peaks in the Mournes, and the revelation of Ben Crom Reservoir and the Silent Valley to the west is particularly impressive.

When you're ready, head south-west from the summit along an informal path. The descent is relatively steep at first, but eases as you near the col beneath Slieve Binnian. Turn left at a junction in the

Above left: On the wide, sloping ledge of the first belay stance of *FM* in the Mourne Mountains.
Above right: FM's granite slabs provide solid friction all the way up. (Daniel Sercombe, iclimbedamountain.wordpress.com)

CARRAUNTOOHIL – Howling Ridge

A classic mountaineering rock climb that follows an exposed and scenic ridge to finish at Ireland's highest summit.

👍 Great for

- Finding a unique way to reach the country's highest point
- Testing your self-control in the face of massive exposure

☁ Conditions

- Dry rock and good visibility all the way to the summit

🗺 Trip Details

- Grade of climb: *VD*
- Length of climb: 8 pitches
- Whole trip distance: 10.5km (6½ miles)
- Whole trip time: 7–8 hours
- Whole trip ascent: 900m (2,950ft)
- Maps: OSi 1:50,000 sheet 78, OSi 1:25,000 *MacGillycuddy's Reeks*, or Harvey Superwalker 1:30,000 *MacGillycuddy's Reeks*.

🏛 Access

- The route starts and finishes at Cronin's Yard, at the end of the road in Hag's Glen. There is a €2 charge for using the car park here, while excellent facilities include a tearoom, camping, showers and toilets (see croninsyard.com).
- Grid Ref: V 836 873
- GPS: 52.026536, -9.695809

A ridge with a view: below the arête a 500m vertical abyss drops to Lough Gouragh.

The most famous easy mountaineering route in Ireland, Howling Ridge is exposed, committing and exhilarating. It starts at an altitude of 650m, halfway up the forbidding north-east face of Carrauntoohil. Following a well-defined line up a steep rock ridge, the biggest impression left by the route is of awesome exposure. The climbing may not be technically hard, but the constant gaping abyss to Hag's Glen some 500m below can't help but sharpen the wits.

The route begins with an ascent to the Heavenly Gates, following a faint trail that is sometimes used as an alternative walking route to Carrauntoohil. From here the technical climbing stretches for over 300 vertical metres, alternating between sections of *Hard* scrambling and *VD* rock climbing. Some parties secure the entire route with a series of climbing pitches, in which case there are around eight pitches. Others are happy to move together over the easier scrambling sections, and only set up belays to secure the steeper rock steps. The best option is to bring a

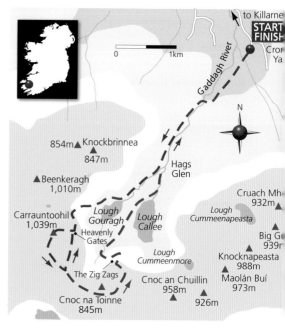

Beside one of the pinnacles at the top of Howling Ridge.

Howling in the Snow

Howling Ridge was first climbed while it was covered by snow and ice in February 1987. It was pioneered by two local mountaineers, Con Moriarty and John Cronin. The route gets its name from Moriarty's dog, Grimsel, who was left at the Heavenly Gates at the base of the route. The dog's howls could be heard echoing around the ridge throughout their groundbreaking ascent.

full complement of climbing gear, including plenty of slings, and make the decision about how to proceed once you see the challenge in front you.

Friction is generally good, and you'll find protection where you need it. It is important to note, though, that the route is notorious for loose rock. Some cracks actually bulge outwards and release gear when pressure is applied. Make sure to test all holds and all gear placements before you commit to them and, if you're not happy, find an alternative route. Also be sure to make an early start to reduce any time pressure. An average time for the climb itself is 2–3 hours, though as much as 8 hours has been recorded.

Guided Excursions

There are several renowned mountain instructors who will happily guide you up Howling Ridge. Try **Piaras Kelly** (tel: 087 744 0523; www.kerryclimbing.ie), **John Healy** (tel: 087 677 7503; www.simplymountains. com) or **Con Moriarty** (tel: 087 221 4002; www. hiddenirelandtours.com), one of the route's first ascenders. If you have no previous experience a two-day course is recommended, which costs around €200 per person.

The Walk In

From Cronin's Yard car park, head through the metal gate and join a wide track. Pass through two more gates, then begin the gradual climb up the valley beside climb the Gaddagh River. After roughly 1km, cross two green metal bridges, following signs for 'Carrauntoohil Mountain'.

Keep left at a path junction and continue along the west bank of the river for 1.2km. The main path now crosses the stream flowing out of Lough Gouragh. Instead of crossing here, follow the stream's western bank almost as far as Lough Gouragh. Shortly before the lake, veer right and join a faint, stony path that climbs south-west in a rising traverse, heading towards the rugged lower slopes of Carrauntoohil.

The path negotiates a series of rock ledges before reaching a flattish platform known as the 'first level'. From here, climb south-west to the foot of an imposing black cliff. Here the path splits; the right fork leads up to O'Shea's Gully, while this route ascends a loose gully to the left. Follow the trail to a narrow notch between two crags; this is the Heavenly Gates, and the official start of the Howling Ridge climb (grid ref: V 807 844).

The Climb

The route begins on the uphill side of the Heavenly Gates. The first pitch consists of around 40m of *Hard* scrambling. This brings you to the base of the first rock step, where the difficulty increases to *VD* for 5m. Here you get your first real taste of the immense exposure that characterises the remainder of the route. The challenge is to keep calm enough to appreciate the incredible location.

A similar pattern is repeated for next part of the route: *Hard* scrambling, followed by a shorter section of *VD* climbing to overcome a steeper rock step. More scrambling then brings you to one of the route's most distinctive features, a buttress known as **The Tower**. This is a *VD* slab beside the apex, where the diagonal rock strata slant awkwardly down to the left. Balance delicately up this, then negotiate another *Hard* scramble to reach **The Finger**, a formation that resembles a closed fist, with one extended finger pointing down the valley.

Shortly after The Finger you reach **The Bridge**, a short but dramatic arête that spans the top of a gully. The exposure beneath this angled slab is massive, but confidence is key and there is nothing technical about the crossing.

You have now joined the ridge known as Primroses. Climb two more rock steps to reach a cluster of angular pinnacles protruding from the apex

Here be monsters: the warning sign near the summit of Carrauntoohil.

of the ridge. A short distance above this the difficulties ease and the slope turns into an easier-angled mixture of rock and grass.

Pack up your gear whenever you feel comfortable and scramble the final 150m to the top. Shortly before the summit you have the pleasure of passing a low warning sign marked with a skull and crossbones – a photo opportunity as mandatory as the one beside the large metal cross at the summit.

The Walk Out

There are several options for descending from Carrauntoohil back into Hag's Glen. Most people begin by heading south then south-east along the main access path. The safest and easiest return route is via **The Zig Zags**. Continue south-east past the col at the top of the Devil's Ladder, then climb over the grassy hummock of Cnoc na Toinne (845m). At grid reference: V 814 835, look out for a small cairn on the left marking the top of The Zig Zags. This grassy path descends north through steep switchbacks and deposits you at the head of Hag's Glen. Turn right here and join the main track that heads past Lough Callee back to Cronin's Yard.

Alternatively you can make a more direct, but more exposed descent via the **Heavenly Gates**.

For this route, don't drop as far as the Devil's Ladder col, but look out for a level terrace in the slope around 200m before it. Turn left here, traversing along a faint path towards a large rock outcrop. The path consolidates on the left side of these boulders, then cuts across the steep slope with a precipitous drop below. Pass through the rock cleft of the Heavenly Gates, then continue down a steep, loose gully to the base of a black cliff. Turn right here and continue to descend north-east, negotiating an awkward rock step before returning to shore of Lough Gouragh. Rejoin to the main Hag's Glen track, then retrace your outward journey back to the start.

Crowning achievement: beside Carrauntoohil's summit cross.

COASTAL WALKING

IRELAND'S COASTLINE is arguably its finest natural asset. Bold headlands, towering cliff lines, golden beaches and hidden coves are just some of the myriad treasures scattered along the seashore.

As with many beautiful landscapes, much of the best scenery lies off the beaten track, and can only be appreciated by those who explore on foot. There is simply no other way to reach the top of the country's highest sea cliffs or to marvel at its most remote beaches except to walk there. Coastal walks don't have to involve a significant height gain to be dramatic – they're such a great blend of wild ocean atmosphere and rugged terrain that, in many ways, they epitomise everything that is unique about Irish walking. Standing at the tip of a chiselled headland 5km from the nearest road, you can appreciate the raw power of nature and the beauty of Ireland in a way that few others can.

Coastal walks encompass a wide diversity of routes. There are easy routes along low, sandy shorelines as well as tougher hikes to coastal summits. A handful of mountain routes require previous hillwalking experience, but most are less technical, crossing lower ground or following signed trails. Most dramatic are the cliff walks, where you can stroll along the edge of sheer precipice, with the waves pounding

Above: Easy coastal routes explore sandy shorelines, like the Ards Peninsula in Donegal.
Previous page: Most coastal walks can be completed all year round. A winter hiker explores the sea cliffs of north Mayo.

An Incredible Coastline

As the crow flies, Ireland measures just 450km from north to south. Yet the Marine Institute has calculated that the coastline stretches for an incredible 7,500km. On the west coast in particular, the shoreline is sometimes fragmented into such a maze of bays, headlands and islets, it's hard to tell where the mainland ends and the labyrinth of islands begins.

against the rocks several hundred metres below. It's impossible to complete these walks without a feeling of exhilaration, and the comparison with a landlocked country couldn't be greater.

Ireland's Coastline at a Glance

Broadly speaking, the Irish coastline is a tale of two halves. While the east coast is low and sheltered, the west is rugged and sometimes inaccessible. In recent years the west coast has adopted the moniker The Wild Atlantic Way, an epithet designed to emphasise the untamed nature of that seaboard.

The character of the west coast is partly explained by the force behind it; while the Irish Sea is on average just 120km wide, the Atlantic Ocean extends for some 3,000km, allowing huge swells to gather force before crashing into the shore. The relentless impact of the waves sculpts the land, shaping rock and mountain alike. Millennia of erosion have left a tremendous variety of natural rock architecture, including sea stacks, arches, pinnacles and blowholes. Some formations are so tenuous it seems they won't survive the next storm, while in other places entire hillsides have been chiselled away, exposing rock strata twisted and folded into improbable patterns.

The cliffs themselves reach 600m high and are amongst the tallest in Europe. Slieve League in Donegal (see page 62) and Croaghaun on Achill Island vie for the title of highest Irish sea cliff, depending on how you define the term 'cliff'. In places like the Cliffs of Moher (see page 65) the coastal precipice is not as high but it is more prolonged, stretching for miles with a thrilling vertical drop to the ocean below.

onto the land above. If you have a choice, walking around low tide is generally best because it gives you more options for progressing along the coast.

Other routes pass along the top of steep cliffs. It's an exhilarating experience to walk along a cliff edge, with a gaping abyss to one side and the waves crashing against the rocks hundreds of metres below. Yet this exposure includes an inherent danger. Few cliff edges are fenced or protected in Ireland and it is up to walkers to exercise their own judgement in terms of safety. The best advice is to stay well back from the edge, be particularly aware of seaward-facing slopes if the ground is wet or slippery and avoid cliff routes altogether in strong winds.

Though most coastal walks can be completed year round, the season will have a significant impact on your experience. Late spring and early summer are the most colourful periods, when coastal flowers like thrift and sea campion are in bloom. Seabirds gather at nesting sites between April and July, and popular breeding spots positively buzz with avian activity during this time. There's more human activity too, as beaches fill up with holidaying families.

By winter the flowers have gone, the bird ledges are empty and the ocean becomes more agitated. The first big swells of the autumn usually hit around October, and storms can remain a regular occurrence right through to spring. These storms bring waves up

The tremendous rock architecture of the west coast includes sea stacks, arches, pinnacles and blowholes.

Even the west coast is not all steep and rocky, however – the headlands are interspersed by gentler, lower landscapes. Sandy beaches are common, both in the form of wide, family-friendly holiday strands, and remote coves that barely see a soul all year. Ireland's beaches are every bit as beautiful and plentiful as in countries like Spain and Greece, it's just the climate that keeps the sun loungers at bay.

The Basics

The routes selected for this bucket list are scattered along Ireland's northern, western and southern shores. On lower routes, it's sometimes necessary to consider the height of the tide before you set out. At low tide you may be able to stride across a firm, sandy beach, but at high tide the sand is covered and you're forced

The hike to Croaghaun on Achill Island involves a tougher coastal hillwalk.

to 20m high crashing into shore, especially in places where the continental shelf lies close to land. You should avoid all coastal walks in these conditions, because air gusts and spray reach far higher again, and there have been several incidents where people have been swept off the rocks and perished.

Essential Equipment

One of the great things about coastal walking is that virtually everyone can do it, and it doesn't have to be hard to be impressive. The amount of preparation required depends on the nature of the terrain you'll be crossing. If you plan to tackle a coastal summit, you should take all the precautions necessary for a hillwalk. Wear sturdy boots and carry a map, compass, extra clothing, food and water (see page 4 for more details).

For lower, shorter walks, you can reduce the amount of equipment you carry. A pair of sports shoes can be more appropriate than boots, and a

map may not be necessary if the route is signed. It is still advisable to carry a waterproof jacket, snack and mobile phone, just to be prepared for the Irish weather and other eventualities.

In case of emergency, dial 999 or 112 and ask for mountain rescue or the coastguard.

Finding Out More

Books: *Ireland's Wild Atlantic Way: A Walking Guide* by Helen Fairbairn details 30 of the best walking routes along Ireland's west coast.

Online: www.wildatlanticway.com provides general information about travelling and staying along Ireland's west coast.

www.easytide.com is one of the best resources for online tide times. Select the closest spot on the map to your location to see a seven-day tide chart. Between the end of March and the end of October, use the drop-down menu to add one hour to the times.

There's no other way to reach Ireland's most remote beaches except to walk there. Melmore Head in Donegal.

CAUSEWAY COASTAL PATH

This magnificent, signed path explores
the most famous stretch of coastline
in Northern Ireland.

Great for

- Marvelling at unique geological formations
- Mixing fabulous coastal scenery with
  historic sites

Conditions

- Calm or moderate winds and good visibility

Trip Details

- Distance: 15km (9½ miles)
- Time: 5–6 hours
- Ascent: 200m (660ft)
- Maps: OSNI 1:25,000 *Causeway Coast and
  Rathlin Island* or *Glens of Antrim,*
  OSNI 1:50,000 sheet 5

Access

- **To the start:** The route starts at the parking
  area for Carrick-a-Rede rope bridge.
  This National Trust site is signed from the B12
  just east of Ballintoy village.
- Grid Ref: D 052 448
- GPS: 55.238943, -6.347355

- **To the finish:** The walk finishes at the car
  park for the Giant's Causeway. The causeway
  is well signed along the B146, around 3km
  north of Bushmills.
- Grid Ref: C 945 439
- GPS: 55.232943, -6.516253

The route finishes at the 40,000 hexagonal columns of the Giant's Causeway.

Causeway Coastal Path, County Antrim

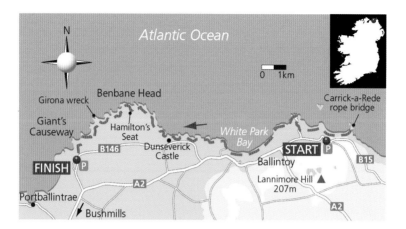

This highly enjoyable walking route is the most fulfilling way to explore the unique natural attractions of the north Antrim coast. The 40,000 hexagonal columns of the Giant's Causeway form the most famous feature of the route, but the whole coastline is so striking you'll come away with countless other memories besides.

The walk described here follows the best section of the two-day Causeway Coast Way. It starts at the thrilling Carrick-a-Rede rope bridge and traces the shoreline west past sandy beaches, secluded harbours, sheer cliffs and historic landmarks. Despite its linear format, return transport is not a problem. The start and the finish points are linked via frequent buses – use the Ulsterbus Causeway Rambler shuttle service during the summer, and the Antrim Coaster service at other times of the year.

The path is signed throughout, and frequent access points mean you can split it into sections to suit your own preferences. Note that the shoreline at either end of White Park Bay is impassable at high tide, so make sure to the check tide times before you set out. There's also a charge for visiting the rope bridge at the start of the walk and for entering the Giant's Causeway visitor centre at the end.

The Walk

If this is your first time visiting Carrick-a-Rede, a trip across the thrilling 20m-long rope bridge is highly recommended and will add 2km to the day. Pay your dues at the entrance kiosk and follow a well-benched path east from the car park. Few people make it across the chasm without a quickening of the pulse. The island is particularly attractive in early summer, when puffins and gulls can be seen nesting on its cliffs.

Return to the car park, then begin the route itself. Follow the path west along the clifftop, with Rathlin Island and Scotland's Mull of Kintyre both visible across the sea. When you join a minor road, turn right, descending to the quiet, picturesque harbour at Ballintoy. The road ends here, but the route continue west along a track, then a footpath. Pass a series of stacks and islands to reach the top of a stone beach. A brief boulder hop around the base of a cliff now brings you onto the 2km sweep of golden sand at **White Park Bay**.

Cross the beach to the cliffs at its western end. Here you have to clamber across more boulders to reach Portbradden, an idyllic collection of houses fronted by a small harbour. St Gobban's Church lies

Game of Thrones

The popular fantasy TV series *Game Of Thrones* made extensive use of the Causeway Coast for filming purposes. And no wonder! The scenery is stunning. If you're a fan of the programme, keep an eye open for numerous locations featured in the series. Key sites include Pyke and the Iron Islands (Ballintoy Harbour), Renly Baratheon's camp at The Stormlands (Larrybane, beside Carrick-a-Rede), and the clifftop towers of House of Greyjoy (a few kilometres west at Dunluce Castle).

Carrick-a-Rede Rope Bridge sways at it spans the 20m gap to a tiny island.

beside the second house; it is no larger than a garden shed and holds the accolade of smallest church in Ireland.

Continue through a natural rock arch and follow the path around Gid Point, crossing a mixture of rock and grass as you trace the indented coastline. Pass Dunseverick Harbour to reach The Sloc, a popular spot for swimming and rock jumping (see page 136). Several more stiles then bring you to the ruins of 16th-century Dunseverick Castle.

The grassy path continues north-west from here, climbing towards **Benbane Head** and Hamilton's Seat, the highest part of the route. You are now tracing the cliff line some 100m above the ocean and there are wonderful views west along the rugged coastline. Midway between Hamilton's Seat and the Giant's Causeway you come to Plaskin Head. This marks the final resting place of the *Girona*, the most famous ship of the ill-fated Spanish Armada of 1588.

It is not long now before you arrive at the **Giant's Causeway**. If you don't want to visit the site itself, continue along the cliff path to the visitor centre. Alternatively, a steep descent down the Shepherd's Steps will bring you to the basalt columns at the shore. Legend dictates that the Irish giant Fionn MacCumhaill built the causeway as part of a bridge to Scotland, but scientists maintain that the hexagonal structures were created by cooling lava flows around 60 million years ago.

To finish, follow the 1km tarmac driveway from the causeway to the visitor centre, which is situated at the top of the hill to the west.

The golden sands of White Park Bay lead to Portbraddan, a tiny hamlet nestled at the base of sheer cliffs.

SLIEVE LEAGUE

These awesome sea cliffs are amongst the highest in Europe, with a classic hiking route to the top.

👍 Great for

- Catching your breath on first sight of the seaward abyss
- Standing atop some of the wildest coastline in Europe

☁ Conditions

- Calm or moderate winds and good visibility

🗺 Trip Details

- Distance: 10km (6 miles)
- Time: 3½–4½ hours
- Ascent: 500m (1,640ft)
- Map: OSi 1:50,000 sheet 10

▦ Access

- The route starts and finishes at Bunglass car park. From Killybegs, head west along the R263. Pass through the villages of Carrick and Teelin, then turn right onto a steep road signed for Bunglass. Pass though a gate (being careful to close it behind you) and continue to the parking area at the end of the road.
- Grid Ref: G 558 757
- GPS: 54.627161, -8.684329

Looking back towards Bunglass from the summit of Slieve League.

The classic view of the Slieve League cliffs from Bunglass, at the start of the route.

Slieve League is home to some of the highest and most impressive sea cliffs in Europe. Viewed from inland, the first impression is of an unremarkable whaleback of a mountain. Move to the seaward side, however, and you cannot help but be awestruck by the drama

and scale of the cliffs plunging into the Atlantic below. Thousands of years of wave action have eaten away at the mountain's south-western side, leaving sheer rock faces and precipitous slopes that stretch for 2km at a height of over 500m. It's a fantastic scene, with few rivals in the country in terms of sheer grandeur.

The good news for walkers is that this is also one of the most popular hillwalks in Donegal, and there is a well-trodden route to the summit. Yet despite the number of visitors, this is not an easy route – it has more in common with a mountain ascent than a low coastal path. There is a constructed trail for the first stretch, but beyond that you'll be following an informal path up sometimes steep slopes. Much of the distance is spent beside a sheer and unprotected drop, so avoid walking in poor visibility or strong winds, and take the utmost care near the edge.

The Walk

The route starts with a bang straight from Bunglass car park. If you've never been here before, the sudden sight of the cliffs falling half a kilometre to the ocean is utterly absorbing. Little wonder that this place is

Near the top of Slieve League. Does coastal scenery get more magnificent than this?

known as *Amharc Mór*, or 'The Big View'.

Begin by taking a well-constructed flagstone path that leaves from the north-eastern corner of the car park. The trail is maintained for the first section, where the number of passing feet is greatest. Head north-east around the cliffs, climbing several flights of steps to reach the top of Scregeighter (308m). The path now becomes more informal, though it remains obvious underfoot. Swing north-west and climb along the cliff edge to **The Eagles Nest** (323m), where the drop to the ocean is almost vertical.

The path now moves away from the cliffs and crosses a couple of small rises. Climb diagonally across the heather-covered slopes of Crockrawer to reach a ridge with fine views at 435m. At one point the ridge narrows to an exposed rib of rock, half a metre wide, with dangerous drops on both sides. Although the OS map marks **One Man's Pass** higher up the mountain, many Irish walkers believe the label has been misplaced, and this is the true location of the pass. In dry, calm conditions the arête offers a straightforward scramble, but you need to have a good head for heights. Alternatively, take the easy path on the right, which avoids all the difficulties and rejoins the crest of the ridge a little higher up.

The ridge broadens now and you emerge onto Slieve League's peat-covered eastern summit (560m). The true summit lies a kilometre further north-west, across another **fine ridge** (this is the section that has

Mountain Worship

Unlikely though it may seem, the remote and inhospitable upper slopes of Slieve League have been a place of religious worship for millennia. If you look down the eastern slopes as you near the summit, you should spot the ruins of a stone chapel and several beehive huts, the remnants of an early Christian monastery. Nearby lie some even older remains, which suggest the mountain was a pilgrimage site during pagan times too.

been wrongly marked on the OS map as One Man's Pass). The ridge here is enjoyably airy, but can be crossed without breaking stride. Again, an alternative path on the right avoids all the exposure.

A trig pillar marks the official highpoint at 595m, and there are fabulous views in all directions. On a clear day it's possible to identify landmarks in several counties, including Croagh Patrick on the southern side of Donegal Bay.

When you've fully enjoyed the panorama, simply reverse your outward route back to Bunglass below.

CLIFFS OF MOHER

This signed path passes above Ireland's most famous sea cliffs, with magnificent coastal scenery from start to finish.

Great for

- Thrilling views across plunging cliffs and thrusting headlands
- Enjoying the connoisseur's way to visit this famous coastline

Conditions

- Calm or moderate winds and good visibility

Trip Details

- Distance: 13km (8 miles)
- Time: 3½–4½ hours
- Ascent: 240m (790ft)
- Maps: OSi 1:50,000 sheets 51 and 57

Access

- **To the start:** The route starts in Doolin village. Either park in a long lay-by just west of the bridge over the Aille River in Fisher Street, or 1km north-west along the R479 at Doolin Community Centre.
- Grid Ref: R 068 965
- GPS: 53.012508, -9.384638

- **To the finish:** The walk finishes at a large car park beside Moher Sports Field, just south-east of Hag's Head. Alternatively you can get 700m closer to the route by continuing to a private car park at Kilconnel, which costs €2. From Liscannor, head west along the R478 for 2km, then turn left and follow signs for the Cliffs of Moher Coastal Walk.
- Grid Ref: R 027 885
- GPS: 52.938500, -9.448881

Looking south along the cliffs from near Aill Na Searrach.

Ireland's most famous sea cliffs are over 200m high and plumb vertical.

For most people, the Cliffs of Moher need no introduction. One of the most spectacular stretches of vertical cliff line in Ireland, it prides itself as the country's premier natural tourist attraction. The visitors come to gaze across an Atlantic rock face that stretches for over 8km at more than 100m high, and reaches its highest point at 214m.

By far the best way to appreciate the cliffs is to follow the footpath that runs along the top of the precipice. This offers the opportunity to explore the entire 14km of coastline between Doolin and Hag's Head, allowing you to experience the coast's quieter charms as well as the busy section around the visitor centre.

As with all linear routes, you do have to consider transport logistics to get back to the start. The simplest option is to use the **Cliffs of Moher Coastal Walk Shuttle Bus** (tel: 087 7755 098; www.cliffsofmohercoastalwalk.ie). This runs at least six times daily from Easter to October, with stops in Doolin, Liscannor, Kilconnel (beside Hag's Head) and the Cliffs of Moher Visitor Centre. A one-way trip between Kilconnel and Doolin costs €7. Park your car at one end of the route, then take the bus to the other end and walk back. At other times of the year, Bus Éireann's service No. 350 runs along the R478 between Liscannor and Doolin between three and five times daily (tel: 091 562 000; www.buseireann.

Signalling Napoleon

When you reach Hag's Head you won't miss Moher Tower, a three-storey, stone signal tower that crowns the headland. This was part of a network of 81 watchtowers constructed all around the Irish coast between 1804 and 1806, to help repel a possible French attack during the Napoleonic Wars. The towers were abandoned after Napoleon's defeat at Waterloo in 1815.

ie). Flag the bus down en route or arrange a special drop-off with the driver.

The route is well signed and follows an obvious trail that is constructed in most places. Unconstructed sections can be muddy and slippery however, so good footwear is advised. Much of the trail also passes along the edge of a sheer drop, with nothing to protect you from the void below. Avoid walking in high winds and exercise extreme caution near the cliff edge.

The Walk

Begin at the road junction on the eastern side of the Aille River bridge in Fisher Street, Doolin. From here, follow the road south-west. At the top of the rise, where the road veers left, continue straight ahead, passing a metal gate and joining a farm track.

trail disappears underfoot. Signs direct you along a fence to a cattle pen at the top of the field. Squeeze along the right side of the pen to reach a track near the R478 road.

Rejoin the constructed pathway and turn right across another field to return to the clifftop. Here, the first, breathtaking view across the **main cliffs** is suddenly revealed. The rock face is now 200m high, and plumb vertical or even undercut.

The route becomes more crowded as you enter the grounds around the Cliffs of Moher Visitor Centre. Here you pass O'Brien's Tower, a viewing point that dates from 1835. The path is heavily constructed now, with a protective line of stone slabs on the seaward side. Descend to a hollow, with the visitor centre 100m to the left. Entry to the centre is free, and there are toilets and a café should you need them.

The coastal route continues south along a brief stretch of tarmac, but the view is still incredible, with 5km of headlands visible between O'Brien's Tower and Hag's Head. As you exit the southern end of the visitor centre grounds, the trail dwindles again to an unprotected, earthen footpath. The path can be muddy here, so take care if it's slippery underfoot. The cliffs gradually lose height now, though there are plenty more good views all the way to **Hag's Head**, which is crowned by a partially ruined Napoleonic signal tower.

From Hag's Head, follow the path as it descends inland to a stone track, then continue onto a tarmac lane. The private car park at Kilconnel is located nearby, while Moher Sports Field, with its large, public car park, is some 700m further down the road.

Just before a second gate, turn right and cross two stiles. This brings you to a gravel footpath that runs above the rocky shore. After another 500m you pass the archaeological remains of a portal tomb in a field on the left, with an adjacent stile that allows you to examine the site.

The path veers inland now and climbs across a hillside to reach a higher section of cliffs. Continue ahead, passing above **Aill Na Searrach**, site of some of the biggest wave surfing in Europe. The next landmark is an open field, where the constructed

The view back over the main cliffs as you approach Hag's Head.

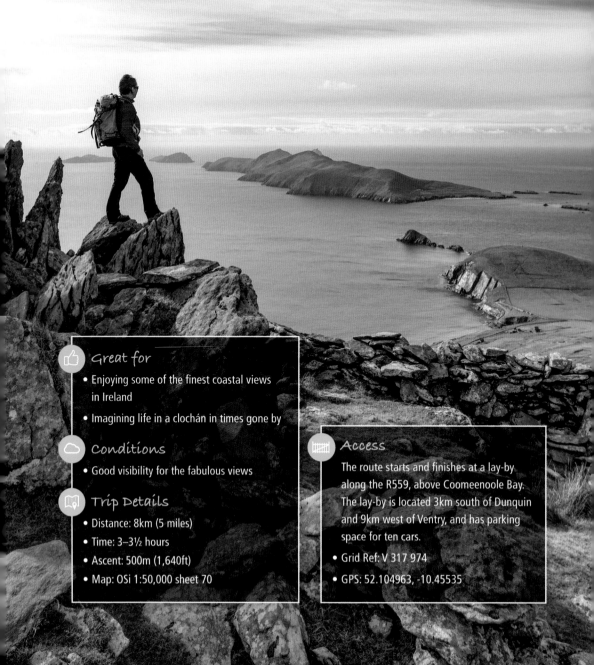

MOUNT EAGLE

Ancient ruins, spectacular island views and a mountain summit all feature on this fantastic little route at the tip of the Dingle Peninsula.

Great for

- Enjoying some of the finest coastal views in Ireland
- Imagining life in a clochán in times gone by

Conditions

- Good visibility for the fabulous views

Trip Details

- Distance: 8km (5 miles)
- Time: 3–3½ hours
- Ascent: 500m (1,640ft)
- Map: OSi 1:50,000 sheet 70

Access

The route starts and finishes at a lay-by along the R559, above Coomeenoole Bay. The lay-by is located 3km south of Dunquin and 9km west of Ventry, and has parking space for ten cars.

- Grid Ref: V 317 974
- GPS: 52.104963, -10.45535

Above: Descending back along the Dingle Way to the finish.
Opposite: There are fabulous views across the Blasket Islands from 424m Binn an Choma.

It is hard to think of a route that packs more variety into 8km than this one. It's essentially a short hillwalk, and includes all the sense of achievement of reaching a 516m summit. Yet the trip up and down the mountain includes such diversity and is enlivened by so many fabulous coastal views that you can't fail to finish it with a smile.

The walk follows paths for the first and final thirds of the route, but the middle section crosses open mountain terrain. Route finding is relatively simple here, though you'll need decent boots, and a compass and map in poor visibility. If the idea of climbing across open mountainside seems daunting, consider an out-and-back ascent along Mount Eagle's south-west ridge. This option follows a mountain path all the way, yet still allows you to appreciate the best views.

The Walk

From the lay-by, head south along the road for 60m. Look for a track on the left, guarded by a metal gate. There is a large stile beside the gate, and a waymarking post indicating the Dingle Way walking trail. This is your access point on and off the mountain. Cross the stile and follow a grassy track as it zigzags up the hillside. After several hairpin bends, the track

The Fahan Clocháns

The remarkable collection of antiquities known as the Fahan group includes at least 460 stone forts, dwellings and monuments. Most prominent from this route are the clocháns – beehive-shaped stone huts – some 414 of which cluster around the south-eastern slopes of Mount Eagle. Some of the earliest examples may have been built by early Christian monks but most are thought to date from the 12th century, when local farmers were marginalised by Norman invaders.

straightens and heads around the south-western shoulder of the hill. Here you cross another stile. The return route descends alongside the stone wall on your left, and if you want to stick to an obvious path and make an out-and-back trip to the summit, you should turn left here. To continue on the full circuit, keep following the Dingle Way and turn right along the wall instead.

You are now following a footpath east around the base of Mount Eagle, with a stone wall on your right. There are great views south to the conical outcrops of the Skellig Islands, and south-east across Dingle

Bay. A kilometre of so beyond the stile you'll begin to notice several curious stone formations in the fields below the path. These are the **Fahan clocháns** – stone huts that once housed a whole family each. The larger, circular stone structures are old ring forts.

Cross a mountain stream – Abhainn an Ghleanna – and continue along the path for roughly 400m. Now look for a stone wall that descends down the mountain from the left. Turn left here, and climb across open hillside on the right side of the wall.

The ascent is moderately steep, and easiest if you stick to the grassy strip beside the wall. At the top corner of the wall, climb diagonally right (north-east) towards the top of the shoulder, now crossing ankle-deep heather and moorland grass.

Roughly 1km beyond the wall the ground evens out, and you reach the concrete trig pillar that marks the **summit** of Mount Eagle. The views are good, but for an even better panorama, head north-west for 250m to the rim of the corrie holding **Mount Eagle Lough**. Here you can enjoy an expanded panorama that encompasses both the lake and the mountains of the Dingle and Iveragh Peninsulas, with many of Ireland's highest peaks displayed across the skyline.

When you're ready, return to the summit trig point. Now head south-west, following a line of wooden posts onto a path along the south-west shoulder. The trail leads along the crest of an increasingly well-defined ridge, descending through a really pleasurable

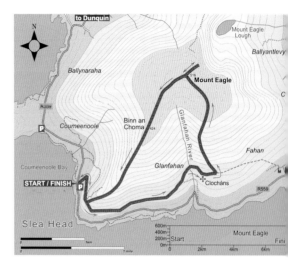

section of walking. By the time you reach the jagged outcrop of 424m **Binn an Choma**, the view over Coumeenoole Bay and Great Blasket Island is nothing short of spectacular.

Descend to a stone enclosure and pass around its right side, ignoring an orange arrow directing you left. Follow a broken stone wall down the ridge, then, just before you pass under a power line, cross to the left side of the wall. Descend along the wall until you reach a stile, which you should recognise from your outward journey. Turn right here, cross the stile, and retrace your initial steps back along the Dingle Way to the start.

Several 12th-century clocháns belonging to the Fahan group can be seen beside the route.

THE SHEEP'S HEAD

Follow signed paths around the tip of this remote peninsula, with wild scenery and fantastic coastal views throughout.

Great for

- Standing at the very end of an isolated peninsula
- Striding along an easy ridge with coastline on both sides

Conditions

- Calm or moderate winds and good visibility

Trip Details - Lighthouse Loop

- Distance: 4km (2½ miles)
- Time: 1–2 hours
- Ascent: 150m (490ft)

Trip Details – The Poet's Way

- Distance: 12.5km (8 miles)
- Time: 3½–4½ hours
- Ascent: 320m (1,050ft)

Access

- Both routes start and finish at a car park at the western tip of the Sheep's Head Peninsula. To access the area, follow the road along the southern side of the peninsula, passing through the village of Kilcrohane. From here, follow signs for 'Sheep's Head', continuing for a further 9km to reach the car park at the end of the road.
- Map: OSi 1:50,000 sheet 88
- Grid Ref: V 733 340
- GPS: 51.545871, -9.826562

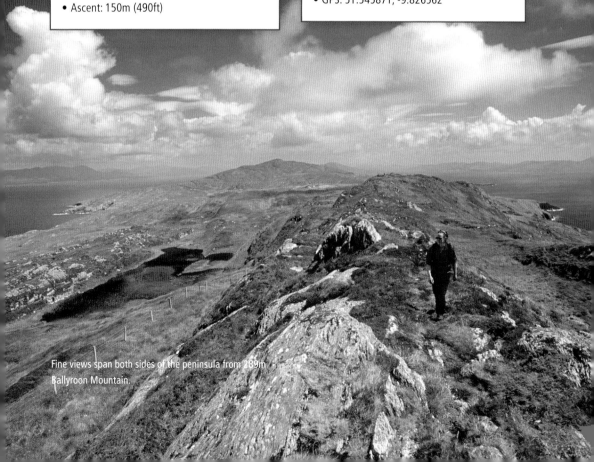

Fine views span both sides of the peninsula from 289m Ballyroon Mountain.

The Sheep's Head is the most isolated peninsula in south-west Ireland. Its wild, primeval atmosphere combines with fabulous coastal views to make it a wonderful place for a walk.

Two different circuits are described here, both fully signed, and both exploring the final few kilometres of land before the promontory finally concedes to the sea. Both follow part of the longer Sheep's Head Way, and are fully furnished with signposts, stiles, and footbridges. The short option – the Lighthouse Loop – is marked by blue arrows. It circumnavigates the far western tip of the peninsula, and encompasses what is arguably the most impressive section of the longer route. The Poet's Way is signed by red arrows. It begins by covering the same ground, but extends further east along the flanks of the headland, giving a better overall impression of the area and including an enjoyable traverse of Ballyroon Mountain, whose scenic summit provides the modest highpoint at 239m. Whichever route you choose, note the terrain underfoot is rugged and undulating, crossing thick moorland grass punctuated by outcrops of rock. Good boots are recommended for both outings.

The Walk

The long and short circuits follow the same route for the first 3km. From the car park, begin by continuing west along the road for 50m, then veer right onto a gravel footpath. This trail carries you across a delightful expanse of rugged upland, then passes the southern shore of scenic **Lough Akeen**.

At the end of the lake, cross a wooden footbridge, then climb to a helicopter landing pad encircled by white stones. **Sheep's Head Lighthouse** lies part way down the slope to the right of the helipad – you can access the building by descending a flight of concrete steps.

Return to the helipad and turn left onto the path that runs along the northern side of the peninsula. There are several wet hollows here that you may have to skirt around. Pass along the top of some 100m-high cliffs, then climb gradually to a trail junction. The short Lighthouse Loop turns right here, weaving across rock-studded ground to return to the car park.

To stay on the longer Poet's Way, keep straight ahead along the coast. Rocks become less frequent

Sheep's Head Lighthouse

In 1968, when Sheep's Head Lighthouse was built, there was no road to the end of the peninsula. It took over 250 trips by helicopter to transport the building materials from Kilcrohane. The beacon marks the entrance to Bantry Bay and though the structure itself is just 7m tall, the height of the cliff beneath it means the light sits 83m above sea level.

now, and you pass through swathes of thick grass. Descend past a pretty **sea inlet** decorated with a waterfall and a pair of rock arches, then continue over several grassy rises.

The route is fully signed and forms part of the longer Sheep's Head Way.

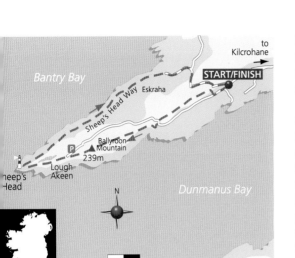

Soon the hamlet of Eskraha comes into sight ahead. Cross a stile and follow a track beneath the buildings. Turn left onto a minor road, then 100m later, turn right over another stile and climb steeply beside some fields.

This brings you to the spine of the peninsula, where you join a lane and follow it left for 50m.

Now turn right, returning to open terrain. The trail soon begins to contour along the southern side of the hill. Negotiate several more stiles and pass two small loughs before descending to a road.

Head left along the tarmac for 20m, then turn right onto a lane. The lane soon dwindles to a track, then shrinks to a footpath as you begin the ascent of **Ballyroon Mountain**. Climb along the apex of the ridge, with boulders and rock outcrops pushing through the grass below. The gradient is relatively benign, and fine views span both sides of the peninsula. As you near the summit, you pass a pile of rocks that is actually a ruined signal tower dating from the early 19th century. The tower was intact until 1990, when it was blown down in a gale.

Continue ahead to reach the official summit, which is marked by a trig point and fabulous views both north and south across the Beara, Iveragh and Mizen Head Peninsulas. The descent takes you past a square, concrete building, which was a look out post during the Second World War. From here it's just a short distance back to the car park where the route began.

Lough Akeen sits amid rugged upland near the tip of the peninsula.

ISLAND-HOPPING

WITH A COASTLINE measuring 7,500km, you'd expect Ireland to have a few islands. Well, it has more than a few; in fact, it has over 570. Around 30 of these are currently inhabited. A few more were once occupied but now lie abandoned, while the remainder exist as entirely natural outposts that have never seen more than the briefest of visits by humans.

With such a wealth of natural resources, Irish island-hopping is a fascinating pastime. The weather may not be as reliable as in Greece, but the islands themselves are every bit as interesting. Each one exudes its own special atmosphere, centred around its intimate connection to nature and the elements. All sorts of wildlife thrive out here, from seabirds nesting on precipitous cliffs, to seals basking on rocky reefs and whales cruising past in offshore waters. Even on populated islands the wildlife usually outnumbers the people. The pace of life is significantly slower, culture and customs survive that have been lost on the mainland, and there is a sense of escape from the hustle and bustle of modern humanity.

It would be an absorbing project to try and visit all of Ireland's islands, but most people content themselves with sampling just a few. The four islands chosen for this bucket list are amongst the most intriguing, and make fascinating places to start. Once you arrive, the only way to explore most of these outposts properly is by foot. Each description includes a walking route that helps you uncover the island's best features.

You'll also find numerous other islands detailed elsewhere in this book, including Inishmurray on page 201. Transport can be arranged to all these places, and they make a great next step on your Irish island odyssey.

Given the eroding force of ocean swells, it comes as no surprise that the majority of Ireland's islands lie off its exposed Atlantic coast. Here the relentless battering of the waves has combined with the idiosyncrasies of geology to create of host of different islands, each one unique in character and form.

Some of the closer islands have tidal causeways, and are actually separated from the mainland for only part of the time. Omey Island in County Galway falls into this category. At low tide you can walk or even drive out across a sandbar, but you'll need to keep an eye on the time; stay too long and you'll find yourself cut off until the tide recedes again.

Others islands are separated by permanent channels, but lie so close to the mainland they are connected by bridge. Valentia Island in Kerry and Achill, Ireland's largest island, are good examples here. The convenience of travelling to and from these places means they are essentially extensions of the mainland, and maintain relatively high populations of people.

Sometimes even a relatively short channel is treacherous at water level, yet the construction of a permanent bridge is uneconomic. The famous rope bridge at Carrick-a-Rede – now in fact a sturdy metal suspension bridge – is one solution to this problem (see page 59 for a walk here). Another unique solution has been found for Dursey Island in Cork, where a cable car has been erected across the channel. This is the only cable car in Ireland – indeed the only cable car spanning an ocean chasm in Europe – and the experience of swooping high above the sea is unparalleled.

Ireland's Islands Fact File

Largest island: Achill – 143 square kilometres
Most remote inhabited island: Tory – 12km offshore
Highest island peak: Knockmore, 462m, on Clare Island
Most popular island attraction: Dun Aengus fort, on Inis Mór

Above: Many islands have a long and poignant human history. The deserted village on Inishkea South.
Main image: Clare Island is the country's most mountainous island, reaching 462m at the summit of Knockmore.

Above: Every island has a unique character. Exploring the rugged west coast of Arranmore in Donegal.
Below: If you have your own boat you can travel to the islands independently. Eagle Island, in County Mayo.

Of course, there are many other islands that lie far offshore, sometimes separated by many kilometres of turbulent seas. These remote outposts often boast spectacular coastal scenery, and have hardy inhabitants who persevere despite the hardships of their location.

Human History

Many Irish islands have a long history of human settlement, reaching back as far as Neolithic times. This reflects the fact that Ireland's earliest inhabitants were seafarers, dependent on the sea for much of their livelihood. However, many of the most visible remains date from the early Christian period, around the sixth century. This was the era of saints and scholars, when islands provided ideal locations for the establishment of monasteries, offering both a humble, contemplative existence and freedom from persecution.

By the 800s the Vikings had arrived, often using the islands as a base for launching their raids. A more settled period followed, and by 1841, there were over 34,000 people living on Irish islands. The Great Famine struck harshly and island populations continued to decline in subsequent years. Services like electricity and medical care were also slow to arrive in such remote communities and by the 1950s and

1960s, prolonged periods of bad weather made the Irish government embark on a programme of forcible evacuation of many islands. Population numbers have continued to dwindle ever since, and today the country has fewer than 8,500 island residents.

Practicalities

The main issue in terms of visiting the islands is getting there. With the exception of Dursey, all the islands described in this section necessitate a boat journey. If you have your own boat – whether a sea kayak, yacht or RIB – you can travel independently, and the journey is likely to provide at least half the excitement. If not, then you'll need to rely on a local boat operator.

All islands are exposed to adverse sea conditions. This storm wave is crashing 75m high above Mayo's Eagle Island.

All the main inhabited islands, and some of the more popular unsettled ones, have a scheduled ferry service. Contact the operator in advance to check departure times and reserve a place. All services are dependent on weather and sea conditions, so double-check sailing times again on the day before travelling. During bad weather it is not uncommon for ferries to be disrupted or cancelled altogether.

Also check the forecast for the duration of your stay. If the weather changes dramatically, your return passage may be cancelled and you could find yourself stranded until conditions improve. In general, the best time to travel is from Easter to September: the sea is calmer, there are more birds and flowers, and ferry services are most frequent.

All the trips described here can be completed in a single day. If you have the time, though, it's always worth extending your visit to stay overnight. This gives a far better impression of the realities of island life, and allows you time to soak up that special island atmosphere.

The provisions you need to bring depend on the island. Some large, inhabited islands have a well-developed tourist infrastructure, with a range of shops, restaurants and accommodation. If this is the case, you won't need to carry much with you. Other islands have no facilities at all. Bring all your own supplies, including food, water and toilet paper. Shelter may be limited, so carry both sun cream and warm, waterproof clothing to protect yourself in all weather conditions. Hiking shoes are generally the best option for your feet.

Many of the populated islands have designated campsites, and wild camping is generally tolerated on the uninhabited ones. Please camp discreetly and follow the principles of Leave No Trace (see www.leavenotraceireland.org/seven-principles). Also make sure ferry operators know if you intend to stay overnight, so they are not concerned when you don't turn up for the evening ferry.

Getting there can be half the fun. On the ferry to the Saltee Islands in Wexford.

TORY ISLAND

This remote north-west outpost boasts a spectacular coastline and unique island atmosphere.

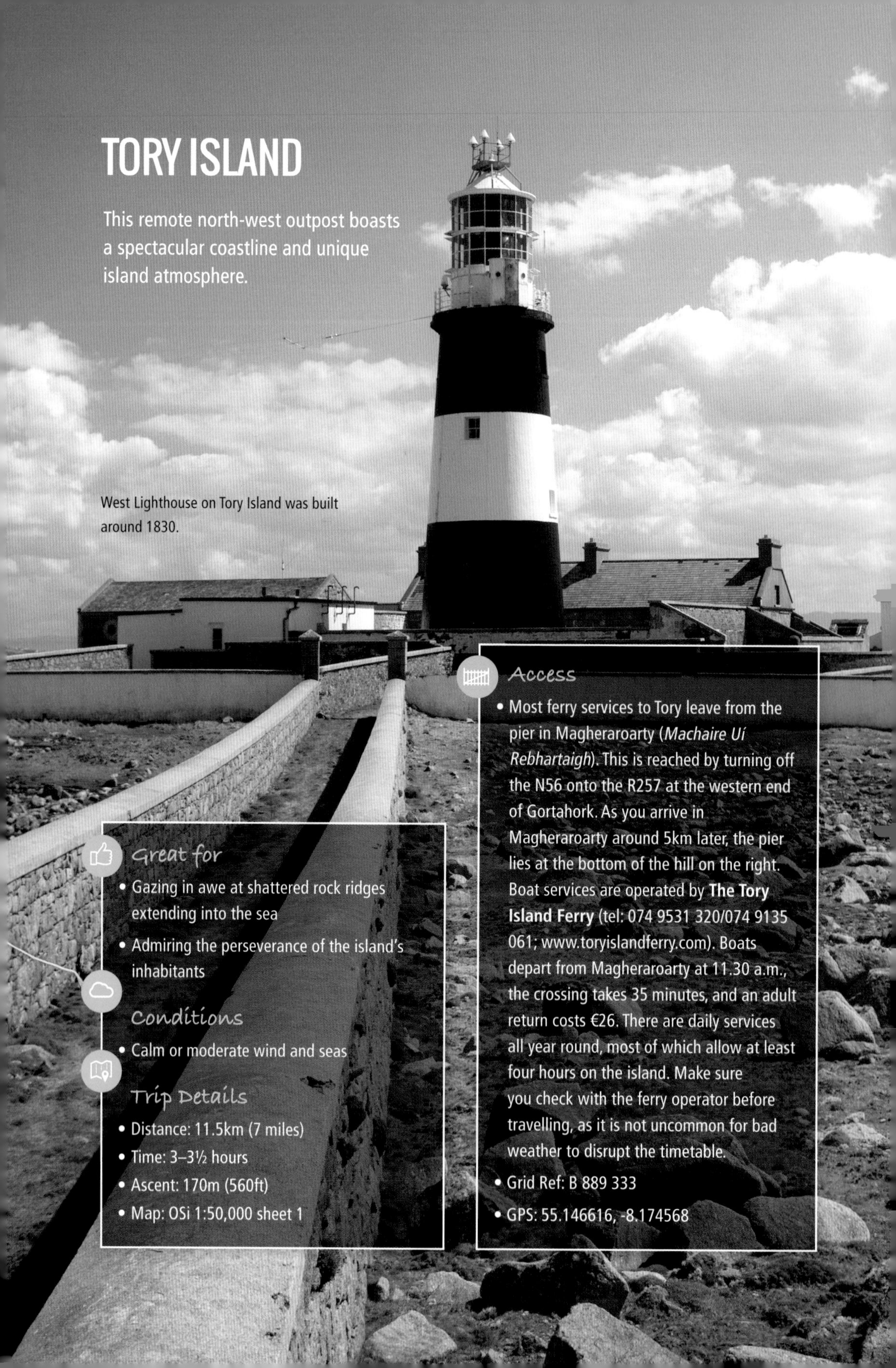

West Lighthouse on Tory Island was built around 1830.

Great for

- Gazing in awe at shattered rock ridges extending into the sea
- Admiring the perseverance of the island's inhabitants

Conditions

- Calm or moderate wind and seas

Trip Details

- Distance: 11.5km (7 miles)
- Time: 3–3½ hours
- Ascent: 170m (560ft)
- Map: OSi 1:50,000 sheet 1

Access

- Most ferry services to Tory leave from the pier in Magheraroarty (*Machaire Uí Rebhartaigh*). This is reached by turning off the N56 onto the R257 at the western end of Gortahork. As you arrive in Magheraroarty around 5km later, the pier lies at the bottom of the hill on the right. Boat services are operated by **The Tory Island Ferry** (tel: 074 9531 320/074 9135 061; www.toryislandferry.com). Boats depart from Magheraroarty at 11.30 a.m., the crossing takes 35 minutes, and an adult return costs €26. There are daily services all year round, most of which allow at least four hours on the island. Make sure you check with the ferry operator before travelling, as it is not uncommon for bad weather to disrupt the timetable.
- Grid Ref: B 889 333
- GPS: 55.146616, -8.174568

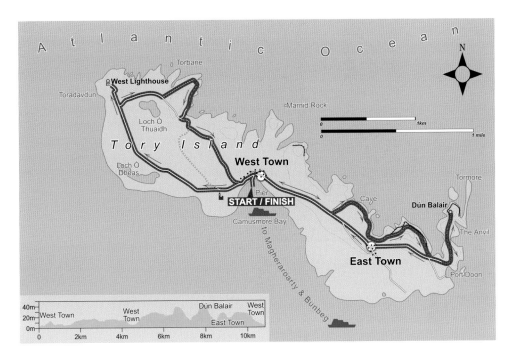

The storm-battered island of Tory lies 12km off the coast of Donegal and is the most remote inhabited outpost in Ireland. At 5km long and 1km wide, it is also one of the country's smallest populated islands, and an evocative and intriguing place to visit.

Most human activity on Tory centres around West Town, where the ferry docks. Birds are far more numerous than people, though, and the large population of summer seabirds includes a circus of puffins. Tory is also home to the largest concentration of corncrakes in Ireland, and the distinctive, rasping call of this endangered bird can often be heard around West Town.

The best walk on the island is a figure-of-eight circuit with two distinct loops. The first, western half of the route is signed as the Tory Island Loop Walk. Yet the eastern side of the island boasts the most dramatic coastline, so a second, unsigned loop to the island's north-eastern tip is also recommended. The sheer cliffs and razor-sharp arêtes that cluster here provide the scenic highlight of the day. This section takes you along the top of steep drops, so take care near the edge and avoid the area in high winds.

Life on the Edge

Tory's isolation makes it particularly susceptible to the impact of Atlantic storms. After a ferocious, eight-week onslaught in 1974, the government made plans for the permanent evacuation of the island. This never happened, thanks to a local campaign that raised funds, established an electricity supply and created a proper ferry service. A community of around 140 inhabitants still perseveres, and the island remains a central part of the Donegal Gaeltacht, renowned for its unique form of Ulster Irish.

The Walk

From the ferry pier, walk up into **West Town**. The village's two main monuments are visible immediately. Above the slipway is a 12th-century tau cross, one of only two T-shaped cruciforms in Ireland. A small distance away lies a ruined sixth- or seventh-century round tower. These two sites are all that remain of a monastery founded here by St Colmcille, but largely destroyed by English troops in the 1600s.

Tory's north-east coast provides spectacular views to the headland of Dún Balair.

Pass the tau cross, then turn left and head west along the road. Before long you pass the round tower, then a small stone enclosure on the left known as *Móirsheisear*, or the Church of the Seven. This commemorates seven islanders who drowned when their currach capsized.

Turn left at the next junction and follow the lane for 1.5km to reach the **lighthouse**, which was built between 1828 and 1832. At the lighthouse gate, the route turns right and continues along a track. Before you leave, it's worth walking to the western end of the lighthouse, where a small graveyard contains eight bodies recovered from the British navy vessel HMS *Wasp*, which sank close to Tory in 1884.

The track away from the lighthouse is partially paved by rough, granite cobbles. Pass Loch Ó Thuaidh, then turn left beside the ruins of a former barracks. A side loop takes you around a headland and past a small slipway before returning to the track, where you turn left.

Follow the track back into West Town. The signed walk ends here, but this route turns left and continues south-east along the road towards East Town. After 1km, leave the road and head left to reach the cliffs, which lie just a short distance away. Pass a large hole in the ground, where a cave roof has collapsed. Then follow the cliffs south-east around a deep inlet, and onto a wild promontory with stunning views east to the headland of **Dún Balair**.

Descend carefully along a grassy slope, then cross the narrow isthmus that connects Dún Balair to the rest of Tory. Turn north here and climb the increasingly rocky slope to the summit cairn. This is the highest spot on the island at 83m and provides a superlative viewpoint, with the whole of Tory laid out before you. To the north, a huge blade of rock extends far out to sea, with several weathered pinnacles ranged along the crest. The whole scene is remarkably impressive. The summit of Dún Balair also marks your turning point. Descend to the road and turn right, walking through East Town and back to the ferry pier where you started.

Top: Fishing boats and the harbour at West Town on Tory, where the ferry docks.
Bottom: Dún Balair is a superlative viewpoint, with the whole of Tory laid out before you.

GREAT BLASKET ISLAND

An atmospheric route through a deserted village and along the mountainous spine of this wild Atlantic outpost.

👍 Great for

- Standing at a 292m summit with slopes dropping away to the ocean
- Spending quiet time in the deserted village, imagining life a century ago

☁ Conditions

- Calm seas and good visibility

📖 Trip Details

- Distance: 9km (5½ miles)
- Time: 3–3½ hours
- Ascent: 450m (1,480ft)
- Map: OSi 1:50,000 sheet 70

🏛 Access

- Several operators provide ferries to Great Blasket Island, but scheduled services only run from Easter to September. Most people leave from Dunquin, where the crossing takes 20 minutes and costs €30. Try **Blasket Island Ferries** (tel: 085 775 1045; www.blasketisland.com) or **Larry's Blasket Ferry** (tel: 087 743 5442). Alternatively a 45-minute ferry runs from Dingle town and costs €40 – contact **Blasket Islands Eco Ferry** for details (tel: 086 335 3805; www.dinglebaycharters.com).
- Grid Ref: V 316 999
- GPS: 52.125418, -10.460032

Follow a green track away from the deserted village on Great Blasket Island.

Situated 2km off the tip of the Dingle Peninsula, the Blasket Islands are Ireland's most westerly land mass. The largest island, Great Blasket, measures 6km long by 1.2km wide, and was inhabited until 1953. Even at its peak, this small Irish-speaking fishing community never included more than 175 people. The vast majority of the land is now owned by the state, which has proposed that the island be preserved as a national park.

The ruined stone buildings of the deserted village provide the first, poignant landmark of the route. From this evocative start, you climb up and around the mountainous spine of the island. Though the landscape is wild and remote, the terrain underfoot is relatively easy. Paths and tracks are followed throughout, and the route is suitable for most fit walkers. You also have a high chance of seeing various species of wildlife, including seals, rabbits, seabirds, basking sharks and dolphins. Overall this is an exhilarating and memorable route, which will remain etched on your mind long afterwards.

Note that good weather is essential for this outing, both because the island has limited shelter

Putting it in Context

To get the most out of your trip to Great Blasket, it's well worth reading one of several evocative first-hand accounts by the island's former inhabitants. Try Tomás O'Crohan's *The Islandman*, or Gearóid Cheaist Ó Catháin's *The Loneliest Boy in the World – The Last Child of the Great Blasket Island*. You could also visit the Blasket Centre in Dunquin, which houses a variety of exhibits detailing the long and varied history of these islands.

and because ferry services do not operate in adverse conditions.

The Walk

From the landing stage where you're deposited by the ferry, follow a grassy path up through the **deserted village**. The 1841 census recorded 153 people living here, in 28 houses. Most of the buildings are now roofless stone ruins, though there are a few buildings that have been repaired in recent years.

Taking a rest on the slopes of Slievedonagh.

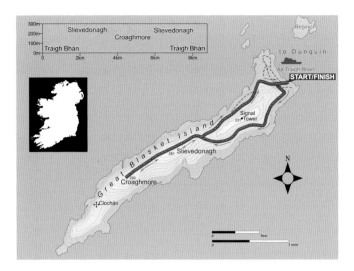

Head towards the upper left corner of the settlement, where you'll find a green track. Turn left here and follow the track, climbing onto the southern slopes of the hill marked on the map as point 231m. After a fairly steep initial ascent, the track evens out and contours south-west. This enjoyable stretch of high, easy walking is further enhanced by fabulous views to the Iveragh and Beara Peninsulas, and to the sharp, distant cones of the Skellig Islands.

At the western side of the hill the track climbs to the ridge top, where you arrive at a junction. Turn left here and head west along a narrow footpath. Soon you pass the site of An Dún, an Iron Age fort that dates from 800 BC. There's little to see above the ground today, but the site attests to the island's long history of habitation.

Continue to follow the path along the ridge, climbing through bracken to reach the broad summit of Slievedonagh (281m). Croaghmore, the island's highest point, is now clearly visible ahead. Descend to a col, with the island narrowing inexorably around you. The northern slopes are now precipitous, and you're walking along a pleasantly **narrow arête** with more gentle slopes to the south.

A final climb brings you to the trig point at the 292m summit of **Croaghmore**. A circle of stones indicates an old clochán below, and fabulous coastal views include the western Blasket Islands of Inishnabro and Inishvickillane.

Though it's possible to continue further south-west towards the end of the island, Croaghmore marks the turning point for most walkers. Reverse your journey along the ridge to the junction in the col just east of Slievedonagh. Turn left here and join a track that makes a gradual descent along the northern side of the island, enjoying more fine views ahead to the mountains of the Dingle Peninsula.

As you return to the eastern tip of the island the deserted village can be seen below, with the beautiful sandy cove and turquoise water of An Tráigh Bhán straight ahead. It's easy to pass any spare time exploring this area before you head back to the landing stage for the departure of your boat.

Nearly there: approaching Great Blasket Island on the ferry.

DURSEY ISLAND

Climb aboard Ireland's only cable car to discover the old villages and mountain ridges of this evocative island.

 Great for

- Admiring the views from a 250m signal tower
- Trusting the cable as you sway high above an ocean chasm

 Conditions

- Calm to moderate winds and good visibility

Trip Details

- Distance: 11.5km (7 miles)
- Time: 3½–4½ hours
- Ascent: 410m (1,350ft)
- Map: OSi 1:50,000 sheet 84

Access

- The route starts and finishes at Dursey Island cable car station. From Castletownbere, head west along the R572 for 22km, following signs for Dursey Island. Park in a large car park at the end of the road. The cable car carries just 6 people, and operates daily except in high winds. From June to September it runs continuously from 9.30 a.m. to 8 p.m., and has scheduled service periods during the rest of the year. For the full timetable, see www.durseyisland.ie. The crossing takes about ten minutes and costs €10 return.
- Grid Ref: V 508 419
- GPS: 51.610252, -10.155059

Walking along the old lane near the start of the route on Dursey.

The old-fashioned cable car ensures an exciting introduction to Dursey Island.

Dursey Island measures 6.5km long by 1.5km wide, and forms a hilly outpost at the tip of the Beara Peninsula. It's separated from the mainland by a channel just 250m wide. Though narrow, this sound has a strong tidal race and is treacherous even in calm conditions. Fortunately, there's an alternative means of transport, in the form of Ireland's only cable car. The experience of swooping across the water in this small, old-fashioned cabin provides a fitting introduction to an atmospheric island.

Dursey's long history of human habitation still continues. Though just two permanent residents remained in the island's three hamlets by 2017, a larger group of islanders return during the summer months. For walkers, the island's sometimes poignant history combines with an open ridgeline and stunning coastal scenery to provide a memorable day out.

Viking Legacy

Despite its apparent isolation, Dursey has been inhabited since the Bronze Age. It features in ancient Irish mythologies, and its name comes the Norse word *Thjorsey*, meaning Bull Island. This is a legacy left by the Vikings, who operated a slave depot here around AD 1000.

The route described here is signed throughout. It takes you along the old road towards the western tip of the island, then climbs over the hilltops on the return. The off-road terrain consists mainly of short grass, but boots are recommended for the occasional patch of bog and rock.

The Walk

From the cable car station, begin by following the single-track lane that contours along the southern side of the island. The first landmark you pass is the stone ruin of St Mary's Abbey, an old monastery and graveyard on the left. Just beyond this, the islet of Illanebeg was the site of an infamous massacre in 1602, when Queen Elizabeth I's forces stormed a fort on the island and killed over 300 islanders, many of whom were simply thrown off the cliff.

After 1km you pass the hamlet of Ballynacallagh, the first of Dursey's three settlements. During the summer, the island's population is swelled by a number of seasonal residents, and there's an interesting juxtaposition between the ruined and renovated cottages, all surrounded by a patchwork of stone-walled fields. The second village, Kilmichael, comes less than a kilometre further on.

Keep left at a fork and continue along the road for another 3km, climbing gently to the third hamlet of

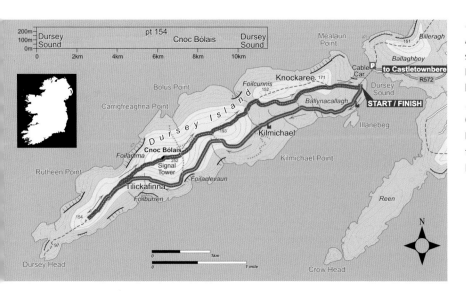

Below left:
A remarkably intact signal tower marks Dursey's 252m high point.
Below right:
On a fine day, Dursey offers fabulous views like this one.

Tilickafinna. The return route turns right at a signpost shortly before the end of the road, but it's worth continuing along a grassy track at least as far as the rise ahead. This **154m summit** provides fine views over the western tip of Dursey, with its three attendant islets, The Cow, The Calf and Bull Rock. Bull Rock, the northernmost island, holds a large sea arch, and was once believed to be a doorway to the Otherworld.

It is possible to continue all the way down to the western tip of Dursey, but many people are happy to turn around at point 154m. From here, retrace your steps back to the signpost, then turn left onto the 'Mountain Route'. This informal path climbs the hillside towards the highest point on the island.

Near the top of the slope, on the left, the remains of the word EIRE can be seen written in white stones on the ground. This served as a navigational marker for pilots during the Second World War. The 252m summit of **Cnoc Bólais** also holds a remarkably intact signal tower dating from 1804, and provides incredible coastal views in all directions.

Descend eastwards from the summit, crossing a green metal stile in the col below. Another gentle ascent and descent bring you over the next rise, then you cross another stile in the subsequent saddle. Continue to follow the path around the southern side of the next hill, where a signpost indicates a choice of routes. You could drop back to the road for the final kilometre, but the more interesting option is to keep left and continue along the Mountain Route. Climb around the southern slopes of Knockree to reach the **crest of a ridge**, where a wonderful bird's-eye perspective across Dursey Sound is revealed. From here, a final short descent to the right brings you back to the cable car station.

GREAT SALTEE ISLAND

Great Saltee is one of Europe's most important bird sanctuaries, and as close as you can get to a wildlife safari in Ireland.

 Great for

- Laughing at puffins, the clowns of the sea
- Close-up encounters with a large and raucous gannet colony

 Conditions

- Dry weather between May and July

 Access

- Boats to Great Saltee leave from the harbour in Kilmore Quay, around 20km south-west of Wexford town.
- Map: OSi 1:50,000 sheet 77
- Grid Ref: S 965 032
- GPS: 52.172821, -6.589052

Puffins can be seen darting in and out of their burrows at the top of the Saltee Island cliffs.

Puffins: the Sea Parrot

Of the 375 species of bird that have been recorded on Great Saltee, puffins are the most endearing. Some 2,000 of these comical birds nest here each summer. Their parrot-like beaks grow dull during winter months, but turn bright orange during the breeding season. Adult puffins form partnerships for life, seeking each other out on the same cliff each year, and incubating a single egg at the back of a burrow in the ground.

If you fancy a safari but don't want to fork out for a ticket to Africa, why not look closer to home? But where could you find safari conditions in Ireland? Top of the list must be Great Saltee Island, 5km off the coast of County Wexford. You won't see lions or leopards, but you will have close encounters with comical puffins, raucous gannets, fluffy chicks and fearsome shags. This is a sight, sound and smell sensation that makes any zoo pale in comparison, and as a showcase of wild birdlife, there are few places as impressive in the country.

Great Saltee is a relatively small island, at 219 acres, yet at the height of the breeding season it's home to some 50,000 seabirds. You can wander within metres of the birds and their nests, so much so that you have to take care not to step on chicks or eggs.

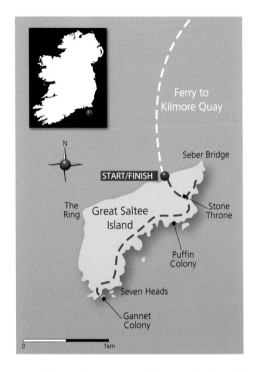

To get the most from your trip, time your visit for peak breeding season, from early May to late July. Bear in mind that there are no facilities and no shelter here, so make sure to bring plenty of food, drink, sun cream and warm and waterproof clothing. Binoculars and a bird identification book are optional extras.

If you're an experienced sea kayaker it's possible to paddle from Kilmore Quay to Great Saltee. The tides can be tricky however, and you'll need to watch out for several hazards including an underwater reef known as St Patrick's Bridge. When the island's owners are in residence a flag will be flying from the flagpole, and visits must be restricted to 11 a.m. – 4.30 p.m. Note, too, that camping and campfires are both prohibited.

Guided Excursions

Most people reach the island by climbing aboard the **Saltee Island Ferry** (tel: 087 252 9736), run by Declan Bates. Contact him in advance to book your passage. Services leave at 10 or 11 a.m. and return mid-afternoon, allowing around five hours on the island. The trip costs €25 per adult, with children half price.

It's a sound and smell sensation to stand beside the gannet colony at the south-eastern tip of Great Saltee Island.

A path leads through bracken, passing above bird-filled bays along the shore on Dursey Island.

The Trip

There's no quay on Great Saltee, so boats draw as close as they can to the shore, then use inflatable RIBs to shuttle visitors to dry land. The odds are you'll still have to clamber across boulders to reach the beach however, so it's worth bringing waterproof sandals to avoid wetting your shoes.

Once on terra firma, head inland up a flight of concrete steps. Follow an obvious, grassy path to a high point in the centre of the island. Here you'll find a **stone throne**, one of several accoutrements added by Michael Neale, a colourful character who fulfilled a childhood dream when he purchased these islands in 1943, then crowned himself Prince Michael the First.

From the throne, head east to reach the coast near a sea stack that is white with gannets. The chasm below is home to many of the island's grey seals, a population that numbers up to 120 animals. Already there are plenty of seabirds, but for the best experience, begin to walk south along the coast. Here you'll find a **puffin colony** gathered around the top of a steep cliff. With their waddling gait, short wings and colourful bill, these charming birds will keep you enthralled for hours.

Continue to follow the cliffs south-west. For the next 500m or so, the coast oscillates past a series of promontories and bays, the cliff ledges providing perfect nesting sites for large colonies of razorbill and guillemot.

Follow the footpath south through flowers and bracken, climbing towards the highest point of the island at 58m. The narrow, rocky path now clings to the clifftop, with a couple of exposed scrambling moves required in places. Amongst the rocks you may see fluffy gull chicks, while green-eyed shags hiss aggressively as you pass.

An onslaught of noise and smell heralds your arrival at the south-eastern tip of the island. This is the main **gannet colony**, where generations of birds have constructed a tight cluster of nests. Each nest is carefully located just beyond pecking distance of its neighbours. It's possible to approach within metres of these elegant birds, which have a wingspan of up to 2m, making them the largest seabird in the North Atlantic.

When you're ready, simply retrace your steps to return to the ferry.

INLAND CANOEING

The Blackwater River in Cork cuts a verdant corridor between beautiful wooded banks.

IRELAND has a remarkable array of inland waterways, and the best way to explore them fully is by open canoe. Whether you're heading out for a few hours or for a multi-day adventure, the essence is to glide silently across rivers and lakes, journeying along the water and feeling like an integral part of the nature around you. It's about the joy of simple strokes, darting kingfishers and evening campfires. If you want to travel in harmony with the planet, this is how to do it.

Despite being a country ripe with opportunity, open canoeing is not a well-developed pastime in Ireland. Enthusiasts from North America can't understand it – we have interconnected lough, river and canal systems that stretch across the country, yet barely anybody out exploring them.

Canoeing isn't a hard sport – you can head off on your own after learning just a few basic strokes. Do it solo, with friends or bring the whole family – the choice is yours. And if you have a touring or sea kayak, there's nothing to stop you completing similar trips in those boats too.

Ireland's Waterways at a Glance

Canoeists are spoilt for choice in Ireland. There are myriad loughs in every county, joined by a vast network of rivers and canals. Long-distance paddlers will find multiple cross-country itineraries, including the Shannon and Erne systems, which combine to offer over 350km of waterway between Counties Donegal

The World's First Boat

The canoe was the first true boat to be used by humans. The earliest known example is the Pesse canoe, which was uncovered in the Netherlands and dates from between 8200 and 7600 BC. Other examples have been found throughout history and in every part of the world, falling into three basic types: bark canoes, skin boats and wooden dugouts.

and Limerick. Side links via the Royal and Grand Canals and the River Barrow extend the possibilities to Dublin and Waterford. The wide range of routes is a legacy of our history: before the advent of road transportation, Ireland's waterways provided one of the primary means of shipping goods around the country.

Before heading out, choose what sort of water you want to explore. Rivers generally have some amount of flow, helping you cover ground more quickly, while tree-lined banks provide good shelter from the wind. Do your research carefully, though, to find out about any rapids or weirs along the route. Loughs can be great fun too, especially if there are plenty of islands to explore and camp on. Don't underestimate the potential for bad weather on big lakes, however; in windy conditions you can find yourself wrestling to

Meet like-minded enthusiasts at events such as the Ulster Canoe Festival each September.

Canoes are great for touring waterside sites. Ross Castle, County Kerry.

keep the boat straight, while waves start to break all around. Sheltered coastal inlets are another option, though you should have more experience – and a proper sea kayak – to venture out onto the open sea.

Wherever you paddle inland, please be aware of the problems associated with invasive aquatic species. Ireland is currently battling invasions of several non-native plants and animals, which spread disease and harm local wildlife. Some water bodies are already polluted with these organisms, while others remain pest-free. To avoid spreading the problem, all water users are asked to be extra vigilant when moving between different locations. Clean, wash and dry all your equipment thoroughly after each outing, checking all nooks and crannies for species that may be secretly hitchhiking on your boat. For more details, see www.invasivespeciesireland.com.

Boats and Paddles

There is some degree of semantic confusion in Ireland over the difference between a canoe and a kayak; most people use the term 'canoeing' to describe

A Canoeist's Prayer

God grant me the serenity to portage those sections I must, the courage to run the rapids I can, and the wisdom to know the difference.

both. Yet there's a significant difference between the two activities. A kayak has an enclosed cockpit that your feet slip inside. Kayakers sit down low and use a double-bladed paddle. Canoes – also known as Canadian or open canoes – are taller boats with a long top opening. Canoeists adopt an upright sitting or kneeling position, and propel themselves with a single-bladed paddle.

Modern canoes can be made from a variety of material, but these days, most people start in a plastic boat. There is a whole range of different sizes too. If you're thinking about paddling either tandem (with two people) or with a family, you'll need a boat about 17ft long. Longer boats are quicker and easier to paddle straight, and hold more gear, though they're

susceptible to being blown off-course by the wind. If you're planning to do a lot of soloing (paddling on your own) and prefer a more manoeuvrable craft, consider a boat as short as 13ft.

Apart from the boat, the other most important piece of kit is your paddle. These can be made from wood (most popular), plastic (cheap and cheerful) or carbon fibre (mainly for whitewater). Length is important here – a taller person needs a longer paddle. To calculate the right length for you, sit inside a canoe and measure the vertical distance from your nose to the waterline. This measurement should be the same as the distance from the paddle grip to the top of the blade.

Other Equipment

It goes without saying that everybody who partakes in watersports should be a confident swimmer. Wear a buoyancy aid at all times, plus a helmet and wetsuit or drysuit if you're tackling whitewater.

Other equipment will depend on the length of your excursion. For a day trip, a map, packed lunch, mobile phone and spare clothing may suffice. Overnight trips take rather more preparation, with camping gear and supplies packed into barrels or dry bags and secured inside the boat. Unless you can devise a circular route, shuttles between the start and finish points must be organised too. Two vehicles or a bike can be helpful here.

Emergencies

In case of emergencies on the water, call 999 or 112 and ask for the police, ambulance or coastguard. The coastguard can also be contacted directly on VHF channel 16.

Getting Started

The person who sits at the back of a canoe (in the stern) is the one who steers, while any passengers at

From top: Descending Lucan weir during the Liffey Descent, Ireland's biggest whitewater race; For overnight trips, pack your gear into barrels or dry bags secured inside the boat. Crom Estate, Upper Lough Erne; Battle of the rapids: in the heat of the action at the annual Mourne Whitewater Race, County Tyrone. (Graham Service)

A perfect autumn day for a paddle on Lough Erne.

the bow or in the centre provide the engine. It helps if everyone aboard knows a few strokes, but it's essential for the stern paddler, the 'J-stroke' being the most important one to master. You will find numerous canoe tutorials online, but it's invaluable having someone to show you the basics.

If you have no previous experience, begin by contacting someone who does. There are numerous clubs, outdoor centres and commercial operators around Ireland, all willing to help you get started. Either pay for a guided trip or instruction course, or join a club to learn organically from more experienced paddlers. Check www.canoe.ie or www.canoeni.com for lists of groups and operators.

Extending Your Skills

After mastering the basics, consider taking a training course to extend your knowledge and ability. If you progress though Canoeing Ireland's Open Canoe Skills levels 2, 3 and 4, you'll be a pretty competent paddler by the end. There are also several canoeing events, such as the Ulster Canoe Festival in September, where you can get together with like-minded enthusiasts and learn new techniques.

By the time you have Level 3 skills, you should be ready to enter the country's whitewater races. With courses that descend rapids and weirs, these make an exhilarating day out. The biggest race of all is the Liffey Descent, an annual event that covers 28km and ten weirs. With around 1,000 participants each year, the scene at the bottom of some weirs is little short of carnage. Safety cover is excellent, however, and it's an event that every Irish paddler should aspire to completing at least once in their careers.

Finding Out More

Books: *Irish Canoe Classics: 34 Great Canoe & Kayak Trips* by Eddie Palmer and Tony Monaghan details many of the best outings on Ireland's loughs, rivers and sheltered coastlines.

Online: www.canoe.ie is the website for Caneoing Ireland, while **www.canoeni.com** and **www.cani. org.uk** cover Northern Ireland.

www.waterwaysireland.org provides route maps and practical information about many of the major water thoroughfares across the country.

www.iww.ie describes all the whitewater rivers around the country, some of which are suitable for open boats.

LOUGH ERNE

This fantastic three-day trip across Upper and Lower Lough Erne features great campsites, a host of historic landmarks, and an enjoyably challenging navigational journey.

👍 Great for

- Getting into the flow of a multi-day canoe-and-camp experience
- Testing your navigation amongst the islands of the Upper Lough

☁ Conditions

- Calm winds, or up to a moderate wind from the south

🗺 Trip Details

- Distance: 40.5km (25 miles)
- Time: 3 days
- Maps: OSNI 1:25,000 Activity Map *Lough Erne*, OSNI 1:50,000 sheets 17 and 27

🚪 Access

- **To the start:** Start at the public jetty in Crom Estate. Crom is owned by the National Trust and has an entrance fee of £5 per person during opening hours, though the entrance gate remains open out of hours too. Crom is signed from the villages of Lisnaskea and Newtownbutler on the A34.

- Grid Ref: H 370 238
- GPS: 54.162394, -7.434188

- **To the finish:** The route finishes at Trory slipway, 5km north if Enniskillen. From Enniskillen, take the A35 Omagh road, and turn left just before you reach the first roundabout.

- Grid Ref: H 226 477
- GPS: 54.378378, -7.652072

Beside Crichton Tower, near the start of the route at Crom.

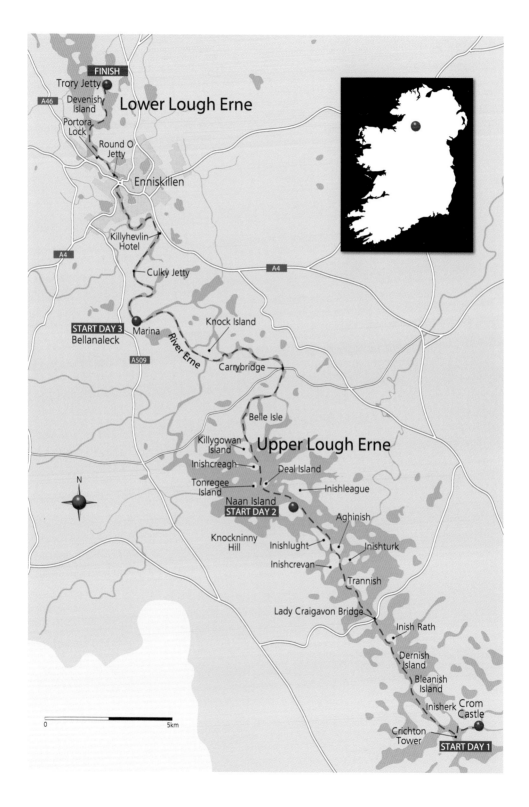

FINISH

Trory Jetty

A46

Devenish
Island

Portora
Lock

Round O
Jetty

Lower Lough Erne

Enniskillen

Killyhevlin
Hotel

A4

A4

Culky Jetty

Knock Island

START DAY 3
Bellanaleck

Marina

River Erne

A509

Carrybridge

Belle Isle

Killygowan
Island

Upper Lough Erne

Inishcreagh

Deal Island

Tonregee
Island

Inishleague

Naan Island
START DAY 2

N

Aghinish

Knockninny
Hill

Inishlught

Inishturk

Inishcrevan

Trannish

Lady Craigavon Bridge

Inish Rath

Dernish
Island

Bleanish
Island

0   5km

Inisherk   Crom
Castle

Crichton
Tower

START DAY 1

If you have never done a multi-day canoe trip before, this is the perfect place to start. It's a well-documented trip along one of Ireland's most popular waterways, and the odds are you'll see other boating traffic along the way. There are plenty of nooks and crannies for a canoe to tuck into, and the wide variety of natural and historic landmarks ensures each day brings a different adventure.

Day one is all about exploring the countless uninhabited islands of Upper Lough Erne, and testing your navigational skills as you weave between them. On the second day you wind along the river section that connects the two loughs, stopping at waterside marinas to refuel as necessary. The final day brings you through the gateway of Enniskillen, to emerge onto the expanse of the Lower Lough.

The sense of journey is strong throughout. From the start at Crom Estate, with its 17th-century castle and island folly of Crichton Tower, to the finish at Devenish Island, home to a unique sixth-century monastery, there are countless waterside sites that tempt you to stop and investigate further. The only way to explore this watery wonderland is by boat, and gliding slowly and silently across it in a canoe is the best experience of all.

Planning

Any three-day boat trip demands a lot of logistical planning. In this case, practicalities are helped by the fact that the outing is part of the 50km Lough Erne Canoe Trail, which is well documented online; see the canoe trail section of www.canoeni.com. The journey suggested here gets its own write-up too – click the Itineraries link and continue to the 'Tower to Tower' route to see full details. The website also lists all amenities such as toilets, campsites and accommodation that can be found along the route. Note that many public facilities are open only between April and October each year.

For a wilder experience, camping is also possible on several uninhabited islands on the Upper Lough. Good options include **Aghinish Island** (Grid Ref: H 314 306; no facilities; landing with firm, flat grass on the north-western tip of the island) and **Naan Island** (Grid Ref: H 302 320; public jetty with wild camping and fire pit). As always, if you decide to camp wild,

please respect the environment and other users and follow the principles of Leave No Trace (see www.leavenotraceireland.org/seven-principles).

How far you choose to go each day will depend on the weather and your level of canoeing experience. Most recreational paddlers cover around 3.5km per hour when soloing, and 4.5km per hour tandem. With so many campsites en route, you can move at your own pace, taking two, three or even four days to complete the route. A fairly leisurely three-day trip is described below, though you'll need to allow an extra hour or two each day for stops.

The linear format also means you'll have to organise a shuttle between start and finish. Vehicles can be left in public car parks beside both jetties, and it takes around 1½ hours to complete the 77km (48-mile) round trip between both points.

Navigation

The main challenge of the route is navigation. This is particularly important on the Upper Lough, where the islands look remarkably similar. A copy of the waterproof OSNI 1:25,000 Activity Map *Lough Erne* is invaluable here; it's designed for boaters, and numbers all the navigational markers along the route. If you get lost, simply head to the closest red-and-white marker post, read its number and locate your position on the map. There are some places without markers for several kilometres, however, so nothing really replaces

Lunch stop at the jetty on Inish Rath, the Hare Krishna island.

Wild camping on the second night, opposite Bellanaleck marina.

ongoing vigilance to keep track of your position.

The 1:25,000 map also marks all the relevant slipways, jetties and campsites. Its scale sometimes makes it unwieldy, so it can be helpful having a copy of the route at 1:50,000 scale too. Don't forget to bring a compass – ideally fixed to the front of your boat – to help with orientation. Of course, there are many possible routes across the Upper Lough, and you can easily devise your own itinerary around the islands.

Note that your speed will be significantly affected by the direction and strength of the wind. The Upper Lough is most exposed, especially at its northern end. Avoid paddling here in strong winds as waves can build up, hampering progress and even becoming dangerous.

In normal water conditions here is little flow anywhere on the route, though a gentle current forms through the central river section in high water. The current becomes strongest under the bridges in central Enniskillen, though it shouldn't cause problems for most paddlers.

Guided Excursions

Probably the best canoe and kayak services in the area are provided by **Share Discovery Village** (tel: 028 6772 2122; sharevillage.org), which you pass on the first day of the trip. They hire boats as well as arranging guided trips.

The Paddle

Day One – Crom to Naan Island
12.5km, 3–4 hours

From the slipway in Crom Estate, paddle west along the shore for 800m to reach the first landmark: the remains of 17th-century **Crom Castle**. It's well worth landing on the pebble shore beneath the ruins and getting out to explore the site properly. An obvious second stop is then **Crichton Tower**, 500m offshore on Gad Island.

From Crichton Tower, the easiest route lies to the west of Inisherk, Bleanish and Dernish Islands. The next island north, Inish Rath, is home to a community of Hare Krishna followers. If you want to explore the island, pull up on the jetty on the western shore. A notice says visitors are welcome to wander freely, and you may be offered food by the residents. Donations are gratefully accepted.

The concrete span of Lady Craigavon Bridge acts as a gateway to the northern part of the lough. The main navigation channel heads north-east here, but a quieter and more direct route for canoes lies to the north-west. Head along the western shore of Trannish Island, perhaps stopping at the bothy halfway along. It's just possible to squeeze through the reed bed between Inishturk and Inishcrevan, or else stick to more open water along the eastern side of Inishturk. Now head north-west past Aghinish (with remote, wild camping possible at its north-west point), then Inishlught. Your goal for the evening is **Naan Island**, recognisable by the large floating jetty that protrudes from its eastern shore.

Naan can be busy in peak season. Its popularity is well justified – there are perfect tent pitches and a ready-made fire pit beneath the trees to the left of the jetty. In high summer, you may find more solitude back on Aghinish.

Day Two – Naan Island to Bellanaleck
15km, 4–5 hours
The main challenge on day two is to find the correct entrance to the **river system** connecting Upper and Lower Lough Erne. Use a combination of map, compass and marker posts to guide you. This stretch

also crosses the most open water of the route, so be wary of strong winds.

Perhaps the easiest route is to begin by paddling north-west, then veer north between Deal and Tonregee Island. Here you rejoin the main navigation channel. Pass the eastern shore of Inishcreagh and Killygowan Island, then follow the markers north-west into the mouth of the river. A handy landmark is the square white wall of Belle Isle water recoding station, which marks the right-hand side of the river entrance.

The narrow confines of the river stand in contrast to the open expanse of the lough. Continue downstream for 3km to reach the village of **Carrybridge**, whose jetty-lined banks make a convenient place to break for lunch.

Keep to the main channel as the river sweeps west from Carrybridge. The shortest route lies to the south of Knock Island, where several large signposts help keep you on track. Pass under a road bridge and continue downstream to **Bellanaleck**, a handy stopping point for the second night. The toilets, showers and village lie on the west bank, while the best camping is beside a fisherman's car park on the east bank.

Day Three – Bellanaleck to Trory
13km, 3–4 hours
This is the easiest day of the trip in terms of navigation. Continue downstream from Bellanaleck, winding

Perfect paddling conditions near Culky jetty.

Beneath the watergate of 16th-century Enniskillen Castle.

round several wide bends in the river. After 2.5km you pass Culky jetty on the left – another possible wild camping spot for self-sufficient paddlers (there are picnic tables but no other facilities). Roughly 2km further on, manicured lawns and a large building on the right mark Killyhevlin Hotel, another possible egress point with its own jetty.

A wide S-bend brings you past extensive reed beds and into Enniskillen itself. As you near the town centre, the river splits around Castle Island. It's possible to land on the eastern bank of this island, and even to camp overnight, though the urban surrounding offers a rather different experience.

Pass Castle Island on its western side; the eastern side is blocked by a floating walkway. Immediately beyond the island lies 600-year-old **Enniskillen Castle**, with its turreted watergate. The castle has been recently renovated and houses several museums. It is open from Monday to Saturday all year round, and daily from June to September.

Pass beneath two road bridges, keeping to the left to find the gentlest flow in high water. Just past a corner, the Round O jetty is home to several public amenities including a toilet block. This is also a departure point for summer ferries to Devenish Island.

The banks become more natural again as you pass through an area of woodland. Keep left now in preparation for **Portora Lock**, which arrives 1km beyond Round O. This is the only lock on the Erne system, which circumvents a weir designed to regulate the level of the Upper Lough. The lock is free and open

daily, with passage controlled by a lock-keeper. Odds are you'll have to share the ride with a motorboat or two, but the vertical drop is relatively benign at just 1m.

After emerging from the lock, follow the eastern bank for 1km, then squeeze through a gap in the reeds known as Friar's Leap. This provides entrance to the wide expanse of the Lower Lough. Directly ahead is **Devenish Island**; cross the channel and paddle along the eastern shore to reach the jetty. Don't miss the opportunity to explore this unique and atmospheric site. The monastery here was founded in the sixth century by St Molaise, though the various churches date from different periods. Highlights include a perfectly preserved round tower, and an intricately carved 15th-century stone cross.

When you're ready, simply paddle 1km north to Trory slipway, where your vehicle should be waiting.

Stopping to explore the monastic site on Devenish Island is a great way to finish the trip.

SHANNON CIRCUIT

This circular trip combines a lough and canal with a quiet, tree-lined paddle along Ireland's longest river.

Great for

- Experiencing the natural Shannon far from noisy motorboats
- Dropping between the narrow walls of your first lock

Conditions

- Calm or moderate wind

Trip Details

- Distance: 19.5km (12 miles)
- Time: 4½–5½ hours
- Maps: OSi 1:50,000 sheets 26 and 33

Access

- The circuit starts and finishes at Drumshanbo Lock. This is located along the R280, on the western edge of Drumshanbo village. Drop your boats on the northern side of the road beside Lough Allen, then leave your vehicle in the car park on the southern side, where you disembark at the end of the trip.
- Grid Ref: G 967 109
- GPS: 54.047877, -8.050587

The start: launching into Lough Allen from the jetty at Drumshanbo Lock.

A Powerful History

Lough Allen Canal was constructed in 1822 to help transport coal from the Arigna mines to Dublin. In 1887 most of this traffic shifted to the region's new narrow-gauge railway, and commercial canal trade ceased altogether in 1930. The canal then fell into disrepair until its restoration in 1996. Lough Allen still has links to power generation because it acts as a storage reservoir for the Shannon hydroelectric scheme, supplying water for Ardnacrusha Power Station some 150km downstream.

At 360km, the River Shannon is the longest river in Ireland. Some paddlers make it their goal to paddle the entire watercourse from source to sea, but most are happy to sample a shorter stretch. This trip joins the river just 29km downstream of the Shannon Pot, concentrating on the only section that is consistently navigable for canoes and kayaks, yet free from the tyranny of motorboats.

The route provides the rare pleasure of a circular outing, and includes an impressive amount of scenic variety. It begins with a 2km crossing of Lough Allen, then follows the gentle flow of the Shannon as far as Battlebridge. Here you make an abrupt turn onto the restored Lough Allen Canal, whose placid waters carry you back to the start.

The natural diversity of lough, river and canal environments is further enhanced by several landmarks. You'll need to portage a dam and negotiate two locks, and for lunch you can choose between a waterside pub at Battlebridge and picnic tables at the nearby lock. Overall, it's hard to imagine a more interesting circuit.

If you want to vary the route, it's also possible to continue downstream along the Shannon Blueway, which links Battlebridge to Carrick-on-Shannon. While the water here is still flat, the river becomes wider as you join the main cruising thoroughfare. Passing motorboats create wakes and reed beds restrict access to solid banks, a situation that continues for much of the remainder of the river.

Guided Excursions

If you don't have your own boat, don't worry; several local companies offer guided trips. **Adventure Gently** (tel: 085 182 1547; adventuregentlyireland.com) organises open canoe outings along the section described, while **Leitrim Surf Company** (tel: 086 349 4013; www.leitrimsurf.ie) ply a similar route on stand-up paddleboards (SUP).

The Paddle

Launch your canoe from the floating jetty on the Lough Allen side of Drumshanbo Lock. Begin by following the navigational markers north across the lake for almost 2km. The first challenge is to locate the point where

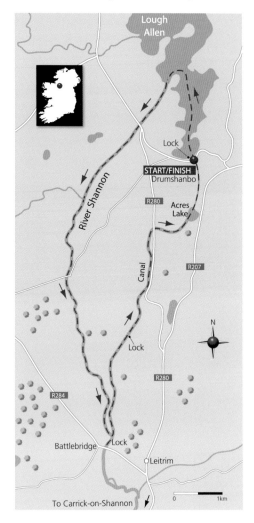

Both the river and the canal offer quiet, tree-lined paddling.

the Shannon leaves the lough. It's tucked away on the left behind the promontory of Holly Island, shortly before the long, wooded headland of Inishfale Island protrudes three-quarters of the way across the lake. You will need to look almost behind yourself to spot it, but the metal gantry holding the **sluice gates**

is an obvious landmark once you're looking in the right direction.

Approach the dam and land just before it on the left, at the bottom of a grassy slope. Carry your boat 80m to the top of the slope, then cross the lane with the help of two concrete stiles. You can now relaunch

Returning to the Shannon after portaging the sluice gates.

on the downstream side of the dam. The water is fast flowing beneath the gates, but you can avoid the current by sticking close to the bank.

A gentle-to-moderate flow now carries you all the way to Battlebridge. The banks are a mixture of open pasture and woodland, with a natural and unspoilt atmosphere pervading. Care is needed in a couple of places to avoid trees that infringe from the bank.

You can gauge your progress from the bridges you pass. There are two bridges in the first kilometre, then a space of 4km to the next one at Drumherriff. Another 4km brings you past a low footbridge (which would be dangerous in flood conditions), to the five stone arches of Battlebridge. The current can be strong beneath this final bridge, though there are no actual rapids.

Around 300m beyond Battlebridge, you have a choice. If you fancy a pub lunch, turn right into a calm channel leading to a small marina and slipway. You are now at **Battlebridge Caravan & Camping Park** (tel: 071 965 0824; www.battlebridgecaravanandcamping. ie), and straight ahead is **Beirnes Pub**, which serves good food in both its atmospheric interior and outdoor terrace.

To continue on the route, keep left instead and pull up at the jetty beneath **Battlebridge Lock**. This marks the turning point of the route, where you swing north onto Lough Allan Canal. Picnic benches beside the jetty offer another good option for a break.

This is the first of two locks you pass, and most paddlers portage them using the steps and jetties provided. If you're suitably confident, though, it's a memorable experience to go through one. The lock-keeper is often stationed at Battlebridge, so chat to him about passing though.

The locks are open daily, from 9 a.m. to at least 6 p.m. between April and September, with more restricted operating hours during the winter. There is a charge of €1.50 per passage. If the lock-keeper is not around, call tel: 071 9641 552, and he should arrive within a few minutes. Once the gate is open, enter the lock and hold one of the metal chains that hang down the stone walls. Keep a loose grip on the chain, letting it slide through your fingers as the water level changes. Wait till the outward gate is fully open before exiting the lock.

Exiting Drumleague Lock along the return canal section.

Having successfully passed Battlebridge, there's a 2km paddle along the canal to **Drumleague Lock**. A recreational towpath runs along both banks here, so you may be accompanied by walkers and cyclists. Past Drumleague, the next landmark is the narrow stone archway of Drumhauver Bridge. The waterway becomes quieter now, the still water and wooded banks creating a verdant corridor that feels both natural and peaceful.

You now arrive at Acres Lake, a small lough with a marina and toilet block on its eastern shore. Keep to the western bank of the lake and follow the navigational markers back onto the canal. After a final 1.5km you arrive at the stone bridge beside Drumshanbo Lock. Pull up at a wooden canoe step on the left just before the bridge, then follow the access trail to your vehicle above.

KILLARNEY LAKES

This fabulously varied route crosses all three lakes of Killarney
and is perhaps the most scenic one-day canoe trip
in the country.

Great for

- Ducking your head to pass beneath countless rock tunnels
- Floating amid the wild grandeur of the Upper Lake

Conditions

- Calm winds

Trip Details

- Distance: 15.5km (10 miles)
- Time: 4½–5½ hours
- Maps: OSi 1:50,000 sheet 78, OSi 1:25,000 *MacGillycuddy's Reeks*, or Harvey Superwalker 1:30,000 *MacGillycuddy's Reeks*.

Access

- **To the start:** The best access to the Upper Lake is from a lay-by along the N71 Killarney–Kenmare road. It is around 12km south of Killarney, and 400m south of a rock tunnel. Parking space is limited, so get there early.
- Grid Ref: V 918 818
- GPS: 51.977840, -9.576316

- **To the finish:** The trip finishes at Ross Castle, which is signed west off the N71 Kenmare road, just south of Killarney town centre. Continue to the end car park, which has convenient access to Boat Alley.
- Grid Ref: V 951 888
- GPS: 52.041626, -9.529403

A riverlike section leads to The Long Range.

For centuries, the three lakes of Killarney have been a central pillar of Irish tourism. All the hype can be rather off-putting, but the fact remains that these are fabulously scenic places. Once you're out on the water you will quickly find yourself alone, enjoying perhaps the most beautiful and varied one-day canoe trip in the country.

The outing has so many highlights it's hard to know where to start. First comes Upper Lake, which is enclosed by the country's highest mountains and

Perfect paddling on Killarney's Upper Lake, with Torc Mountain reflected ahead.

Watch out for the Grade 2 rapid beneath Old Weir Bridge.

exudes a wild grandeur that is unparalleled in Ireland. Then there's the trip along a riverlike link section, with narrow rock gaps and an easy rapid thrown in for effect. Ancient bridges then lead to Muckross Lake and Lough Leane, where shoreline attractions include numerous limestone outcrops, all pockmarked by caves and weathered into fantastic formations. By the time you finish at 15th-century Ross Castle, you can't help but feel the trip really epitomises the essence of Irish inland canoeing.

The route's linear format means you will have to organise a shuttle. From April to October you can use the convenient **Killarney Shuttle Bus** (tel: 087 138 4384; www.killarneyshuttlebus.com) to get from Ross Castle to Torc Waterfall. From there, it's a manageable 6km bike ride to the start beside Upper Lake.

Note that before you launch your own boat on the Killarney Lakes, you must first obtain a canoe permit. The permit is free, and designed to prevent the spread of invasive species that have an adverse impact on aquatic wildlife.

The day before your arrival, call the national park ranger on tel: 064 663 5215, and arrange a time to collect your permit the following day. You must then power wash your boat, both inside and out. In Killarney, Hegarty's garage, located a short distance south of the Gleneagle Hotel along the N71, has a convenient, coin-operated wash station. Take your power-washing receipt to the ranger station, and exchange this for a permit. The ranger station is located further south along the N71, in a large, unmarked stone building on the left, around 200m before the entrance to Muckross House. Ring the bell beside the front door for attention.

Guided Excursions

Given the beauty of these lakes, there are surprisingly few companies running commercial canoe trips. **Outdoors Ireland** (tel: 086 860 4563; www.outdoorsireland.com) and **Cappanalea Outdoor Centre** (tel: 66 9769244; www.cappanalea.ie) are two of the main operators. Expect to pay €80–100 per person for a full-day trip. All equipment is provided and no previous experience is necessary.

The Paddle

From the lay-by, follow a footpath to the lakeshore. You're on the bank of a small bay, so after launching, paddle north for a few hundred metres, past Stag Island. The lake is already sublimely beautiful, with rocky crags along the shore and mountains all around.

Exploring the limestone caves along the northern shore of Muckross Lake.

It is nice to begin by heading west for a short distance, to enjoy the full view along the **Upper Lake**. When you're ready, turn around and retrace your route east, this time keeping to the lake's northern bank. Pass a curiously shaped peninsula with three rocky arms, then head north across an almost enclosed bay. You are now looking for a 10m-wide rock portal known as **Coleman's Leap**, which is the lough's only exit point. The gap only becomes visible when you're right beside it, and feels like a secret entrance from a fairytale.

You have now entered a riverlike section, where the channel averages around 50m wide. Bent waterweeds are testament to a gentle flow, which helps your downstream progress. After 2km the channel widens and you enter the Long Range. Cross to the north-western corner of this, passing a car park on the eastern bank that can be used as an alternate access point.

The water becomes shallow as it exits the Long Range; keep to the centre for the deepest passage. You are now back in a riverlike channel, with the next few hundred metres dominated by a sheer prow on the left known as the Eagle's Nest. Follow the water as it zigzags around four hairpin bends, then straightens up for the approach to **Old Weir Bridge**.

This double-arched bridge spans a Grade 2 rapid, so you may want to get out and scout this section. Pull into a large eddy on the right just before the bridge, and follow a path up through the heather, then back left to reach the rapid. In normal conditions the line is pretty straightforward, and shouldn't cause too many difficulties.

Immediately beyond the rapid lies the Meeting of the Waters, where all three lakes converge. Your onward route lies to the right, but it's tempting first to tie up beside a set of stone steps and take a break at **Dinis Cottage café**. Set in an 18th-century hunting lodge, the windows of this teahouse feature guest names etched with diamond rings, stretching back as far as the mid 1800s.

Back on the water, you now enter the open space of **Muckross Lake**. The route exits this lake via Brickeen Bridge, just 600m to the north, but first it's worth detouring east to explore the limestone crags that line the lough's northern shore. These outcrops have been eroded into a series of caves and other formations, some of which you can paddle right inside.

When you've explored sufficiently, pass under Brickeen Bridge and enter Lough Leane, the largest of Killarney's three lakes at 19 square kilometres. If there's any wind, the water here is likely to be most affected. Turn right after the bridge and follow the southern shore of the lake for around 2.5km, passing a series of bays and headlands. There are more limestone caves here too, but for the best formations, strike out north across the lough.

Plot a route past Ash Island, Jackdaw Rock, Elephant Rock and Swallow Island. These are all **limestone formations** are that either fringed by caves and tunnels, or have arches cutting right through the middle of them. With some careful manoeuvring you can weave around and under the rocks, enjoying an aqueous maze that's unique on Irish inland waters.

After exploring Swallow Island, head north into a low bay. At the bay's north-western corner you should see an old signpost marking the boating channel to Ross Castle. Squeeze through the narrow passage known as Boat Alley, and get out at a small wooden jetty on the left, shortly before a stone bridge. Ross Castle car park is now just a few metres away.

RIVER BARROW

This historic waterway offers passage via either locks or weirs, and is set within a beautiful verdant valley.

 Great for

- Enjoying the sense of journey along a historic waterway
- Revelling in the excitement of shooting multiple weirs

 Conditions

- Low to medium water levels, calm or moderate winds

 Trip Details

- Distance: 20.5km (13 miles)
- Time: 5–6 hours
- Map: OSi 1:50,000 sheet 68

 Access

- **To the start:** The trip starts in the village of Goresbridge, which is located along the R702. There is a car park on the western side of the bridge, with an adjacent jetty and slipway.
- Grid Ref: S 684 536
- GPS: 52.630425, -6.990618

- **To the finish:** The journey finishes in St Mullins, which is signed off the R729 between New Ross and Graiguenamanagh. From the old abbey beside the village green, follow a lane steeply downhill to reach the riverside car park and slipway.
- Grid Ref: S 728 378
- GPS: 52.487735, -6.929323

Start point: beneath the 18th-century arches at Goresbridge.

If you like shooting the Barrow weirs, you're a prime candidate for the Liffey Descent, Ireland's greatest annual canoe and kayak race. This takes place in September each year on the outskirts of Dublin, and negotiates ten weirs over a 28km course. For full details, see www.canoe.ie/liffey-descent. There used to be a similar event called the Barrow Descent over the section of river described here, but it hasn't been held since 2013.

At 192km, the Barrow is the second longest river in Ireland. The section between Athy and St Mullins is actually a navigation, with locks that bypass every rapid and weir. Commercial goods were transported here by barge from 1761 to the 1950s, with a connection to the Grand Canal providing a link between Waterford port, Dublin and the River Shannon.

Today the river is the preserve of leisure boaters, with small cruisers and barges progressing through the lock system, while canoeists and kayakers choose between the locks or shooting the weirs. Touring canoes often take three days to run the entire 68km stretch between Athy and St Mullins, passing through countryside, towns and villages, and finding places to camp wild along the towpath each night.

If you're looking for a one-day paddle, the section between Goresbridge and St Mullins is the undisputed highlight of the river. Here the Barrow passes through a beautiful valley, with wooded banks supporting a wide range of wildflowers, greenery, insect and bird life. The tranquillity of the flat sections is juxtaposed with the excitement of the locks and weirs, and there's a palpable sense of journey.

Whether you shoot the weirs or use the locks to bypass them will depend on your skill level; previous whitewater experience is necessary to descend the weirs safely. The weirs range in height from 1m to 3m, and all involve straight drops at relatively shallow angles. They are well spaced along the river – at least 1km apart – with flat water at the bottom to allow you to recover your wits.

Passage is generally straightforward in normal summer conditions, when water levels are low and there's no tow-back at the bottom. Please note that the river is an altogether different proposition in high water or flood conditions, and there have been fatal incidents of paddlers caught in powerful stoppers, or tow-backs, beneath the weirs. The description here refers to low water levels; things will look very different in higher flows.

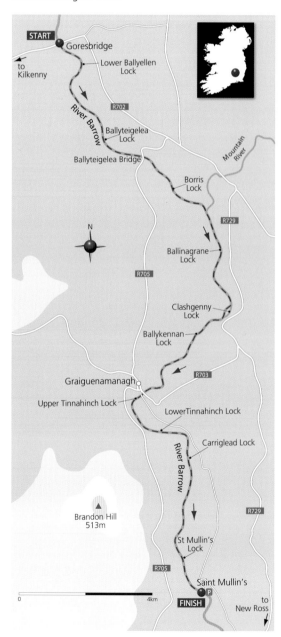

Taking a break on the banks of Mountain River.

All the difficulties can be avoided by using the locks, ten of which are found along this stretch. The navigation is overseen by Waterways Ireland, who recommend that canoes and kayaks portage around each lock using the jetties provided. If your boat is heavily laden, you can bring it through the lock by holding it from the bank with a long rope. To operate the locks yourself you'll need to buy a lock key for €25 from **Waterways Ireland** (tel: 057 935 2300; www.waterwaysireland.org); keys can be collected from their offices in Dublin or Tullamore. Beside each lock you'll also find the phone number for the lock-keeper, who can provide help if you need it.

If you prefer a shorter trip, consider starting or stopping at Graiguenamanagh, or at Ballyteigelea Bridge, where there's a car park on the northern bank. Limited help is also available with the shuttle; Kilbride Coaches (tel: 051 423 633; kilbridecoaches. com) run morning bus services between Goresbridge and Graiguenamanagh from Monday to Saturday.

Guided Excursions

Several local operators offer guided canoe trips along the Barrow. Try **Pure Adventure** (tel: 087 2265 550; www.pureadventure.ie) or **Go with the Flow** (tel: 087 2529 700; www.gowiththeflow.ie). It's also possible to hire canoes from €35 per day with **Paddle your own Canoe** (tel: 087 414 0461; www. paddleyourowncanoe.ie).

The Paddle

Goresbridge slipway lies just downstream of a multi-arched bridge, which dates from 1756. The trip begins gently, with 1km of flat water before you arrive at Lower Ballyellen Lock. All the locks and navigation channels on this section lie on river left, while the weirs lie on river right, angled diagonally across the river. To pass via the lock, keep left along the cut, negotiate the lock, then rejoin the river below the weir. To pass via the weir, keep right and scout along the top of the drop to find the best descent point, then straighten up and go for it. For Lower Ballyellen Weir, the best chute lies about 10m in from the right bank.

The river now enters a verdant valley, with the water forming a peaceful corridor between wooded banks. A 2.5km flat section brings you to Ballyteigelea Lock, where the weir links several islands on the right. The first section of weir on the far right is often easiest if it's not too heavily vegetated.

After another kilometre you pass under the arches of Ballyteigelea Bridge, then reach Borris Weir, which is about 500m wide and often shot over the first section on the right. Around 1.5km downstream, look out for a small stone bridge on the left, which marks the confluence with **Mountain River**. If you pass under the bridge, a sandy bay on the left makes a lovely place for a break.

There are three more locks and weirs between here and Graiguenamanagh, at Ballingrane, Clashgenny and Ballykennan, all located around 2km apart. The first two weirs have several possible lines, while Ballykennan is taken via a chute on the far left. Beneath Ballykennan weir lies 100m of straightforward Grade 2 **rapids**, leading to a second 'eel weir', which is an inverted V shape with channels on the far left and far right. The best line here is far left, which gives another 100m of Grade 2 water.

Roughly 3km of flat water brings you to the pretty market town of **Graiguenamanagh**. The first building on the right is the rowing club, which has diving boards and a slipway out front. This is another good place for a break, with the nearby Waterside Café and Restaurant providing drinks and snacks.

Continue under the arches of Graiguenamanagh bridge, where you're confronted by Upper Tinnahinch lock and weir. The weir is best descended via a chute about 10m in from the right bank. Lower Tinnahinch comes another kilometre downstream, and is also taken via a chute on river right. This is followed by another V-shaped eel weir, again with channels on the far left and far right.

A kilometre later, Carriglead weir is followed by a similar eel weir. Some 3km of flat water then brings you to the final obstacle, at **St Mullins** lock and weir. This marks the end of the navigation for motorboats, as the river is tidal below this point. The weir is taken in the centre via a good chute, but great care is needed here in high water and incoming tides, when the combination of flows creates a sticky stopper that has lead to fatalities.

A final kilometre of water – either shallow or deep depending on the tide – brings you to the finish at **St Mullins**, with its slipway, car park and waterside café. The remains of a seventh-century monastery and 12th-century motte-and-bailey lie just 100m up the exit road, and are well worth exploring before you leave.

There are nine weirs along our route on the Barrow, which are generally low in summer conditions.

SEA KAYAKING

A different perspective on the country's most famous coastline at the Cliffs of Moher.

IMAGINE a remote stretch of coastline in the west of Ireland. The sea cliffs reach 200m high, and stretch around headlands and bays for 30km. All along the base of the cliffs the pounding Atlantic has shattered the rock into a maze of outcrops, with towering stacks, slender pinnacles, deep caves and natural arches scattered all around. In most conditions, exploring this rocky wonderland would be impossible; only a tiny boat could weave amongst such intricate formations, and ocean swells generally prevent small craft from approaching.

But occasionally the sea calms down, and a high-pressure system renders the surface as smooth as glass. This is the cue sea kayakers have been waiting for. For just a few short days it will be possible to get inside the rocky labyrinth, squeezing through tunnels and chasms, threading the arches and touching formations that few people even know exist.

And because you're doing all this by gliding silently at surface level, you're close to marine life too. Chances are that before you finish several seals will have popped up beside you, you'll have examined starfish, urchins and anemones, and, if it's your lucky day, even had an encounter with dolphins or a basking shark.

If conditions allow, perhaps you can extend your trip into a multi-day journey. Pack your hatches with a tent and stove, pick a few offshore islands, and head off for several days of genuine wilderness adventure. For an intimate, independent exploration of the coast and islands, there's simply nothing to rival it.

Irish Sea Kayaking at a Glance

Irish sea kayaking is literally world class, right up there with the earth's top destinations. Yet only recently has word begun to spread about the quality of the paddling on offer here. This isn't surprising, because recreational coastal kayaking is very much a growing activity both here and globally. A few pioneers began extolling its merits in Ireland in the 1970s, but it was 1991 before of the Irish Sea Kayaking Association was

Top: Ready to go. Choose a fibreglass or plastic boat depending on your preferred type of paddling.
Bottom: The green room, Belmullet Peninusla. It's amazing how often you experience a bit of magic on the water.

Though most paddlers stick to shorter trips, some people can't help but go big. The first recorded circumnavigation of Ireland by sea kayak was achieved by Franco Ferrero, Derek Hairon and John Bouteloup in 1978. Since then over 80 people have made their own journeys around the country's perimeter. In 2015 Mick O'Meara from Waterford set a new speed record, completing the 1,500km voyage, solo and unsupported, in just 23 days.

established. The first real guidebook to kayaking the Irish coast was published in 2004, and the number of people involved in the sport has been increasing ever since.

As a rule of thumb, Ireland's Atlantic coast – from Antrim in the north to Cork in the south – offers the most dramatic scenery. This is where you'll find the tallest cliffs, most spectacular formations and highest density of islands. Yet this is also where the sea is at its most challenging in terms of storms and wave height. The east coast is has a lower, gentler charm, and it's not so much swell as wind and currents that cause problems here.

Of course, sea kayaks can be taken on inland waters too. You will find loughs and sheltered estuaries all around the country, and these are great places to learn your strokes, or retreat to when the sea is too rough.

The Boat

Most sea kayaks are 15–17ft long, and there is a huge range of designs to choose from. A wide boat will be more stable but slower and harder to manoeuvre, while a narrow one is fast but tippy. As a beginner you might want to start with a wider boat, then reduce the volume as your stability improves. The boat has to suit your body shape too. Manufacturers usually offer their boats in several sizes, ensuring the right amount of stability for your body weight, as well as comfortable cockpit fittings like foot rests and thigh braces.

A retractable skeg (a fin deployed from the bottom of the boat) is a requisite, to help your boat track

better in windy conditions. Rudders are less well received; the general consensus is that you'll become a more proficient paddler by learning old-fashioned steering techniques rather than relying on a rudder.

The biggest question for many paddlers is what the boat is made of. There are two main options: plastic, or a lighter composite material like fibreglass. The best material for you depends on what sort of paddling you intend to do. Plastic boats are heavier and slower, but far more durable and significantly cheaper (around €1,700 new). If you like rock hopping or landing on pebble beaches, this is the way to go. Composite boats cost more (around €3,000) and are easily damaged by contact with rock. But they're light, sleek, fast and responsive, and great for races or open-water excursions. There's a good second-hand market for most boats, as plastic kayaks in particular last a long time.

Other Equipment

While on the water you should wear a buoyancy aid at all times, plus a wetsuit or drysuit to keep yourself warm in case of immersion. Wear wetsuit booties on your feet, and a helmet if you're rock hopping or going into caves.

The minimum recommended group size is three people. At least one person in the group should carry the following: a first-aid kit, water pump, spare split paddles, tow line, compass and map of the route

Inaccessible cliff lines are often most dramatic. Beneath Horn Head in Donegal.

(carried on the deck in a waterproof map case). You'll need a range of dry bags too, for carrying items like non-waterproof cameras, spare clothing and food. For overnight trips you'll learn the art of minimal packing, with all your camping gear and supplies first placed into dry bags, then squeezed inside the storage hatches. Seeing how well you can live out of such a small space is all part of the fun.

Emergencies

In case of emergencies, the coastguard can be contacted in several ways. Call 999 or 112 on a phone, or use channel 16 on a VHF radio. Note that reception for both these devices may be sporadic in certain circumstances, like under a remote cliff. A personal locator beacon (PLB) relays a distress signal to the coastguard via satellite, and should work so long as you have a view of the sky. Make sure all your communication devices are readily accessible and carried on your person.

Getting Started

The main prerequisite for kayaking is to be a confident swimmer. After that it's a matter of being shown the basic strokes, then spending as much time as possible on the water until your reactions become automatic.

Begin by contacting someone who knows what they're doing. For a handy list of instructors and trip operators, see www.iska.ie. In terms of clubs, many Irish kayak clubs encompass a range of disciplines, including inland and whitewater paddling as well as sea kayaking. In the beginning it doesn't matter too much which sort of kayaking you do, as all the strokes are transferrable. For a full list of kayak clubs around the country, see www.canoe.ie or www.canoeni.com.

Extending Your Skills

Once you've mastered the basics, you can extend your network of contacts by attending a sea kayak gathering. The Irish Sea Kayaking Association organises a number of weekend meets around the country each year, with peer-led trips and skills sessions for both beginners and advanced paddlers. Another good option is the annual Inishowen Sea Symposium, which is run by professional coaches; see www.inishadventures.com for details.

Perhaps the best way to advance your ability and knowledge is to progress through Canoeing Ireland's skills awards. Sea-specific courses start at Level 3, which allows you to participate in group outings. Level 4 is what all keen sea kayakers should aim for, as it equips you to undertake independent sea journeys. Completing a Coastal Navigation course is a requisite part of this exam, and provides indispensible advice on trip planning, forecasting, tides, currents, and generally staying safe in the marine environment.

Only a tiny boat could explore formations like this cave deep inside the Slieve League cliffs.

Finding Out More

Books: The undisputed bible for Irish sea kayakers is *Oileáin* by David Walsh. This comprehensive guidebook describes the entire Irish coastline and 570 islands, with a wealth of practical information throughout. To view the book online, see www.oileain.org.

Online: **www.canoe.ie** is the website for Canoeing Ireland, while **www.cani.org.uk** and **www.canoeni.com** cover Northern Ireland.

www.iska.ie is the online home of the Irish Sea Kayaking Association. Check the 'Useful Links' page for sea area forecasts and online tide times.

SLIEVE LEAGUE & SLIEVE TOOEY

This superlative, three-day trip exemplifies the very best of Irish sea kayaking.

👍 Great for

- Getting personal with some of the most dramatic coastline Ireland has to offer
- Being amazed by the endless procession of stacks, caves, arches and cliffs

☁ Conditions

- Calm sea and wind

🗺 Trip Details

- Distance: 53km (33 miles)
- Time: 3 days
- Map: OSi 1:50,000 sheet 10

🏛 Access

- **To the start:** The trip starts at a slipway on the southern side of Loughros Point. Begin by heading along the N56 to Ardara. Just south of the village, near a sharp bend in the road, turn west onto a minor road signed for Loughros Point. Follow this for 7km, then turn left onto a smaller lane. The slipway is located at the end of this road.
- Grid Ref: G 652 928
- GPS: 54.782335, -8.541015

- **To the finish:** The route finishes at Teelin harbour. This is accessed from the village of Carrick, along the R263. Turn south in the centre of Carrick, following a brown sign for Teelin Pier. Keep straight ahead along this road to arrive at the pier 4.5km later.
- Grid Ref: G 593 752
- GPS: 54.623405, -8.632162

A massive 20m-high arch marks the start of the trip.

This is one of the most spectacular three-day sea kayak trips in Ireland, and amply demonstrates why the country is right up there as a world-class sea-kayaking destination. It's a committing outing along an exposed Atlantic coastline, so not suitable for novices, but in the right conditions the scenery is so consistently magnificent it's a journey you'll never forget.

The guidebook *Oileáin* describes the Slieve League cliffs as 'one of the truly mighty excursions of Irish sea paddling', while the continuation beneath Slieve Tooey is 'dominated by stretches of awesome cliffs, hundreds of metres high. Along the entire length lie mighty sea stacks … almost unknown to the general body of sea going folk'. Many paddlers find the section beneath Slieve Tooey even more impressive than Slieve League.

As well as taking you beneath some of the highest sea cliffs in Europe, you'll pass more stacks, arches and caves than you imagine possible. There's simply no other way to explore most of these formations than by kayak. This is a remote area too, so wild camping where the coast relents is all part of the adventure.

Planning

All multi-day sea kayak trips necessitate a large amount of planning, both in terms of logistics and packing. The most important factor to get right is the sea conditions. This trip is all about getting close to the base of the cliffs, so a calm sea is a prerequisite. In even a moderate swell you won't be able to approach the rock and will miss out on most of the magic. This is an exposed Atlantic coast, so getting a weather window long enough to complete a three-day trip is easier said than done. Ideal conditions come round just a couple of times a year, so you'll need to watch

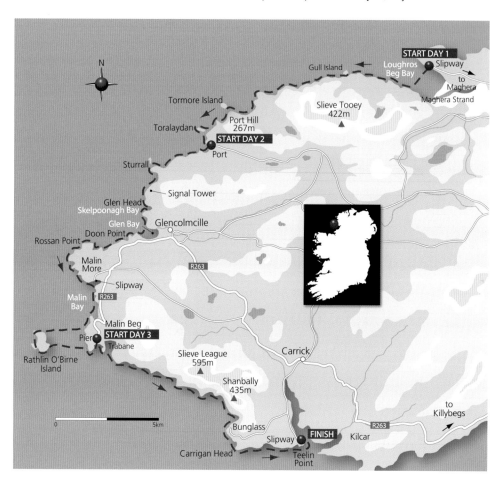

Top: Several towering waterfalls plunge over the Slieve League cliffs.

Bottom: Perfect paddling conditions at Slieve League, beneath some of the highest sea cliffs in Europe.

the forecast carefully and be ready to head off as soon as you see an opportunity arising.

The trip statistics assume a reasonable amount of exploring along the way. The amount of investigating you do affects your speed; recreational paddlers average 6km/h on a straight crossing, but 4km/h is a more reasonable estimate if you're delving into every tunnel and cave. With so much impenetrable cliff line, campsites and egress points are limited. Plan your trip carefully to make sure you reach your destination in reasonable time each day. Tidal flows are relatively weak, reaching a maximum strength of 1.5 knots at springs in Rathlin O'Birne Sound. Note that the current flows north around here and Rossan Point for three-quarters of the time.

The trip is described from north to south, but can be completed just as easily in the opposite direction if the wind favours that approach. The linear format means you'll have to organise a shuttle between start and finish. Vehicles can be left beside both slipways but the connecting roads are slow; allow at least 45 minutes for the 35km one-way trip.

Guided Excursions

Several companies offer guided sea kayak trips along the Slieve League coastline, though prior experience is a prerequisite. **West Coast Kayaking** (tel: 083 437 0893; westcoastkayaking.ie) and **Inish Adventures** (tel: 087 220 2577; www.inishadventures.com) are two local operators who know the area well.

The Paddle

Day One – Loughros Point to Port
15km, 4–5 hours

The first day of the trip is spent exploring an endless procession of arches and caves, before weaving through a labyrinth of sea stacks to finish at the deserted village of Port.

From Loughros Point slipway, begin by heading south-west across Loughros Beg Bay. The extensive sands of Maghera Strand are visible at the back of the bay to the left. Keep left of a stack in the centre of the bay, then aim for the first visible inlet on the opposite shore, where the first stacks are marked on the map. Above this the rugged slopes of Slieve Tooey rise to 511m high.

Taking a break on one of the storm beaches beneath Slieve Tooey.

The first cove sets the scene for the day ahead. It holds several stacks, with one larger islet cut almost in half by a **massive arch** some 20m high. From here the route heads west along the coast, following the precipitous shoreline all the way to Port. There are so many features and formations it's impractical to describe them all, but suffice to say that every inlet and cove is worth exploring to see what lies within.

Around 4.5km from the start you reach Gull Island, which is actually connected to the mainland by a shingle bank. This presents the first opportunity to pull in for a break, though several more storm beaches further on offer similar options. Note that seals congregate in large numbers on some of these beaches during the autumn birthing season, and by October it may be impossible to land in some places. Earlier in the year you'll see numerous seals in the water but the beaches remain largely clear.

West of **Gull Island** a series of slender headlands protrude from the mainland. Several of these have long tunnels cutting through the ends of them, which are just possible to squeeze through if the tide is right. As you emerge from one tunnel, the entrance to the next is lined up ahead. In other conditions the tunnels

act as blowholes, sending massive plumes of spray erupting skyward with every wave.

Around 3km before Port you pass a long shingle beach backed by sheer cliffs. At the western end of this lies the hulking outcast of Tormore Island, Ireland's tallest seastack at 139m. This is the start of another maze of stacks that continues all the way to Port. Along the way you'll pass An Bhuideal, a distinctive outcrop that pairs a triangular cone with a slender north tower. Rock climbing routes snake to the top of many of these stacks – see page 45 for details of the route up An Bhuideal.

Toralaydan Island is the final significant landmark of the day; its landward channel is tidal so you have to detour around it at low tide. A final scattering of stacks ushers you to Port, where you can disembark at a slipway on the northern side of the bay.

Port is an atmospheric place, with its deserted stone ruins and remote location. The best spots for camping lie 100m up the lane, across a footbridge on the right. A small stream provides water, though the large number of sheep means you're advised to boil it before use.

Day Two – Port to Malin Beg
23km, 5–6 hours

The remarkable density of formations continues on the second section. You can choose to visit Rathlin O'Birne Island at the end of this day, or leave it to the start of the next stage.

It's hard to tear yourself away from Port, but you must eventually and continue your journey south-west along the coast. The scenery remains as impressive as before, and after 3km you round the knife-edged headland of Sturrall. The bay on the southern side is enclosed by sheer cliffs some 200m high, and holds one of the most **remarkable arches** along the Irish seaboard, a slender formation reminiscent of Delicate Arch in the desert of Utah. Given the Atlantic swells that regularly careen into this sculpture, it surely can't survive much longer.

Continue south to Glen Bay, which is backed by a sandy beach and the village of Glencolmcille. There's a car park on the southern side of the beach should you need it. Either detour to the beach, or cut across the mouth of Glen Bay and continue towards Rossan Point. The section around **Rossan Point** and Rathlin O'Birne Island is the most exposed of the route. Fortunately, Rossan Point is bordered by a long line of rock outcrops, and you can find shelter in the channel between them and the mainland. There are numerous opportunities here for rock hopping, and it's also worth keeping eye open for basking sharks, which often feed around this headland.

On the southern side of Rossan Point, the small slipway at Malin More is a good place for a break, with wild camping possible here too. It's in the spot marked as Oughig on the OS map. This is where you must make a decision about **Rathlin O'Birne Island** – do you want to visit it today or leave it till tomorrow? If you want to leave it, simply continue south around the mainland, heading directly for Malin Beg harbour.

If you still have energy to spare, follow the coast for another 3km, then cut west across Rathlin O'Birne Sound. The best landing place is a stony beach at the north-east of the island. Get out here and walk along an old track enclosed by stone walls, which brings you across a natural bridge to the **lighthouse**. Incredibly,

Beneath the remarkably slender arch just south of Sturrall.

this was the world's most powerful nuclear-powered light back in the 1970s. It has since harnessed the wind as a power source, before switching to solar today. As well as visiting the lighthouse, it is also worth making a full circumnavigation of the island by sea. Amongst other features, you can paddle right through the 30m chasm beneath the natural bridge near the lighthouse. When you're ready, make the 2km crossing back east to the mainland, aiming for a prominent signal tower on a headland. Malin Beg harbour is located at the back of a sheltered inlet just east of this headland; a white cottage with three chimneys sits above the pier and helps to identify the inlet from the water. The harbour is popular with scuba divers and snorkellers (see page 149), and wild camping spots can be found at the top of the slipway. There's a tap about 500m away, beside the crossroads then slightly to the right. Just left of the crossroads is Malin Beg Hostel (tel: 074 9730 006; www.malinbeghostel.com), while a small shop and café lies along the road to the right.

Day Three – Malin Beg to Teelin
15km, 4–5 hours
The stacks and arches dissipate along this section, to be replaced by the immense drama of Ireland's tallest sea cliffs. A few storm beaches offer opportunities for a break, but there are no escape routes between start and finish. It's another committing yet magnificent day.

Leave Malin Beg harbour and turn left, now heading south-east along the coast. Just around the corner the beautiful sandy beach of **Trabane** cuts an unlikely hole in the surrounding rock. Paddle across the mouth of the bay, then continue around Rossarrell Point, where the main section cliffs stretches straight ahead for 8km to Bunglass.

Port is a remote and atmospheric place to camp for the first night.

There's a huge variety of caves and arches all along this coastline.

Again, each inlet and indentation is worth exploring. There are several places where streams plunge over the cliffs, forming tall **waterfalls** that you can paddle beneath. There are also some large caves that dig deep into the base of the cliffs, and are great fun to investigate.

The first good option for a break is a pebble beach tucked behind a headland at grid ref: G 523 784. Several other storm beaches also lie between here and Bunglass, offering further opportunities to stretch your legs. The **cliffs** themselves reach their highest between the summit of 595m Slieve League and Bunglass. There are several places here where the precipice looms sheer for 300m above you, making you feel most insignificant as you bob in the water below.

The drama begins to ease after Bunglass, as you arc south around Carrigan Head. From here it's still 3.5km to the mouth of Teelin Bay, which is guarded by three headlands and hard to pick out from a distance. It's only as you round Teelin Point that the western arm of the bay is revealed to your left. Stick to the coast as you paddle the final 300m north-west, then finish at a slipway tucked behind the large harbour wall at Teelin.

INISHKEA ISLANDS

From tropical beach and turquoise water to towering arches and a deserted village, these remote islands have it all.

👍 Great for

- Camping wild beside a pristine, white-sand beach
- Discovering the atmospheric remains of a poignant past

☁ Conditions

- Calm wind and sea

🗺 Trip Details

- Distance: 19km (12 miles)
- Time: 5–6 hours
- Map: OSi 1:50,000 sheet 22

🚪 Access

- The crossing to the Inishkea Islands begins from a slipway beside Portmore beach, at the southern tip of the Belmullet Peninsula in County Mayo. From Belmullet town, follow the R313 south towards Blacksod (An Fód Dubh). Around 4km before Blacksod, turn right onto the L5231, signed for Bóthar an Chósta. Continue straight ahead for 3.5km to reach the slipway.
- Grid Ref: F 613 183
- GPS: 54.095545, -10.120385

Threading one of the dramatic arches at the western end of Duvillaun More.

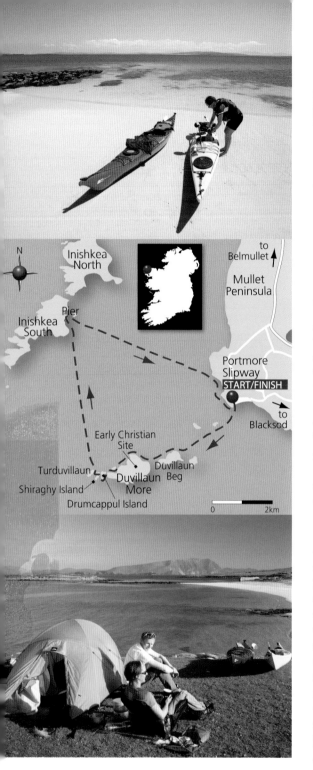

The Inishkeas have been inhabited since at least the sixth century, and in the 1800s some 300 people lived on the two main islands. In 1908 Norwegian fishermen established a whaling station on Inishkea South, slaughtering 60 whales annually for the next three years. The wide platform and rusty machinery on top of the pier show where the carcasses were butchered. Unfortunately, a series of terrible tragedies in the 1920s exposed the perils of island life and the last permanent resident left in 1939.

As well as hand-railing along the coast, the other main theme of sea kayaking is visiting offshore islands. With some 570 islands scattered around the Irish seaboard, the opportunities for exploring this natural wealth by kayak are almost endless.

The Inishkea Islands, off the Belmullet Peninsula of County Mayo, exemplify the essence of Irish island trips. Inishkea South is particularly memorable, with a pristine white-sand beach, a deserted village, and a long and interesting history. Paddling out here, then camping wild for a night or two, is such a wonderful experience it's sure to inspire you to investigate other islands too.

The simplest way to reach Inishkea South is via a straight out-and-back trip from Portmore beach, a return trip of some 15km. Without deviation, the paddle takes less than 1½ hours each way. Even allowing an hour or two to explore the island, this fits comfortably into a day trip. To soak up the atmosphere of the place properly, it's best to stay for at least one night, preferably two. An ideal itinerary would be to explore the Duvillaun Islands on the way out, then set up camp on Inishkea South. On the second day, visit Inishkea North and circumnavigate the south island, then spend another night wild before returning to the mainland on the third day. In fine, summer conditions, it's hard to conceive of a more pleasant way to spend a weekend.

The islands provide some degree of shelter from most swells, so while care is needed along their exposed western coasts, the area between the mainland and the Inishkeas is often relatively calm.

Top: Is it Ireland or the Caribbean? Landing on the pristine, white-sand beach on Inishkea South
Bottom: Inishkea South has a wide choice of beautiful camping spots.

You still need to choose your forecast wisely, though. The biggest hazard is a submerged reef that extends 1.5km from the south-eastern tip of Inishkea North; strong currents and breaking waves form here at low tide. The currents in the channels between the islands behave rather strangely too, flowing strongly and changing direction around two hours before local slack water.

Inishkea South has a good pier, and several of the deserted cottages have been renovated by descendants of the original inhabitants. During summer weekends you are likely to be sharing the island with others, though there's plenty of room to find your own space. Solitude is likely outside peak season.

Guided Excursions

There are no regular kayaking trips to the islands, but sea kayak guides operating in the area include **Paddle and Pedal** (tel: 087 680 8955; www.paddleandpedal. ie) and **Saoirse Na Mara** (tel: 086 1733610; www.irelandwestseakayaking.com). Contact them to discuss guided outings.

If you're not a kayaker, it's still possible to visit the Inishkeas with the help of a local boatman. **Geraghty Charters** (tel: 086 673 6711; www.bruchlannlir.com) and **Dive West Ireland** (tel: 086 836 5983; www. divewestireland.com) can both arrange passage in a motorboat.

The Paddle

From Portmore slipway, paddle out past the little headland that protects the western side of the bay. You should now be able to see the Duvillaun Islands to the south-west. Keep south of the outcrop of Leamareha Island, then pass along the northern shore of Duvillaun Beg, a low, grassy island grazed by sheep during the summer.

Just 400m west of Duvillaun Beg you reach **Duvillaun More**, the largest island of the group, whose history makes it worth investigating further. Land in a rocky cove on the eastern shore, near the end of the track marked on the OS map. You can then walk over rough grassland to explore the island on foot.

Duvillaun More had a population of 19 people in 1821, but was abandoned in 1917. One house near the middle of the island was undergoing renovation at the time of writing. There was a monastic site here between the sixth and tenth centuries, and several ruins and artefacts from the early Christian period lie dotted around the island. The most striking monument is a carved pillar near the brow of a hill, depicting a pre-Celtic cross on one side and a Greek crucifixion on the other.

It is also well worth making a circumnavigation of Duvillaun More by kayak. The cliffs at its western end reach 60m high, and a number of stacks and rocky islets lie scattered off its western tip. In calm conditions you can weave through the chasms and channels, and will discover two **massive arches** as well as several caves hidden amid the labyrinth.

When you're ready, head north towards **Inishkea South**. The main arrival point is the large stone pier tucked behind Rusheen Island in the north-east. If there are any groups on the island who have arrived by motorboat, this is where their vessels will be moored. As a sea kayaker you have the luxury of choice, so can pull up wherever you like. There are good campsites just south of the pier, on the north-easternmost headland, and 2km south around a low bay just east of point 15m.

There's plenty to explore on the island, including the **deserted village** beside the pier and the white-sand beach just north of it. If you head west from the pier you can also climb a hillside covered by old lazy beds to reach a white navigational tower marking the island's 72m high point. Extensive views from here encompass Achill Island and the north Mayo mainland.

A circumnavigation of the island by kayak is recommended; the most dramatic scenery lies along its south-western shore. A short hop will also bring you north-east to Inishkea North, which is lower but holds more evocative ruins in its own deserted village, with a prominent burial mound lying just east of the buildings.

It is hard to tear yourself away from these charming islands, but when you must, a 5km crossing south-east will bring you back to the mainland. Finish by following the shoreline south to return to the slipway at Portmore.

HOWTH AND IRELAND'S EYE

Combine Ireland's Eye with the round of Howth Peninsula for one of the best wildlife and sea kayak experiences on the east coast.

Great for

- Getting close to thousands of nesting seabirds from May to July
- Exploring a wild, rugged coastline surprisingly close to the nation's capital

Conditions

- Calm wind and sea

Trip Details

- Distance: 13km (8 miles)
- Time: 3–4 hours
- Map: OSi 1:50,000 sheet 50

Access

- **To the start:** Start beside Sutton Dinghy Club on the south-western side of Howth Peninsula. There is public beach access here, and if the club is open they should let you launch from their slipway. Parking space is limited however, so try to leave cars in Howth.
- Grid Ref: O 264 378
- GPS: 53.376310, -6.101126

- **To the finish:** Finish at the public slipway beside the lifeboat station in Howth harbour. A large, free car park is conveniently located beside the slipway.
- Grid Ref: O 285 394
- GPS: 53.389817, -6.068550

the main gannet colony lives on this angular sea stack off the north-eastern tip of Ireland's Eye.

A Martello tower marks the north-western point of Ireland's Eye.

Ireland's Eye, the island that lies at the heart of this trip, is one of the natural treasures of the east coast. Lying just 1.5km offshore, it is a wildlife sanctuary and home to thousands of seabirds during the breeding season from May to July. There are seals here too, and the island is only a small distance behind the Saltees in terms of the wildlife experience it offers.

There's no doubt the best way to visit the island is by sea kayak. The trip described here begins on the southern side of the Howth Peninsula, then completes the 'Round of Howth', an anticlockwise circumnavigation of the headland. The crossing out to Ireland's Eye provides the grand finale, before you finish at Howth harbour.

Independent paddlers should plan their trip carefully, ideally launching soon after low tide to avoid battling tidal currents of up to 2 knots that run along the eastern side of the peninsula. The current runs north on the flood (incoming) tide, and south on the ebb (outgoing) tide. Note that several tidal eddies also form along the southern shore of the peninsula, with the current flowing eastwards here for three-quarters of the time. The best way to understand it all is to search online for 'Dublin Bay Tidal Atlas', where you'll find a great You Tube graphic from the Dublin Port Company showing how the currents work.

You will need a shuttle between start and finish, though with just 4km separating these points, the logistics are not overly arduous. If you don't have two vehicles, it doesn't take long to complete the distance by bike, taxi or foot.

Guided Excursions

If you're not an experienced sea kayaker but would like to give paddling a try, this is an ideal place to start. Join one of the guided trips led by **Shearwater Sea Kayaking** (tel: 086 836 8736; www.shearwaterseakayaking.ie). They provide all the equipment, instruction and guidance necessary for beginners to make the crossing to Ireland's Eye, with prices starting from €55 per person.

Alternatively you can forget the kayaking and hop aboard one of the regular ferry services between Howth harbour and Ireland's Eye. **Island Ferries** (tel: 086 845 9154; www.islandferries.net) and **Ireland's Eye Ferries** (tel: 086 077 3021; www.irelandseyeferries. com) are two of the main operators. The trip costs €15 for adults and €10 for children.

The Paddle

At low tide the water in front of Sutton Dinghy Club is reduced to a shallow channel, with large swathes of exposed sand. However it should still possible to launch a kayak at all tides.

Begin by paddling south-east, past an obvious Martello tower. The coast becomes higher and rockier as you progress, with pebble coves nestling amongst the crags. Around Drumleck Point, the distinctive white building of **Baily Lighthouse** comes into view ahead. Cross the rather ominously named Doldrum Bay, which is backed by taller and steeper cliffs. Take care as you round the point beneath the lighthouse as there can be a significant tidal current here, with choppy water in cases of wind over tide.

Of Birds and Monks

Amongst the thousands of seabirds that nest along the cliff-fringed northern shore of Ireland's Eye, the newest arrivals are the gannets. These elegant birds started to breed here only in 1989, and now form the only significant colony between Scotland and Wexford's Saltee Islands. Yet the island is renowned for its history too: ninth-century monks working in a monastery here once produced the Garland of Howth, an illustrated manuscript similar to the Book of Kells and now preserved in Trinity College Dublin.

Pass the lighthouse and begin to head north along the wild, eastern side of the peninsula. The **cliffs** here are steep and rugged, with seabirds nesting all the way along. The ledges are crowded with kittiwakes, razorbills, guillemots and shags, and where the colonies are densest, a cacophony of noise mixes with the pungent odour of guano. Two pebble beaches provide the opportunity for a break, while several small stacks offer a spot of rock hopping.

As you round the Nose of Howth, at the north-eastern corner of the peninsula, the unmistakable profile of Ireland's Eye comes into view ahead. Continue west along the coast for 500m or so. The rocks here are a popular location for swimming and jumping, and on a summer's afternoon it's teenagers, not birds, who crowd these ledges.

When you are ready, make the 1.6km crossing to the eastern shore of **Ireland's Eye**. The southern half of the island is relatively low, but you'll be are drawn inexorably towards the angular **sea stack** at its north-eastern corner, home to the main gannet colony.

Round the stack and continue along the north coast, where the precipitous cliffs are covered with thousands more birds. Around halfway along, look out for puffins standing guard at the entrance to their burrows. There are also several large caves here, which can be explored in the right conditions.

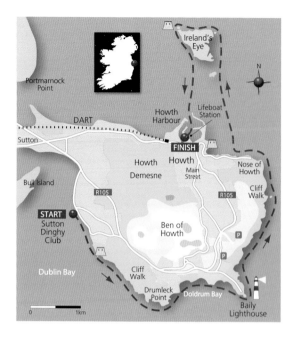

The island's north-western point is marked by another Martello tower. Round this to reach the beaches of the west coast. These are perfect places to pull up and explore the island on foot. Take care during the summer because there are large numbers of herring gull and black-backed gull, both of which nest on the ground. Eggs and fluffy chicks lie scattered amongst the rocks all over the northern part of the island. Further south, a path leads through the bracken to the ruins of St Nessan's Church, part of the old monastery established here in AD 700.

When you're ready, return to the boats and head south across 1km of open water to reach Howth harbour. The lighthouse at the tip of the harbour wall is a convenient navigational guide. Head to the back, right-hand corner of the harbour and exit via the public slipway beside the lifeboat station.

Watch out for tidal currents as you round the headland beneath Baily Lighthouse.

THE COPPER COAST

Explore a fascinating array of stacks and arches along this complex yet sheltered coastline

Great for

- Threading an endless succession of sea arches and rock channels
- Examining a copper deposit that exemplifies the unique geology of the area

Conditions

- Calm wind and sea

Trip Details

- Distance: 22km (14 miles)
- Time: 5–6 hours
- Maps: OSi 1:50,000 sheets 76 and 82

Access

- **To the start:** The trip starts at Newtown Cove car park, located on a sea cliff some 3km south-west of Tramore town centre.
- Grid Ref: X 572 993
- GPS: 52.143726, -7.166354

- **To the finish:** Finish at the parking area for Ballydowane Cove, which is signed from the coast road between Bunmahon and Stradbally.
- Grid Ref: X 407 978
- GPS: 52.132048, -7.405701

Narrow channels weave between the stacks and outcrops.

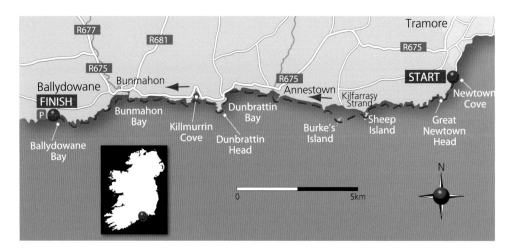

Waterford's Copper Coast is renowned amongst sea kayakers for the intricacy of its rock formations. The cliffs may not be as high or dramatic as some west coast locations, but the rock hopping is excellent and there are as many caves, stacks, tunnels and arches as anywhere along the Irish seaboard. Its position on the south-east coast also means it's relatively sheltered, and kayak guiding companies regularly bring complete novices to explore the area.

The majority of the coastline lies within the UNESCO Copper Coast Global Geopark. This has been formed in recognition of the area's incredible geological heritage; volcanoes, deserts, ice sheets and ocean forces have all combined to create the spectacular array of coves, headlands and islets visible today. At least 36 different minerals have been recorded in veins and seams inside the rock, and a thriving mining industry flourished here during the 19th century. For sea kayakers, the upshot of all this is great scenic variety, plus historic interest in terms of copper-stained cliffs and old mine shafts visible from the water.

There are numerous access points all along the coast, so it's possible to devise an itinerary of almost any distance. If the 22km trip described seems too long, either split the journey across two days, or use alternate egress points at Kilfarassy Strand, Annestown, Boat Strand pier, Kilmurrin Cove or Bunmahon. Frequent beaches also mean there are plenty of opportunities to take a break during the trip itself.

Tidal streams are slight, though you should avoid paddling if there is significant wind or swell coming

A 19th-century Copper-Rush

The copper-mining industry grew up around Knockmahon in the 1820s, and within a couple of decades, it had boomed into one of the most important mining centres in the world. By the 1960s, a shaft at Tankardstown tunnelled some 256m into the cliff, with large interior cables to raise the copper ore. Copper was not the only mineral excavated: at the eastern end of Ballydowane Bay, a ventilation shaft in a sea stack once linked to silver mines dug below the seabed.

The Copper Coast is a succession of rock features of all shapes and sizes.

Exiting the massive sea arch just west of Kilfarrasy Beach.

from the south. The whole point of the trip is to get in close to the rocks, so calm conditions are a prerequisite. It is worth exploring every channel and stack to locate their tunnels, so make sure to allow plenty of time; 4km/h is a reasonable estimate of speed given the amount of exploring you'll want to do along the way. The linear format also means you will have to organise a shuttle. Options include two vehicles, a long bike ride, or catching one of buses that ply the road between Stradbally and Tramore three days a week.

Guided Excursions

Several local companies arrange guided kayak trips along this coastline. Contact **Pure Adventure** (tel: 087 226 5550; www.pureadventure.ie) or **Ardmore Adventures** (tel: 083 374 3889; ardmoreadventures .ie) to discuss the possibilities.

The Paddle

From Newton Cove car park, carry the boats south down a flight of steps to reach a small pebble beach and slipway. Launch here, then begin to follow the coast south-west. The first couple of kilometres consist of low cliffs, and immediately there are opportunities for rock hopping between various outcrops.

After 1km you arrive at **Great Netwown Head**, located immediately beneath the prominent Metal Man sculpture (see page 143 for details). Just where the coast turns west, notice the entrance to a tall,

narrow cavern. If you explore to the back of this passage, two side entrances will appear on the left, allowing alternate exit points. This is just the first of several three-way tunnels you will pass during the course of the day.

A series of cliff-backed coves, each with an array of stacks and outcrops, brings you to the pebble beach at Garrarus. The next big feature is **Sheep Island**, which is attached to the mainland at all but high tide. According to the guidebook *Oileáin*, 'Both halves of Sheep bear more arches and through caves per square metre than any other Irish island.' You can easily spend 15 minutes exploring this outcrop alone.

A kilometre later, out from the sand of Kilfarrasy Strand, the collection of rocks known as Burke's Island is also worth exploring. Don't miss the tunnel that cuts through its south-western corner. The **headland** just west of Kilfarrasy is also bisected by a massive arch and smaller tunnel.

A section of straight cliffs then brings you to the outcrops of Brown's Island, at the entrance to the sandy cove at Annestown. Continue west around Dunabrattin Bay to reach the sheltered harbour, pier and slipway at Boat Strand.

Dunabrattin Head offers another maze of outcrops, then 1km later, you pass the enclosed, sandy horseshoe of Kilmurrin Cove. The cliffs rise again to 50m as you pass beneath the former mine workings at **Tankardstown**. Rectangular holes of old ventilation shafts can be seen high in the cliff face, evidence of the industry that once took place deep within the precipice. At the cliff base, look out for the distinctive green streak of an exposed copper vein. It is well worth landing on the rocks and examining this deposit up close to appreciate the incredible geology of the area properly.

The next sandy beach is Bunmahon, popular with families during the summer. West of here the coast returns to a series of rocky coves and storm beaches, with stacks and outcrops scattered just offshore. Don't miss St John's Island, which has a sea arch cutting through its centre.

The beach at **Ballydowane** provides a fitting finale to the trip, backed by impressive cliffs of red sandstone. Land on the sand near the western end of the beach to access the car park above.

WILD SWIMMING

Choose coastal conditions wisely. Poll na bPeist ('the Worm Hole') on Inishmore is a unique natural swimming hole in calm conditions, but lethal when conditions are rough. (Lukasz Warzecha)

LET'S BE HONEST: there are relatively few days in Ireland when most people choose to swim outside in a swimsuit. Even in August, water temperatures along the Irish coastline average around 15°C. Compare this to a normal indoor pool temperature of 27°C, and it's clear that Irish sea swimming never becomes what you might call warm. Summer lakes and rivers are more hospitable, but only by a small margin.

So what's the solution? Should we steer clear of outdoor swimming? That would be a great shame, because the country's magnificent coastline and countless lakes are a fabulous resource just waiting to be appreciated. Most people prefer a modern solution: climb into a wetsuit and you'll find you can suddenly spend an hour or more in the water rather than running out blue-lipped after five minutes.

Having negated the temperature issue, you can begin to enjoy all the wild-swimming opportunities the country has to offer. As well as endless scenic beaches and lakes, there are thrilling jumps off high rocks, longer swims through arches and into sea caves, and purpose-built diving boards hovering above deep pools – all of which are described in this section.

Sometimes, of course, longevity isn't your primary concern and the exhilarating refreshment of a cold-water dip is exactly what you want. Picture those sunny days when you're all hot and sweaty from some other activity, and cool water immersion will seem such a temptation. The final swim spot featured here falls into this category. Situated two-thirds of the way up Ireland's tallest mountain, it's a bracing plunge into the highest lake in the country. You have been warned!

Irish Wild Swimming at a Glance

Purpose-built swimming pools are a relatively new phenomenon in Ireland. Before that, all swimming took place outside. The lack of indoor facilities explains the historically low number of Irish people who could swim; it was just too cold and unpleasant to learn proper strokes outside. It is only in the last 40 years that most towns have had indoor pools, and teaching children to swim has become the norm.

As more people became confident around water, outdoor watersports increased in popularity. Improvements in wetsuit design have helped too,

Being Cold-Water Aware

Have you ever noticed how you come up gasping after jumping into cold water? This is Cold-Shock Response, where your body makes an involuntary inhalation after a sudden cold immersion. Even at Irish summer water temperatures of 15°C, it is hard to control this reaction. If you are still underwater when your body gasps it is extremely dangerous; this is the cause of around 60 per cent of drownings in Britain and Ireland. Wetsuits insulate you against the shock, but if you choose to swim without one, make sure you get in slowly and habituate yourself gradually to the low temperature of the water.

extending the al fresco swimming season beyond July and August. Now there's a plethora of people involved in outdoor swim-based activities, from triathletes to surfers and snorkellers, as well as a core of enthusiasts for whom the joy of open water swimming is enough in itself and needs no further enhancement.

Some wild-swimming spots are local institutions; people have been taking the plunge from the Forty Foot in Dublin for 250 years. At these places you may find concrete steps descending into the water, with handrails and – if you're really lucky – some sort of shelter to protect you from the elements while you get changed. The country's most popular beaches are also patrolled by lifeguards in July and August. Yet most outdoor swim locations remain entirely unadorned, leaving you to your own devices surrounded by nothing but nature.

The Basics

Conditions are everything in outdoor swimming. The ideal is a flat, calm day where the water is as smooth as glass and the warm sun dries you afterwards. At the other end of the spectrum are those days when wind chills the air and whips the water into an endless succession of peaks and troughs. Your approach and technique will vary accordingly; a smooth crawl stroke is bliss in perfect conditions, but difficult to maintain when surrounded by waves.

Novices will find open-water swimming very different from an indoor pool. The water is colder,

darker and choppier, there are no lanes to follow and no defined edges to the swim area. Some people become anxious about the hazards and creatures that might lurk beneath the surface. If you're concerned, get in slowly, focusing on your breathing. Swim along the shore rather than away from it, lifting your head frequently to take sightings from landmarks to keep yourself orientated, and swim in a straight line. In windy conditions, breathe on your downwind side to minimise the spray hitting your face. Remember that once you leave the shore you won't be able to rest until you return, so don't go too far and stay well within your limits of endurance.

Ideally you should swim with another person, and, as a backup, have someone else on shore who knows where you are. You need to take particular care with sea swimming, when large swells, incoming tides and rip currents all introduce their own hazards. Rivers can be dangerous too; it's amazing how quickly even a strong swimmer becomes tired when battling against a current. Jumping, and particularly diving, into open water also causes accidents. Always check water depth and hidden obstructions first before launching yourself off anything.

Essential Equipment

In theory you don't need any equipment to go wild swimming. Find a quiet spot, strip off your clothes, and the rest will follow. In practice, most people bring a swimsuit and a towel as a minimum.

Depending on how long you want to stay in and your tolerance of the cold (aka your 'wimp factor'), a wetsuit can be a good idea. The thicker the neoprene the more warmth it provides, but also the more buoyancy it adds and the more it hinders proper swimming. If your aim is long distance, go for a triathlon-style wetsuit. These are designed specifically for swimmers, with an aerodynamic coating, more flexible arms and buoyancy panels that support a horizontal position.

Neoprene booties are optional, but will help ease your entry and exit if the ground is rough underfoot. A brightly coloured silicone swim cap should be considered mandatory, both as insulation and to make yourself visible to other water users. Tow floats are another valuable safety tool, again making the swimmer more visible. Most serious swimmers also wear goggles, smeared with a coating of spit to stop them steaming up.

Make sure you are prepared for your exit too, especially if you're staying in long enough to get cold. Warm clothes, a flask of hot drink and a sweet snack will be much appreciated afterwards.

Extending your Skills

Like all outdoor sports, open-water swimming is safer and more fun if you have like-minded people to do it with. Start by contacting your local triathlon club, as many of their swim events take place outside. Find your nearest club on the Triathlon Ireland website, www.triathlonireland.com. Some swimming clubs may have members interested in wild swimming too.

There is also a whole calendar of organised open-water swim events that take place around the country each year. See openwaterswimmer.ie and the open-water section of www.swimireland.ie for details of some of the main ones. Most events offer a choice of distances ranging from a few hundred metres to almost several kilometres, with full safety cover provided.

Finding Out More

Books: *Wild Swimming in Ireland* by Maureen McCoy and Paul McCambridge details 50 of the best swim spots around the country.

Online: **www.outdoorswimming.ie** lists another 200 wild-swimming locations around Ireland. The Irish Water Safety website – **www.iws.ie** – displays safety advice for different water users, while **www.coldwatersafety.org** deals specifically with cold water issues.

Opposite from top: Wild swimming includes different levels of excitement. A big jump into the Blue Pool in Portrush, Antrim; It doesn't get better than this: a perfect dawn dip in Lough Derg, County Clare. (Patrick Bolger); For open-water excursions, dress like a pro with a triathlon wetsuit, bright swim cap and goggles; Some wild-swimming spots are local institutions: the Forty Foot at Sandycove, County Dublin. (Brendan Lyon).

Below: Ireland has countless scenic beaches and lakes that are perfect for swimming. Mullaghmore, Sligo.

THE SLOC, DUNSEVERICK

The combination of sheltered, non-tidal pools and a deep inlet perfect for rock jumping makes this a firm favourite with the whole family.

👍 Great for

- Developing confidence in a range of protected rock pools
- Feeling the surge of adrenaline as you leap from high rock ledges

☁ Conditions

- Calms seas or swell from a non-northerly direction

▦ Access

- Access the area via the A2 road between Ballintoy and Bushmills. Turn north onto the B146, following signs to Dunseverick. In Dunseverick village – around 1km east of the castle – turn onto a minor road signed to the 'Harbour'. The path that leads down to The Sloc is located on the left some 500m later, around 200m before the harbour.
- Map: OSNI 1:50,000 sheet 5
- Grid Ref: C 997 445
- GPS: 55.237269, -6.432556

The sheltered pools of The Sloc are perfect for families and novice snorkellers.

Coasteering groups regularly visit this rock-fringed inlet at Dunseverick, which offers jumps up to 5m high.

This wild-swim spot offers hours of fun for all sorts of watersport enthusiasts, from novice swimmers looking for sheltered pools, to adrenaline-charged rock jumpers. There is also good snorkelling, and scope for longer aquatic excursions for more dedicated ocean swimmers. And the best part is, it's all entirely natural: all the fun of a water park, but without a metal railing or concrete step in sight.

This is a little-known location, largely frequented by locals. The name comes from the Irish *sloc*, meaning sea gully or channel, though some people anglicise it to 'the slot'. Either way, it's an accurate description of the deep, rock-fringed inlet that provides the main focus of the area. The channel is deep enough to allow safe jumping at all tides, and is sheltered from all but northerly swells. Remember to bring wetsuit booties or water shoes to help with all the rock scrambling.

Locals tend to park along the road immediately above The Sloc. The road is narrow here, so a better option is the large car park 200m further on above picturesque Dunseverick Harbour, where facilities include a toilet block. It is worth noting that you will be following a tiny section of the Causeway Coast

From humble beginnings...

Despite its diminutive size, Dunseverick Harbour has been the start of many epic journeys. During the 1800s, local people would leave from here in small fishing boats, being rowed out to join larger schooners bound for Glasgow or Derry. In these cities they would board bigger emigration ships, then make the long and often fraught voyage across the ocean to America, Australia or New Zealand.

Path to reach the coast. If you have time, a walk just 1km east along this path will bring you through a sea arch to the cliff-backed hamlet of Portbradden, at the end of beautiful White Park Bay. For full details of this spectacular walking route, see page 61.

The Swim

From the harbour road, cross a stile and descend a flight of steps to reach the shore. Here you'll find a small patch of sand surrounded by rock outcrops, which forms the main base of the area. Dunseverick

Harbour lies just 200m to the right, while the inlet of The Sloc borders the area to the left.

If conditions are calm enough, proficient swimmers and snorkellers may want to begin at the **harbour** and swim across to the beach, or even around the headland and directly into The Sloc.

Young children and novice snorkellers will prefer the series of safe **rock pools** that lie enclosed within the headland itself. These pools are sheltered from all but the very largest ocean swells, and retain their water even at low tide. The furthest pools, up on the rocks, contain water that is often appreciably warmer than the surrounding ocean. This area is also used by local sub-aqua companies to introduce trainee divers to the underwater world, so on a summer's day there can be a lot of different activities taking place at once.

The largest pool is backed by low rocks, which provide a perfect introduction to the fun-filled pursuit of rock jumping. Once you feel confident, head across to the main event at **The Sloc** itself. Here, a deep channel just 6m wide cuts inland between parallel lines of rock. These basalt outcrops provide countless opportunities for jumping and diving, with ledges spread across all heights from sea level to 5m high.

Pick the size of your challenge, leap in, then scramble up one of several points of weakness and do it all again. Once you've jumped a few times you will understand why this is a popular venue for local coasteering groups. Older children in particular can spend hours here, with shrieks of fear and joy reverberating endlessly until spoilsport adults call them away.

Summer fun at The Sloc.

LOUGH CUMMEENOUGHTER

Scale the slopes of Ireland's mightiest mountain to swim in the highest lake in the country.

Great for

- Looking up from the water to the intimidating peaks looming overhead
- Refreshing yourself after the climb in the best way possible

Conditions

- Dry ground and good visibility for the climb

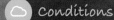

Trip Details

- Distance: 9.5km (6 miles)
- Time: 4½–5½ hours
- Ascent: 570m (1,870ft)
- Maps: OSi 1:50,000 sheet 78, OSi 1:25,000 *MacGillycuddy's Reeks*, or Harvey Superwalker 1:30,000 *MacGillycuddy's Reeks*.

Access

- Start and finish at Cronin's Yard, at the end of the road in Hag's Glen. The car park here costs €2, and excellent facilities include a tearoom, camping, showers and toilets (see croninsyard.com).
- Grid Ref: V 836 873
- GPS: 52.026536, -9.695809

Lough Cummeenoughter: a wild infinity pool.

A Glacial Stairway

The climb to Lough Cummeenoughter takes you through a wonderful succession of hanging valleys, known as the first, second and third levels. These small side valleys are set high above the floor of Hag's Glen, and were eroded from the sandstone bedrock by the thick glaciers of the last ice age. Lough Cummeenoughter fills the floor of the highest corrie, its outlet stream cascading down each step all the way to Lough Gouragh below.

Located at an elevation of 707m, Lough Cummeenoughter is a unique swimming spot. Not only is this the highest lake in Ireland, it's also one of the most dramatic. Nestled at the base of a natural amphitheatre with the country's two tallest peaks towering on either side, Irish swimming doesn't come any wilder than this.

The lake itself is surprisingly hospitable; it has a sandy bed and becomes deep quickly enough to dive into. As you might imagine, however, the main challenge is getting there. A footpath called O'Shea's Gully passes right beside the lake, but this is rough, mountain terrain, and you will need to be suitably prepared for all the eventualities of a steep hillwalk. There are even a couple of rock ledges and easy scrambling moves thrown in for good measure.

Fortunately, the path is one of the most popular ascent routes to Carrauntoohil, so if you head out on a fine summer's day, you should have the reassurance of other walkers around you. Most parties are fixated on the summit, so you may be the only one stopping to swim at the lough. The water remains cool here all year round, but it's wonderfully refreshing to arrive at the lake all hot and sweaty from the climb, and dive straight into the depths. Prepare yourself for a sharp intake of breath; given the length of the walk-in, hauling a wetsuit up to these heights is impractical, and this is likely to be a flesh experience.

The route statistics assume that after your swim, you return the way you came. If you prefer to climb for a further 332 vertical metres to reach the top of Carrauntoohil, this will add at least another 2km and 1½ hours to the day. Either way, there's the option of a second swim in another scenic lake on the way down.

The Swim

From Cronin's Yard, head south through a metal gate and join a wide track. Follow this through two more gates, then begin a gradual climb up Hag's Glen, beside the Gaddagh River. After roughly 1km, cross two green metal bridges, following signs for 'Carrauntoohil Mountain'.

Keep left at a path junction and continue along the west bank of the river for 1.2km. The main path now crosses the stream flowing out of Lough Gouragh. Instead of crossing here, follow the stream's western bank almost as far as **Lough Gouragh**. Shortly before the lake, veer right and join a stony path that climbs to the west.

The path begins with a rising traverse towards the rugged lower slopes of Carrauntoohil. The terrain is rough underfoot, and you'll need to negotiate one steep rock ledge to reach a flattish platform, known as the 'first level'. From here, climb south-west to the foot of an imposing black cliff, where the path splits. Turn right for Lough Cummeenoughter and O'Shea's Gully.

The trail now veers north-west and cuts up a rock crag to reach another hanging valley, known as the

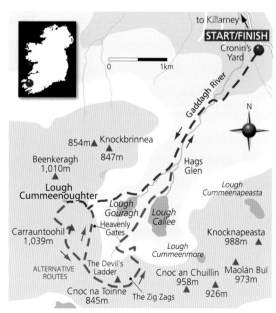

'second level'. Here you join the banks of the outlet stream that drains Lough Cummeenoughter, though the lake itself remains hidden from sight. Follow the left bank of the stream across the hollow and up a short, cliff-like headwall. Hands will be called on to pull yourself up the rock, with the stream forming a waterfall on your right.

You now arrive at the 'third level', the final **hanging valley** of the route. Backed by the vertiginous slopes of Carrauntoohil and Beenkeragh – Ireland's first and second highest mountains respectively – this is an immensely atmospheric location.

It's only as you mount the final rise that **Lough Cummeenoughter** is revealed at the base of the corrie. The path passes along the southern shore; follow this until you find a suitably sandy place to enter the water. The swim itself is exhilarating both in terms of the drama of the location, and the temperature of the water. Try to stay in long enough to float on your back and appreciate the horseshoe of cliffs all around.

After your swim the simplest option is to reverse your route back to Cronin's Yard. Having come this far, though, it's tempting to continue to the summit of Carrauntoohil. To do this, continue along the path, climbing steeply up the loose rock of O'Shea's Gully at the back left-hand corner of the corrie.

At the top of the gully you're met by an incredible view over Coumloughra. Turn left here and make the final, steep climb to the top of **Carrauntoohil** (1,039m). The summit is marked by a conspicuous metal cross, and a suitably impressive 360-degree panorama.

For details of the two main descent options from Carrauntoohil, see **The Walk Out** on page 54. Both routes take you back to Hag's Glen, passing either Lough Gouragh or Lough Callee on the way. These lakes both offer opportunities for a second dip, if you still have the energy.

Top: Exhilaration stems from both the drama of the location and the temperature of the water.
Bottom: Nestling beneath the precipitous cliffs of Carrauntoohil, Lough Cummeenoughter is Ireland's highest lake.

GUILLAMENE & NEWTOWN COVE

A fabulous coastal swim spot with deep-water diving, cliff jumping, and an open-sea excursion to an impressive cave.

👍 Great for
- Launching off the high diving board
- Open-water swimming along the cliffs to a stunning cave

☁ Conditions
- Calm seas, especially for the open-water excursion

⛨ Access
- Park at Newtown Cove car park, which is located on a sea cliff some 3km south-west of Tramore town centre.
- Map: OSi 1:50,000 sheet 76
- Grid Ref: X 572 993
- GPS: 52.143726, -7.166354

Swimmers and jumpers enjoying the facilities at Guillamene.

It is hard to imagine a wild-swimming location that offers more than Guillamene and Newtown Cove in County Waterford. Top-class facilities combine with a fabulous location at the start of the Copper Coast, a celebrated stretch of shoreline littered with rocky cliffs, islets, arches and coves.

There's something here for everyone. Young children venture into the water from a pebble beach, teenagers and adults turn somersaults from the high diving board, while experienced open-water swimmers venture along the cliffs to explore deep into several impressive caves.

The area is home to Newtown & Guillamene Swimming Club, which has been in existence for over 80 years. It's largely thanks to the subscriptions and fund-raising efforts of club members – supplemented by European grant money – that the construction and upkeep of the facilities has been possible.

The Swim – Guillamene

To reach Guillamene, head to the eastern side of the car park, then follow a concrete path across a grass lawn and down a set of steps. The deep water here means this is the traditional diving cove, safe at all tide levels. There has been organised swimming here

The Metal Man

One of Tramore's most famous landmarks is the Metal Man, a painted iron statue that stands atop a high pillar on Great Netwown Head. Constructed in the wake of a tragic shipwreck in 1816, when 363 people lost their lives just off the headland, the sailor points a warning finger to passing ships. For swimmers and kayakers, the statue also marks the great cave that lies at the base of the cliffs below.

since the 1880s; it was designated for men only until the 1980s, and though women are now welcome, the sign has been retained as a historic relic.

Near the base of the cliff you will find a brightly painted changing shelter, along with a variety of ways of launching yourself from the rocks into the sea below. The **high diving board** sits between two and four metres high, depending on the state of the tide. A set of concrete steps and a metal ladder provide less fearsome alternatives.

Inside the big cave beneath the Metal Man. Swim out through the exit on the left.

On the opposite side of the inlet, steps have been cut into the rocks and provide access to another series of unofficial and largely natural dive plinths. Chose any height that suits you, but make sure to jump far out to ensure you land in the water.

The Swim – Newtown Cove

Just south of the car park, more steps lead down to Newtown Cove. Reserved as the ladies' area in times gone by, this is a small sheltered cove backed by a pebble beach, with adjacent pier and slipway. The water here is not as deep as Guillamene, but convenient ladders still make pier jumping popular at high tide.

Impressive though the facilities are around the car park, this is just the start point for experienced open-water swimmers. The real **long-distance challenge** is to explore the coast south-west along the base of the cliffs. Wait for calm conditions before you set out because the shore can be exposed to Atlantic swells. Several rock platforms along the way mean you can haul out and take a rest if you need to.

There are several places where you can swim inside rock outcrops, and within a couple of hundred metres you reach the first cave. In the right conditions, confident swimmers can venture inside these caverns to explore their gaping interiors, the dark confines and reverberating echoes offering a truly awe-inspiring – and slightly humbling – experience.

If you have the energy and experience for a 2km round trip, the best cave lies on the western side of **Great Netwown Head**, just around the corner as the coast begins to turns west. This tall, narrow cavern stretches back for 50m and seems to be a cul-de-sac, until you reach the very end and two side entrances appear on the left. Depending on the tide, it should be possible to stand at the back of the cave. Swim through the first side exit into a cove bound on all sides by steep cliffs, with Waterford's famous Metal Man monument towering immediately overhead. A truly unique swimming experience!

Open-water swimmers take a break beside a cave entrance 500m south of Guillamene.

SNORKELLING

Irish snorkelling at its best.

SNORKELLING is a simple idea: put on some goggles, take a tube to help yourself breathe and go for a swim. It's so easy – people have been doing it for 5,000 years using hollow reeds as breathing aids – yet the rewards of the sport are innumerable, and far outweigh the effort required.

By donning a snorkelling mask, you're literally giving yourself a window onto another world. Suddenly you can see and explore a whole new environment, an underwater habitat that is completely removed from our normal land-based existence. Novice snorkellers are often amazed by their first experience, shocked at the alien-looking plants and creatures that live just beneath the surface, yet remain hidden to most people.

You can snorkel anywhere there's water, though the visibility and range of life is generally better at sea. While you shouldn't expect conditions akin to a tropical reef, Ireland does very well given its temperate maritime climate, and the wonderful geological diversity of the coastline means there are endless coves, bay and harbours to explore.

Ireland's varied coastline provides perfect underwater habitats for marine life.

Irish Snorkelling at a Glance

Ireland's Atlantic coast offers the country's best snorkelling and diving, with excellent visibility in many areas. Some sites are well documented and renowned amongst the sub-aqua community, though there are countless other locations too. It's great fun

Bog Snorkelling

Forget about wildlife on this trip – the water is so thick with muck you can barely see! Along with similar events in Wales, Australia and Sweden, the Irish Bog Snorkelling Championships takes place in County Monaghan in September each year. Competitors must complete two consecutive lengths of a 55m peat trench, wearing masks and snorkels and relying on flipper power alone for propulsion. Some are serious athletes, others dress up in costumes, but there's no denying the fun involved.

to devise your own snorkel safari and spend several days exploring promising-looking coves and inlets for yourself.

The nutrient-rich water of the Gulf Stream sustains a wide variety of marine life. In all, 245 different species of fish have been recorded here, along with 25 cetaceans (whales, dolphins and porpoises) and two species of seal. There's a huge variety of marine invertebrates too, ranging from molluscs, jellyfish, anemones and starfish to lobsters and crabs. The largest crab in Ireland, the spider crab, can have a leg span measuring over 50cm, and is regularly spotted by snorkellers.

The number of people who snorkel regularly is relatively small, and much of the activity is informal in nature. In Counties Mayo and Galway, five coastal sites have been designated as official snorkelling Blueways – safe havens with interesting underwater habitats that are ideal for beginners and experts alike. For more details about these sites, see www.blueway.ie.

There are also several commercial operators around the country who offer guided snorkelling trips, based either on land or from a boat. Search online for 'snorkelling tours Ireland' to find contact details.

The Basics

For the best snorkelling experience, you need to find the holy grail of calm water, good visibility and plentiful marine life not far below the surface. Sunny days are best, because sunlight penetrates through the water and illuminates the features below. The safest sites lie in protected bays, where the water is calm and there isn't much current. Avoid large towns and river estuaries; the water here can be disturbed by pollutants or be murky due to silt. The best areas are usually found around rocky outcrops, where marine life tends to concentrate.

Snorkelling at night is also very rewarding, and is particularly enjoyable on a full moon. You'll see a whole new ecosystem in action, because many marine creatures are nocturnal and remain hidden during the day. Select a spot you're already familiar with, and carry a good underwater scuba torch to illuminate the otherwise dark environment.

While it's great to have encounters with all sorts of marine species, make sure you respect wildlife. Seals, dolphins, crabs, eels and some fish can all react aggressively if put under pressure. Look but don't touch and keep a respectful distance, letting creatures approach you, rather than the other way round.

Like diving, safe snorkelling involves the use of a buddy system. Ideally, two people should enter the water together, while a third person remains on the shore to provide land-based assistance. In case of an emergency, call the coastguard by dialling 999 or 112.

Essential Equipment

In theory, you need just two pieces of kit to start snorkelling: a snorkel and a mask. Given the temperature of sea around Ireland (which ranges from roughly 9°C in March to 15°C in August), you'll also appreciate a wetsuit, with neoprene hood, gloves and booties, if you want to stay in for any length of time.

The most important thing to get right is the fit of the mask. This is something you need to try on before you buy because if it doesn't fit well, you'll be plagued by leaks. Note that masks should be rinsed in fresh water after use, and kept out of direct sunlight to avoid degrading the silicone. The snorkel should have a mouthpiece that fits comfortably and allows you to breathe calmly and efficiently. There are various designs on the market; the best ones are made of silicone and have a purge valve to help clear water from the tube.

In terms of wetsuits, a 5/3mm or 6/4mm suit is recommended. Wetsuits introduce a significant amount of buoyancy, so if you like diving underwater, you'll need to compensate by wearing a weight belt. While not strictly necessary, a pair of fins (or flippers) also facilitates more efficient swimming and more powerful surface dives.

Getting Started

Providing you're a confident swimmer, snorkelling is something you can try without any expert instruction. If you've never used a mask and snorkel before, take it to your local swimming pool for a practice session before heading out to sea. When you're ready to hit open water, make sure conditions are calm and there are no significant currents within your chosen area. High slack tide is generally considered the best and safest time to snorkel.

Your final act before entering the water should be to prepare the inside of your mask to keep it fog-free. Either coat the glass with a commercial anti-fog

If you're lucky you may meet a marine mammal, like this dolphin in Doolin, County Clare. (Lukasz Warzecha)

Bog snorkelling is great fun, but don't expect any visibility! (Colin Gates)

gel, or rub spit across the lenses. Rinse this off then quickly put the mask in place and keep it there. Every time you remove the mask you decrease the efficacy of the de-fog solution.

If you're wearing fins, put them on at the water's edge then enter the sea by walking backwards. The most efficient fin-swimming technique is to kick from the hip without bending your knees, letting the fins provide all your propulsion while your arms remain still by your side.

You may sometimes want to duck dive to examine a creature in closer detail. Begin by taking a deep breath, then when you return to the surface, exhale sharply as if you were spitting out a cherry stone. This will send the water shooting out of the snorkel. Two blasts are often required to clear the tube completely, but with practice the entire manoeuvre can be completed without lifting your head from the water.

Extending Your Skills

If you don't feel confident snorkelling on your own, or want to extend your skills further, get in touch with the Irish Underwater Council (also known as CFT) at www.diving.ie. They run beginners' courses and an Advanced Snorkel Diver course, which will improve both your technique and understanding of the sport. Their website also lists over 80 sub-aqua clubs around the country, many of which welcome

snorkellers as well as scuba divers as members. It's not unusual for people to begin snorkelling, then progress to full scuba diving as their interest in the marine environment increases.

For a better list of clubs in Northern Ireland, also see the diving section of www.outdoorni.com.

Finding Out More

Online: Snorkelling falls within the remit of the Irish Underwater Council. See the snorkelling section of **www.diving.ie** for more advice about practising the sport in Ireland. The Dive Sites section of their website also includes an interactive map of diving locations, some of which are relevant to snorkellers.

The black goby is one of many fish species you might spot on your underwater adventures. (Richard Thorn)

Sea anemones come in all different colours.

MALIN BEG

Highlights of these two renowned snorkelling locations include a rock tunnel, crystal-clear waters and perfect sandy cove.

Great for

- Swimming through a narrow rock tunnel in Malin Beg Harbour
- Gazing across the idyllic horseshoe bay holding Silver Strand

Conditions

- Calm sea and wind

Access – Malin Beg Harbour

- Follow the R263 through Kilcar, Carrick and Glencolmcille, and continue to the hamlet of Malin Beg (*Málainn Bhig*). Once in the village, turn right just past Malinbeg Hostel onto the L5115. Descend for 400m and park in a lay-by above the pier.
- Map: OSi 1:50,000 sheet 10
- Grid Ref: G 493 799
- GPS: 54.665439, -8.786221

Access – Silver Strand

- Silver Strand is marked on the OS map as Trabane. It's located at the end of the R263, where a large clifftop car park gives direct access to the beach.
- Map: OSi 1:50,000 sheet 10
- Grid Ref: G 498 800
- GPS: 54.665414, -8.777391

Main image: The pristine beach of Silver Strand. The best snorkelling lies along the right side of the cove.
Inset: Inside Malin Beg's rock tunnel, whose walls are decorated by starfish.

Enjoying perfect summer conditions at Malin Beg, with the sea stack visible behind.

Malin Beg is a remote hamlet in west Donegal that is renowned amongst the Irish sub-aqua community. These are some of the clearest waters in the country, with visibility averaging around 8m. There are several well-known scuba sites located just offshore, but the harbour itself is also recognised as one of the best shore-dive locations in Ireland, with fabulous underwater scenery submerged by less than 5m of water. The ease of access means snorkelling here is every bit as rewarding as diving and, during the summer months, snorkellers can often be found kitting up on the quay in preparation for their excursion.

From the depths to the heights...

As well as offering great snorkelling, Malin Beg also lies at the western end of the formidable Slieve League cliffs (see page 62 for details). Though most hillwalkers approach Slieve League from Bunglass, it's also possible to set off from Silver Strand car park, and follow the coastal mountains south-west for 6km to reach the 595m summit. The juxtaposition of mountaintop and underwater world will leave you in awe at the natural diversity of this incredible coastline.

The harbour itself lies at the back of a narrow cove, with a central sea stack and nearby rock tunnel providing memorable features to explore. Yet the charms of the area don't end there. Just a kilometre away, Silver Strand (or *Traban*) is surely one of Ireland's most beautiful beaches. A perfect horseshoe of golden sand enclosed by steep green mountains, it would be a great shame to leave Malin Beg without also visiting this natural marvel. The western side of the beach is another recognised snorkelling site, so you can explore two underwater locations in one day, with a picnic thrown in between for good measure.

Both Silver Strand and the harbour face south, and are enclosed on three sides by high headlands. This means they are sheltered from wind and swell coming from any direction other than south. It is quite feasible to find calm, pleasant conditions in these coves even as north- and west-facing shores are battered by waves.

The Snorkel – Malin Beg Harbour

From the parking area, descend to the harbour, where you'll find a steep little slipway and concrete quay. The easiest access is off the slipway, though the quay offers fun jumping options for families.

You'll notice the good visibility as soon as you duck underwater. The snorkelling starts immediately, with a range of rock and colourful seaweeds providing a perfect habitat for marine life. Start by following the right side of the cove out towards the **sea stack**. Along the way you may spot soft corals and sponges, as well as species like pollock, wrasse, plaice, goby, lobster, spider crab and urchin.

Just around the corner, not far from the stack, you'll notice a low **rock tunnel** that bores into the cliff on the right. This chasm is a great place to explore – it's about 10m long and narrow enough that you can touch both walls at once. It leads out into a tiny, enclosed rock cove. Notice how the weed disappears where the light can't penetrate, though starfish seem quite content on the dark rock walls.

The entire harbour area is worth exploring and it is easy to spend an hour or more in the water before returning to the quay.

The Snorkel – Silver Strand

Access to Silver Strand is via a flight of 180 concrete steps set into a steep, grassy slope. Once at the bottom, cross the sand to the right-hand side of the bay, where a jumble of submerged rocks decorate the base of the cliff. The beach shelves gently, so it's easy to walk along the sand into the water. If conditions are calm, it is worth continuing out along the edge of the cove to some large **rock stacks** just around the corner, where the underwater nooks and crannies shelter more life.

As well as exploring the rocky edge of the cove, look out on the sandy seabed for flatfish such as turbot and brill, though these are often well camouflaged and can only be spotted if they move.

Entry point: the small pier and slipway at Malin Beg.

KEEM STRAND

Dive into the turquoise waters of this remote cove to explore an official Blueway snorkel trail, with the added security of summer lifeguards.

Great for

- Watching fish dart around a submerged mountain base
- Revelling in the history and natural beauty of the wonderfully sheltered location

Conditions

- Calm sea and wind

Access

- Head to the large car park above Keem Strand, at the western end of the R319 on Achill Island.
- Map: OSi 1:50,000 sheet 30
- Grid Ref: F 560 042
- GPS: 53.967254, -10.195508

The best snorkelling lies along the cliff base on the southern side of Keem Beach.

Keem Strand is a remote and atmospheric cove so striking it has been designated one of the signature discovery points of the Wild Atlantic Way. With a sandy beach that shelves gently into turquoise waters, this remote spot becomes even more memorable if you don a snorkelling mask and explore its sub-aqua world. Lying at the far western tip of Achill Island, it's something of an adventure even reaching Keem. Achill is Ireland's largest island, but separated from the mainland by a channel just 100m wide, with a simple bridge spanning the gap. It's another 23km to Keem, with the final section of road climbing a spur of Croaghaun Mountain above an unprotected and precipitous drop to the ocean.

The beach itself sits at the back of a horseshoe bay, surrounded on three sides by steep green slopes. As a photo point, it's one of the most picturesque beaches in Ireland. The surrounding hills also act as natural weather break, sheltering the bay from the prevailing wind and swell. It's quite possible for the larger beach at Keel, 8km east, to be beaten by wind-driven spray, while swimming and snorkelling remain perfectly attractive at Keem.

Croaghaun Mountain

If you're feeling energetic, why not combine your snorkel with a coastal walk? Options include a 5.5km circuit that climbs to the lookout post atop Moyteoge Head, just south of Keem Strand, then heads north-west along the ridge to Achill Head. Alternatively, tackle the ascent of 688m Croaghaun and gaze over the massive cliffs that cut into its northern flank. Either way, there's nothing better than descending all sweaty from the slopes and diving straight into the turquoise water below.

Despite its remote location, Keem is a popular spot and has the facilities to match. There's a large car park, and lifeguards provide coastal supervision during July and August. During the summer there is usually a watersports trailer parked at the top of the beach, hiring wetsuits, snorkels and kayaks. Its opening hours can be unreliable, though, so if you want to guarantee your underwater fix, the best advice is to bring your own gear.

The spider crabs at Keem can measure over 50cm wide. (Richard Thorn)

Above: Keem Strand occupies a beautiful cove at the remote western tip of Achill Island.
Below: The sandy seabed at Keem gives the water a turquoise hue.

The Snorkel

Though snorkelling is worthwhile on both sides of the bay, the main trip is the official **Blueway** – a designated snorkel trail that runs along the cliffs on the southern side of the beach (to your right as you look out to sea). There's little to mark the trail on the ground, but the lifeguards will be happy to answer any questions you have. The depth of water here means snorkelling is possible at all levels of tide, while weak tidal currents make it suitable for beginners.

Enter the water from the beach and begin to make your way along the jumbled boulders at the base of the cliff. Kelp grows between the rocks, providing

a perfect habitat for sea life. You can expect to see numerous fish, from relatively large individuals darting between the rocks, to shoals of sand eel flashing silver just below the surface. Sea urchins and spider crabs are also common.

Venture as far as you like around the base of the cliffs before returning to the beach. If you're visiting in May or June, keep an eye open for **basking sharks**. These gentle giants reach 11m long and are the world's second-largest fish. Fortunately, they have no teeth and are harmless to humans, surviving by filtering microscopic plankton from the water.

Achill was once home to the world's largest basking shark fishery, with some 9,000 sharks caught here over 14 years during the 1950s and 1960s. Most were caught from Keem, by men balanced in traditional curragh rowing boats. Display boards in the car park provide more information. Perhaps unsurprisingly, the shark population crashed soon afterwards, and though individuals can still be seen, the species is now considered endangered in the north-east Atlantic. If you are lucky enough to see one, please report your sighting to the Irish Whale and Dolphin Group (www.iwdg.ie) to aid their conservation efforts.

NOHOVAL COVE

This isolated inlet harbours caves, stacks and arches, with an impressive array of marine wildlife thriving below.

👍 Great for

- Swimming deep into caves and around several large sea stacks
- Watching some surprisingly large fish glide through the kelp

☁ Conditions

- Calm sea and wind

Nohoval Cove is a feast of stacks, caves and arches, all rising darkly above turquoise water. (Shutterstock)

🏛 Access

- You will need an OS map or GPS to reach Nohoval Cove, County Cork. It is generally accessed via the R611 Belgooly–Carrigaline Road. The final couple of junctions – to the north-east of the cove – are signed, then a steep, single-track descent brings you to the inlet itself. Parking is limited to a small lay by and a couple of pull-in spots at the end of the road.
- Map: OSi 1:50,000 sheet 87
- Grid Ref: W 734 514
- GPS: 51.715478, -8.384809

County Cork gets its fair share of summer visitors, yet also contains places so far off the beaten track, you wonder if you're still in the same county. Just a stone's throw from hustle and bustle of Kinsale, Nohoval Cove is one of the secret spots. The maze of approach lanes means you woud never happen across it, and once there, it still feels like the edge of the world.

The back of the cove is a narrow inlet, hemmed in on both sides by steep cliffs. Yet a short climb to the adjacent headland reveals a bay filled with more natural drama than you would imagine possible. A feast of stacks, caves and arches lie scattered below, all rising darkly above turquoise water. Once the refuge of smugglers and pirates, it's mainly watersport enthusiasts who visit the cove today, with snorkellers, scuba divers, sea kayakers and cliff divers all revelling in its natural treasures.

Underwater Cork

With a coastline that stretches for over 1,000km, it's no surprise that Cork contains several spots popular amongst snorkellers. Other recognised sites include Robert's Cove, just 7km east of Nohoval. Alternatively, you could head 90km west to Lough Hyne. This small lake held freshwater until 4,000 years ago, when rising sea levels turned it saline. Today it's refreshed twice daily by a seawater current that surges through the rapids of Barloge Creek. The warm, highly oxygenated water and sheltered surroundings create a unique natural habitat, sustaining a variety of aquatic plants and animals found nowhere else in the country.

Above: Seals swim amongst the kelp on the eastern side of Nohoval Cove. (Fáilte Ireland)
Opposite: You can swim into caves on both sides of the inlet at Nohoval.

The unique atmosphere of the place is matched by a wealth of life below the surface, and you will see bigger fish here than at most other snorkelling locations in Ireland. The sea is also the warmest in the country, with an average August water temperature of 16.4°C, over 2°C warmer than the north coast.

Nohoval Cove is accessible at all times, but try to visit around high tide if you want to swim around the stacks. The inlet is generally sheltered too, though it is exposed to southerly and easterly swells.

The Snorkel

As you arrive at Nohoval Cove, the most obvious landmark is the ruin of Nohoval Castle just above the shore. The ocean lies at the end of the road, but is partially obscured by the surrounding valley. The best way to get your bearings is to climb onto the **headland** just east of the cove, where there's a great view over the whole bay. Follow a small footpath that heads left from the road, halfway between the lay-by and the shore. A short, diagonal ascent brings you to a lookout point, where you can see all the main stacks and arches protruding from the shallows below.

When you're ready to start snorkelling, return to the end of the road and get in. At high tide the water rises almost to the track, though you'll have to clamber over a few boulders at lower tides.

There are numerous features to explore within a 250m radius. **Caves** can be found on both sides of the inlet, while the main **stacks and arches** – known locally as 'The Turrets' – are located just around the corner on the left. The depth of water around the stacks will depend on the tide; you can swim all around them at high tide, while a rocky causeway connects them to the shore later on.

Wherever you go within the cove you'll be surrounded by life. The seabed is a mixture of sand, rock and kelp, and provides a perfect habitat for all sorts of creatures. There are particularly large spider crabs, pollock and wrasse, as well as shoals of darting sand eels flashing silver near the surface.

In calm conditions you could also leave the inlet and follow the shore around to the left. After a ten-minute swim you'll reach a cove that is home to a seal colony. It's a wonderful experience to watch these mammals in their natural environment, but remember not to approach too closely as they can react aggressively. Let them be the ones to approach you if they want to.

Explore the nooks and crannies for as long as you like, then return to your entry point to finish.

HOOK HEAD & SOLOMON'S HOLE

Hook Head offers two unique snorkelling spots, with a natural rock arch and the world's oldest lighthouse as backdrops.

Searching for spider crabs in the natural pool beneath Hook Head Lighthouse.

Scuba divers rate Hook Head amongst Ireland's top places to dive. It offers plenty of scope for boat diving, with several wrecks fringing the west coast of the peninsula. But the area is also known for its shore dives, and along with the clear water and abundant sea life, it's this accessibility that makes the area appealing to snorkellers.

Most of the best sites are concentrated at the southern tip of the peninsula, within a couple of kilometres of Hook Head Lighthouse. If you only have time for one outing, concentrate on the area immediately adjacent to the lighthouse. This is a popular tourist site so don't expect solitude, but it does provide a unique place to explore.

The Snorkel – Hook Head Lighthouse

Begin by walking to the end of the road beside the lighthouse. Continue onto the path that runs around the southern wall of the building, but after just 10m, veer right along the edge of a chasm. Cross the rocks

The World's Oldest Lighthouse

Hook Head Lighthouse is the oldest operational lighthouse in the world. There has been a beacon on the headland since the fifth century, originally in the form of a nightly bonfire. The lighthouse itself was built in the 1200s, and operated by monks for the first 400 years. The signal is now automated, but coastal erosion means the building is unlikely to survive another 800 years into the future.

for a further 50m to reach a large **natural pool** that's almost enclosed by the surrounding reef.

The rocky setting protects the pool from waves and currents, but you should still avoid swimming in stormy conditions. The pool itself offers great snorkelling at all but low tides. You should see plenty of underwater life amid the kelp and rocks, with some remarkably

At mid tide there's plenty of headroom beneath the arch at Solomon's Hole.

large spider crabs. The reef here is limestone, which is easily eroded, so numerous gullies, chasms and holes provide shelter for fish. It's a novel experience to lift your head and see the unmistakable tower of Ireland's most famous lighthouse looming above.

In calm seas it is possible to venture beyond the pool to the coastline beyond, but beware that a tidal race runs past this headland, so only attempt open-water excursions at slack water (an hour before low and high tide).

The Snorkel – Solomon's Hole

The other most interesting snorkelling site in the area is Solomon's Hole, which should be explored at mid to high tide. From Hook Head Lighthouse, you can reach this spot either by foot or by car. To walk there, head along the path that skirts around the southern walls of the lighthouse compound, then continue north-east along a delightful section of the Wexford Coastal Path. This grassy trail leads along the top of the foreshore, and brings you to Solomon's Hole after 2km.

Alternatively, drive the 2.5km and park at Slade Harbour. Head through a stone archway at the south-eastern corner of the harbour, then cross a stile and head south along the Wexford Coastal Path. After roughly 300m, shortly before the next stile, you will notice the numbers 11 and 12 painted on the shore-side rocks. Solomon's Hole lies beneath the arch just right of number 12.

This excursion is more memorable for its remarkable geology than its underwater life. The hole itself is a small enclosed pool that has formed beneath a natural **rock arch**. A sloping ledge allows easy access to the back of the pool, which deepens as it nears the arch. At mid tide there's plenty of headroom to swim underneath, but at very high tide you may have to duck underwater to pass through.

On the far side of the arch, the channel narrows to a slender gully, 12m deep but just 2m wide. Divers attest to the lobsters, crab and wrasse that shelter here. In calm conditions you can exit the gully and explore the coastline beyond, before squeezing back though the chasm and under the arch to finish. Before leaving, make sure to walk over the top of the arch too, just to say you've explored it from every possible angle.

Like snorkel locations all over the world, sunshine at Hook Head helps to make underwater features more visible.

OFF-ROAD CYCLING

Ballinastoe, in County Wicklow, is just one of several great mountain bike centres around Ireland. (Neal Houghton)

THERE ARE NUMEROUS excellent road-biking routes all round Ireland, but they are not the subject of this bucket list. The emphasis here is on wild adventures, which means getting off the road to places where you can cycle free from the pressure of motor traffic. This sort of biking is a breath of fresh air, both literally and metaphorically. There's no looking over your shoulder, worrying about the speed the next vehicle will pass at. There's no noise or air pollution and no stress. It's just you, your bike, the trail and the scenery, and you'll be amazed what a liberating way it is to travel.

On a bike you cover ground much more quickly than by foot, enjoying a real sense of journey as you travel across the landscape, yet you're going slowly enough to appreciate the little things too, climbing off the saddle to examine some flowers or taking a break while you appreciate a particular view. Whether you're on your own, with family or friends, this is a lovely way to explore the countryside.

In Ireland, off-road biking falls into two main categories: greenways and mountain biking. Greenways are purpose-made trails designed for leisure cyclists and walkers. They tend to be largely flat with wide, solid surfaces, and offer traffic-free touring routes across some of the most scenic parts of the country. They demand no particular expertise and are popular with families.

Mountain biking ups the ante somewhat. The trails are narrower and have a rougher surface, but if you proceed carefully the easier routes still lie within the reach of all proficient cyclists. The more technical trails involve steep descents, tight corners and rock drops, and demand more experience and expertise. Whatever level you ride at, mountain biking is an exhilarating

Other Irish Greenways

If you like greenways, you could also try the Great Southern Trail Greenway. This runs for 36km from Rathkeale to Abbeyfeale in south Limerick, following the route of the old Limerick–Tralee railway. See www.southerntrail.net for more details. In Northern Ireland, check the Newry Canal Towpath, which runs for 32km from Newry to Portadown, or the 34km Lagan and Lough Cycle Way around Belfast.

sport and can be really satisfying when you get into the rhythm and flow through a well-designed section of trail.

Irish Off-Road Cycling at a Glance

Ireland's first purpose-built mountain bike trail centre opened only in 2007. This was located in Ballyhoura Forest, in Limerick, which still offers the most extensive network of trails in the country.

The sport has exploded in popularity since then, and there are now 11 official Irish mountain bike venues. Five of these are in Northern Ireland: as well as Rostrevor, which is featured on page 165, there are professionally designed trails at Castlewellan, Davagh Forest, Barnett Demesne and Blessingbourne. The Republic has seven designated trail centres. Besides Ballyhoura (see page 177), there's Ticknock, Ballinastoe, Derroura, Portumna, Bike Park Ireland and Glencullen Adventure Park.

Greenways are an even newer phenomenon. The first was the Achill–Westport Greenway (see page 168), which was completed in 2010. The huge success of this project has been a catalyst for further development, and there are now a host of new greenway routes that have either been completed very recently (see the Waterford Greenway on page 228) or are in the planning process. The most ambitious project to date spans half the country from Dublin to Athlone, and is described on page 172.

Of course there are opportunities for off-road cycling away from official centres too. The vast network of bog tracks in rural counties are a particularly good resource for those with a decent map. So long as you avoid private property and minimise erosion, there's nothing to stop you devising your own route into the wilds.

Essential Equipment

Whatever sort of cycling you do, you should always wear a helmet. Make sure it fits properly and complies with the EN1078 European Standard. The helmet should sit just above your eyes to protect your forehead, not on the back of your head as is commonly seen.

Greenways are so flat almost any bike will do, but you'll appreciate a more technical spec for mountain

Opposite from top: Devise your own off-road circuit along the country's bog tracks. This one is on Achill Island; River and canal towpaths offer an easier cycling experience. The Barrow towpath near Graiguenamanagh, County Kilkenny. (Jason Baxter); Pump tracks and skills courses are great places to practise off-road techniques; Get off the road and see where you end up. Killiney Hill, Dublin. (Jason Baxter).

Below: Enjoy long-distance views from Derroura mountain bike trail in County Galway.

biking. Things like disc brakes, a wide range of gears and front shock absorbers will all be appreciated on these trails, along with chunkier tyres that provide better traction. Unless you're getting into specialist downhill riding, bikes with rear suspension are not required for most Irish trails.

Expect to pay around €250 for a hybrid bike suitable for smooth surfaces, and €500 for a decent entry-level mountain bike. If you don't have a bike, don't worry: most greenways and trail centres have relatively inexpensive bike hire shops nearby.

If you ride often you'll appreciate a pair of padded shorts and gloves. A pump and puncture-repair kit or spare inner tube are also recommended. Wear appropriate clothing to protect yourself against the elements, and don't forget food and drink. An 80kg cyclist burns around 650 calories per hour, so you'll need regular snacks to keep your energy levels up. Mobile phones are also invaluable in dealing with any mishaps that may arise. Carry your gear in pockets or in a small backpack, but keep things to a minimum as heavy bags make cycling awkward.

Getting Started

Most people learn to ride a bike as a child, a skill that stays with them for the rest of their lives. Even if you have cycled only infrequently since then, you should be able to manage a greenway. The surface here is so flat and the dangers so limited that this is a perfect place to build confidence. Pick a section of an appropriate length – 20km or even 10km might be enough for your first outing – and take all the time you need to enjoy the experience.

Mountain biking is one of the most technical forms of cycling, yet there are many trails around the country that are suitable for novices. Most trails are graded according to a colour-coded system: green trails are easiest, blue runs are moderate, red means difficult and black routes are extreme. If you're even a semi-proficient cyclist you should be fine with green routes, and it won't be long before you're hitting the blues too. Many trail centres also have short pump tracks (skills courses), which can be an ideal place to find your feet.

It won't take long to appreciate that good mountain biking demands specific skills in terms of cornering, weight distribution, gear selection and braking. The 'attack position' – standing up on the bike with pedals level, knees and elbows bent, and fingers covering both brakes – is one of the first skills you should learn, and will make the world of difference to your control.

If you're a complete beginner, get somebody more experienced to show you a few basics. You'll find plenty of skills videos and tutorials online. Then get out there and experiment with different positions and techniques. Don't let minor tumbles put you off. These are generally not serious in nature, and are part and parcel of mountain biking.

Extending Your Skills

Once you've gained a bit of confidence, why not make contact with your local cycling club to see if they do any off-road riding? There are over 450 clubs registered with Cycling Ireland, spread all around the country. The club locator map, in the membership section of www.cyclingireland.ie, will help you find the one closest to you. Otherwise, if you live near one of the trail centres, there's bound to be a club associated with it.

Mountain bike skills courses run by professional coaches are also recommended. These are held at many trail venues and outdoor activity centres. If you get really keen you may even want to start competing. The annual Biking Blitz (www.bikingblitz.ie) is a beginner-friendly series of events with a 'Baggy Shorts' class for novices. Age categories go from under-six upwards, so the whole family can give it a go.

Finding Out More

Online: www.cyclingireland.ie is the sport's governing body for the island of Ireland both on and off the road.

www.irishtrails.ie provides an index of off-road routes in the Republic, listing both greenways and mountain bike venues. Select the category 'Off-Road Cycling Trails' on the home page. For Northern Ireland, **www.cycleni.com** has a similar off-road listing detailing both family routes and mountain bike trails. **www.mountainbikeni.com** concentrates specifically on mountain biking in the north.

ROSTREVOR MTB TRAIL

The fun and exhilaration of this epic singletrack descent more than justify the effort of the climb.

Great for

- Zipping down endless singletrack as you weave across forest and hillside
- Enjoying the views from a genuine mountain climbed entirely on your bike

Conditions

- Dry ground and good visibility for the views

Trip Details

- Distance: 27km (17 miles)
- Time: 3–4 hours
- Ascent: 550m (1,800ft)
- Maps: OSNI 1:50,000 sheet 29, or OSNI 1:25,000 Activity Map *The Mournes*

Access

- Rostrevor Forest is located within Kilbroney Forest Park. The park entrance is signed off the A2 road 1km south of Rostrevor town centre, partway between Newry and Kilkeel. Park in one of two bottom car parks, located on the left just inside the forest entrance. The bike centre is located in the second, 'main' car park. Alternatively, to reach the upper trailhead, continue past the lower car parks then swing right and follow the steep scenic drive to the top.
- Grid Ref: J 186 178
- GPS: 54.097358, -6.187284

Enjoy expansive views over Carlingford Lough from the Cloughmore Climb.

The viewpoint at the sharp switchback known as Kodak Corner. (Chris Hill)

Rostrevor is regarded as one of the best mountain bike centres in Ireland. Its attractions are twofold. First come the trails themselves, which offer 49km of epic riding along largely purpose-built, singletrack routes. Second is the location. Beginning from the shores of Carlingford Lough and rising almost to the 485m summit of Slievemartin in the Mourne Mountains, the rides include several lofty panoramas and do true justice to the term 'mountain' biking.

This isn't a beginner's venue, however – novices would be better off on the green or blue trails at nearby Castlewellan Forest Park. Rostrevor offers nothing below red grade, with a 27km red trail, 19km of black, and two specialist downhill trails rated at the extreme grade of orange.

Hunted like a Hound

Rostrevor is home to one of the most unusual mountain bike events in the Irish calendar – the annual Red Bull Foxhunt. This has taken place every year since 2011, and involves some 450 amateur riders massing on the start line. A bugle sounds, and the race is on to descend the 5.6km course as fast as possible. This pack of 'hounds' is chased by three 'foxes' – often current or former world downhill champions – who are detained for a further eight seconds before they set off in pursuit. The ensuing chaos is legendary.

While experts will appreciate the technical features and jumps of the harder trails, the red route is renowned amongst intermediate-level riders for its quality and variety, and is achievable by most proficient bikers. The features here are not overly fearsome, and can be rolled as quickly or as slowly as you like. Expect medium-sized steps, sections of boardwalk and occasional moderate rock drops, set both within thick forest and across open hillside.

Non-climbers will also be relieved to know there's an option of starting at the top car park, thereby reducing the overall ascent by 210m and the distance by 4.5km. You can either park your own vehicle here or leave your car at the bottom and avail of the uplift service operated by **East Coast Adventure** (tel: 028 4173 8516; www.eastcoastadventure.com), who run the bike centre located in the bottom car park. A single uplift costs £5, or else it's £17.50 for a half-day service. The same company also hires bikes, with hard tails available from £30, and full suspension from £45.

Other facilities at the bottom car park include a campsite, café, children's playground, toilets, showers and a bike wash. Before you set out make sure to buy a trail map from either the bike shop or campground reception. This costs £2 but will help you keep track of your progress along the trail, and identify several possible shortcuts in case you need them.

The Ride

Every bike trail in Rostrevor is signed by coloured arrows on wooden posts. Follow the red arrows for this route, beginning from the bottom car park on a path shared by the black trail.

The trip begins with an ascent that has been described as 'lung-busting', as you gain over 400m in altitude in the first 9km. Forest tracks are followed for the first 2km, then a brief respite in the gradient leads to another climb past the upper car park. If you have chosen to drive this far, join the trail in the upper right corner of this car park.

You now begin what is known as the Cloughmore Climb, following a singletrack trail through the forest on western slopes of Slievemeen. Several clearings allow expansive views over Carlingford Lough, providing confirmation of how much height you've gained. The most famous viewpoint comes at a sharp switchback known as **Kodak Corner**.

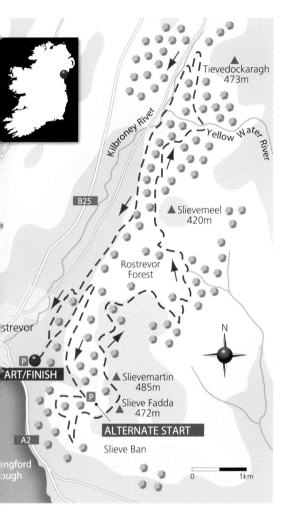

steps and a couple of moderate rock drops keep you on your toes as you zigzag through the forest, before a long, twisting section of **boardwalk** brings you to a forest track. Follow the markers through a couple of junctions, then head back across the open slopes of Slievemeel, surrounded in late summer by blooming heather.

Two further forest sections provide more **singletrack fun**, punctuated by a ford across the Yellow Water River. It's not long now before the trail swings south and begins to head along the Kilbroney valley back towards the start. If you still have the energy there's plenty more singletrack along the Home Run, while a gently descending forest track runs parallel to the trail and offers an easier alternative for tired legs. Don't miss the final kilometre of trail, however, where a fast, free-flowing section to the right of the track provides an exhilarating finale.

The trail finishes by depositing you back at the bottom car park, where most riders head straight to the café to recover.

The route includes long sections of singletrack trail weaving through the forest.

Another kilometre of forest remains before the boughs begin to thin and you reach the tree line. The trail now sweeps in a semicircle around the upper slopes of Slevemeen and Slievemartin. At one point you pass a stile on the right, with a walking trail and line of fence posts heading uphill beyond it. It's well worth leaving your bike here for a few minutes and walking 300m to the trig point at the top of **Slievemartin**. Fabulous summit views encompass most of the peaks of the Mourne Mountains, including Slieve Donard to the north-east.

Back on the bike trail, the gradient soon switches to downhill and the fun really begins. It comes as a relief to let the bike roll across a high, open section before plunging back into the trees. Frequent small

ACHILL–WESTPORT GREAT WESTERN GREENWAY

The most scenic greenway in Ireland, this innovative cycle trail runs through a wild Atlantic landscape.

👍 Great for

- Appreciating ever-changing views over wild mountain and coastline
- Whizzing across inhospitable bog with firm track beneath your wheels

☁ Conditions

- A dry day without too much wind

Trip Details

- Distance: 42km (26 miles)
- Time: 4–5 hours
- Maps: OSi 1:50,000 sheets 30 and 31

Access

- **To the start:** The greenway starts in the large car park for Achill Island Hotel/Óstán Oileán Acla. This is located beside the R319, at the mainland end of the bridge over Achill Sound.
- Grid Ref: L 740 999
- GPS: 53.933258, -9.919781

- **To the finish:** The best place to finish is Westport Quay, where vehicles can be left in a large quayside car park. The quay is signed along the R335 on the south-western side of Westport town.
- Grid Ref: L 980 845
- GPS: 53.800223 -9.548640

Between Achill and Mulranny the route traces the shore of Bellcragher Bay, with the Nephin Beg Mountains rising ahead.

also brings exposure to the elements, so make sure to dress appropriately.

Bike Hire

There are several bike hire outlets along the greenway, including **Clew Bay Bike Hire** (tel: 098 24818; www.clewbaybikehire.ie) and **Greenway Bicycle Hire** (tel: 086 0382 593; greenwaybicyclehire.com). Most companies offer bikes, baby trailers and child seats, as well as helmets and locks. Many have different outlets along the route, or provide shuttle bus services to bring you back to base. Expect to pay around €25 for an adult's bike or €15 for children, with a shuttle bus journey included.

The Ride

From Achill Island Hotel, follow the waymarks onto the main road and turn right. The first 800m follows the R319 road with no special provision for bikes, so care is needed here. The greenway then turns left up a short lane, and then sharp right onto the firm track that will continue for most of the rest of the day. The only interruptions come in the form of two or three gates and numerous cattle grids, which control access to the surrounding farmland. The gates require dismounting to negotiate while the grids can be ridden across with care.

The scenery is immediately impressive, with just a few fields separating you from the shore of **Blacksod Bay**. After 6km the trail sweeps south, and you pass Dánlann Yawl Art Gallery, which has an adjacent coffee shop and offers the first opportunity for a break.

The greenway passes the picturesque harbour at Newport.

When it was completed in 2011, this wonderfully scenic route along the northern side of Clew Bay was the longest greenway in Ireland. It was an innovative project that proved so popular it inspired similar ventures all around the country. Today more than a quarter of a million people use the trail annually, all attracted by the well-benched, traffic-free track and consistently beautiful views over wild mountains, green pastures and Atlantic coastline.

The route follows the line of the old Midlands Great Western Railway, which closed in 1937. It can be completed in either direction, though the best approach is west to east, with the prevailing wind at your back. There are numerous access points, so it can be broken into smaller sections to suit your party. The natural breaks come at Mulranny, after 13km, and Newport, after 31km. From Achill to Newport the scenery is consistently impressive, but many people choose to finish in Newport. The final section from here to Westport runs beside the main N59 road and is less attractive, and only really recommended for purists determined to complete the full route.

The trail is fully signed and almost entirely off-road, with a surface of fine gravel as far as Newport, then tarmac beyond that. It's largely flat but does include a few gradual climbs, with several sharp ascents around Westport. There are numerous options for making detours or taking refreshment in nearby cafés, pubs and hotels. The open terrain ensures good views but

A Belated Success

The single-gauge Achill–Westport railway opened in 1894. It was one of the country's Balfour Lines – never expected to make a profit, but designed to regenerate disadvantaged districts. Even then it never reached its expected passenger figures, and closed after 43 years. The irony is that having been converted into a modern greenway, it is achieving its goal of regeneration. It now sustains up to 100 jobs and adds over €7 million a year to the local economy.

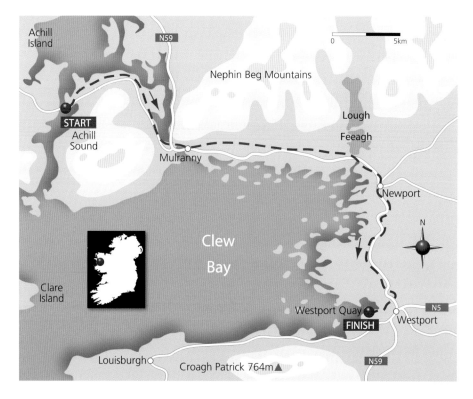

The scenery becomes wilder as you cross a sharp humpback bridge over the Cartron River and continue south-east across open moorland. The main focus of attention is now to the east, where the wild peaks of the Nephin Beg Mountains rise across Bellcragher Bay. Here you leave the Corraun Peninsula and join the mainland proper. A long, steady climb through beautiful woodland brings you to a row of holiday homes beside Mulranny Park Hotel. Just beyond this lies the old Railway Station House, which has been renovated as a service centre for greenway users. Bike hire, toilets and showers are just some of the facilities on offer.

Mulranny is a major access point for the trail; turn right beside the station house to reach the hotel and N59 road. If you want to add a detour of 2km, cross the road in front of the hotel, then carry the bikes down a flight of woodland steps. You can now cycle along a Victorian causeway spanning Trawoughter Bay, and enjoy a picnic at Mulranny's sandy beach. Return to the station house to resume your journey.

Continuing east along the route, it's not long before you leave Mulranny and climb onto wild moorland on the lower slopes of the mountains. The elevated position allows fabulous views over **Clew Bay** to the south. This wide Atlantic inlet is decorated by myriad islands, many of which are submerged drumlins left over from the last ice age. The unmistakable cone of Croagh Patrick rises skyward on the opposite shore. It's a beautiful vista, and one that stays with you for most of the way to Newport.

Refreshment opportunities along this stretch include Nevin's Newfield Inn, reached via a detour to the right some 7km beyond Mulranny. You now begin a long, gradual descent to the Burrishoole Channel, a tidal river. Pass through twisty red railings, then turn left over the distinctive Burrishoole Bridge, whose seven stone arches date from the 18th century. The route now crosses to the southern side of the N59. An optional, 1.5km detour to the right here brings you to the 15th-century ruins of Burrishoole Abbey, which is well worth investigating if you have the energy.

The official trail runs beside the road for a kilometre, then joins the tarmac for the final approach

to **Newport**. This small, attractive town has a wide selection of shops, pubs and cafés.

If you're continuing to Westport, cross the Black Oak River via the main road bridge. To the left you can't miss the seven-arched viaduct built to carry the old railway across the water. The greenway follows the N59 out of town, then moves to a dedicated tarmac cycleway on the left side of the road. There are no services along this stretch, and the trail sticks close to the road for most of the way to Westport, with the exception of a short section in the middle.

As you approach **Westport**, the greenway climbs gently through woodland and passes through a series of stone arches. You now join a private driveway and arrive at the Attireesh access point (grid ref: L 995

857). The official route turns left here, climbs a very steep hill, then embarks on a rather convoluted and confusing loop around the eastern and southern side of the town, before finishing at Westport Quay.

An easier option for reaching the quay is to turn right at Attireesh and follow this road to the N59. Cross straight over the N59, heading towards Carraholly. Roughly 500m later, then turn left into the northern entrance of Westport House. Follow this roadway through the park, past two minor junctions. Now turn right and left, heading towards the park's southern exit. This brings you over the Carrowbeg River to Westport Quay, with the large quayside car park located directly ahead.

Above: Crossing 18th-century Burrishoole Bridge around 3km before Newport.
Below: The trail's elevated position allows fabulous views south over Clew Bay.

DUBLIN–ATHLONE GREENWAY

Follow Ireland's longest greenway on a journey along the Royal Canal and an old trail line.

👍 Great for

- Cycling halfway across the country without touching a road
- Imagining the industrial heyday of both the railway and canal

☁ Conditions

- No specific requirements

📖 Trip Details

- Distance: 126km (78 miles)
- Time: 1–3 days
- Maps: Given the simplicity of navigation, the best map is OSi 1:250,000 Ireland East, which shows the whole route on a single sheet.

Access

- **To the start:** The official start point is the first lock of the Royal Canal in Dublin. This lies 500m north of Connolly Station, along Amiens Street. The best place to leave a car is at Connolly Station car park.
- Grid Ref: O 168 356
- GPS: 53.356615, -6.244614

- **To the finish:** The route finishes at Athlone train station. This is located on Southern Station Road in the town centre, and has an adjacent car park.
- Grid Ref: N 043 418
- GPS: 53.426881 -7.935741

Passing over the first of two aqueducts soon after Longwood.

Greenways have become something of a buzzword in Ireland in recent years, with new projects springing up almost annually. The most ambitious proposal to date is a greenway that would bisect the entire country, stretching from Dublin to Galway. This would link into a pan-European cycle trail extending the width of the continent from Galway to Moscow.

It is a fine idea, and it was relatively easy to get from Dublin to Athlone, in the middle of the country. Several pre-existing paths, like the Royal Canal towpath, could be repurposed here. But beyond Athlone the route was not clear, and would have to cross a patchwork of private land. Achieving agreement proved difficult, and this section of the route has been shelved for now. The cross-country dream remains intact, but in the meantime cyclists will have to be content to get halfway. Even at half its planned distance, the route is 126km long, and is Ireland's longest continuous off-road cycle route by a significant margin. Completing it is a great achievement.

While the scenery could hardly be described as dramatic, it is very pleasant, with plenty of pastoral countryside. During the summer you can expect to see numerous wildflowers bordering the trail, along with butterflies and water birds like herons, ducks and swans. This is a journey through Ireland's industrial heritage too, centred on the canals and railways that were so important in the 19th century.

Practicalities
The greenway is 3m wide and flat throughout, with a tarmac surface in urban areas and firm, fine gravel across rural sections. If you're very fit it is possible to cycle the entire route in a single day, though many people prefer a slower pace and split the journey across two or more days.

There are train stations at the start and finish, and at several intermediate points along the way, including Maynooth, Kilcock, Enfield and Mullingar. This makes it easy to break the trip into smaller chunks, and greatly facilitates a one-way ride. Simply begin at one station, ride to another, then hop onto the train to return to the start. Note that the carriage of bikes is often restriced during peak periods, and all bikes must be booked in advance. For more information,

Highs and Lows of a Flat Canal

The Royal Canal was designed to transport goods between Dublin port and the River Shannon, but was beset with problems as soon as construction started in 1790. The first 24km took five years to complete and consumed all the company's money. From then on, a mountain of debt accrued. By the time the canal finally reached the Shannon some 27 years later, it had cost £1.5 million – almost €100 million in today's money. The advent of the railways in the mid 19th century dealt canal trade a heavy blow, though the waterways struggled on until the 1950s. Many became blocked and overgrown before a restoration programme was established. In 2010, after 60 derelict years, the refurbished Royal Canal finally reopened as a leisure amenity.

see the Travel Information section of www.irishrail.ie.

At the time of writing, path-building work was still incomplete between the M50 and Clonsilla, at a 4km section known as the Deep Sinking. It may be several years before a new, smooth surface arrives here. In the meantime access is still possible, though you'll be following a rougher trail along this stretch. If you're concerned, confirm the current situation online before you set out.

The Ride
Section 1: Dublin to Enfield – 44km
The route begins along a wide pavement in the urban heart of Dublin city. It starts by following the southern side of the Royal Canal, but switches banks multiple times as you progress along the route. Navigation is spectacularly straightforward: simply follow the waterway all the way to Mullingar. The Dublin–Sligo railway line also runs parallel to the route for most of the way.

In the first 8km you pass 11 locks, 18 bridges and several unmistakable Dublin landmarks including the bulbous steel stadium of Croke Park. The surroundings are certainly urban, but adjacent parks and playing fields provide welcome greenery. You then cross the **M50** on a spectacular aqueduct constructed during

Once you join the Old Rail Trail, the canal is replaced by an old train track.

the canal's restoration in 1999 – the first aqueduct built in Ireland for almost 200 years.

West of the M50 the canal passes though a narrow limestone cut known as the Deep Sinking, where the towpath passes 10m above the water. Back in the 19th century this section sometimes proved fatal for draught horses towing barges through the chasm below. The bedrock means resurfacing is more technical here, and though the trail is passable, this section is likely to remain rough until 2019.

The landscape gradually becomes more rural now, with fields bordering the path. The stretch between Leixlip and Kilcock can still be noisy with traffic, however, as the R148 road is never far away.

In Leixlip you cross **Ryewater Aqueduct**, which carries the canal over the River Rye. There are numerous aqueducts along the route, all providing such smooth passage over rivers, valleys and roads that you would barely know you were crossing them. The ease of travel belies the effort of construction;

this one is 30m high and took six years to build in the 1790s. The canal was originally routed further north along an easier course, but the Duke of Leinster demanded it be diverted past his ancestral home in Maynooth. Engineering complications caused by the detour include this aqueduct, the Deep Sinking, and 11 additional locks, the extra cost of which amounted to almost a third of the entire construction capital.

Soon you arrive in **Maynooth**, 24km from the start. (To access the town centre, turn right at the first road bridge. The train station lies across a footbridge just beyond the watery expanse of Duke's Harbour.) The trail is largely straight now to the town of Kilcock. Soon after this you pass Fern's Lock, the 17th lock of the route. This is the start of a 32km stretch known as the Long Level, where the ground is perfectly flat and there are no locks at all. Construction of the canal was still problematic, however, and as the route passes through Cappagh Bog and confronted numerous issues with subsidence. Today the trail is attractive and tree-lined almost all the way to Enfield, some 20km beyond Maynooth.

To reach Enfield train station, turn left at the town bridge and walk up onto the main street, then turn left onto the station road 120m later.

Section 2: Enfield to Mullingar – 42km
If you're accessing this section from Enfield train station, walk to the end of the station road and turn right. At the canal bridge 120m later, turn left and descend onto the greenway.

The waterway and towpath now snake their way west, passing under the modern R148 road at Moyvalley. Furey's Bar, on the waterside here, offers friendly refreshments. The route now diverts away from main roads for almost 20km, passing through one of

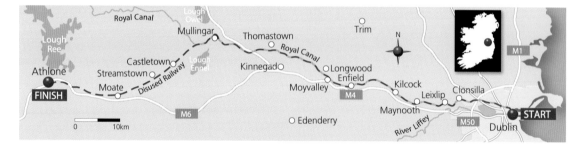

Moate station in County Westmeath is a charmingly preserved collection of 19th-century railway buildings.

the prettiest and most remote sections of countryside on the route.

Near the start of the section at Longwood you pass two aqueducts, the first carrying you over a road, the second crossing an impressive triple-arched bridge over the **River Boyne**. Soon after this you pass Hill of Down, where there's another waterside pub. The canal and railway now part company for the only time in the route.

The countryside is more open now, and can be exposed until you reach the woodland around Hyde Park demesne. This is followed by **Thomastown Harbour,** some 24km from Enfield. Here the canal begins to climb to summit level, passing through a series of eight locks, all spaced 400m apart. Not long after this you pass beneath the N4 road, where Mary Lynch's pub offers another option for a break.

The canal continues through fields near the N4 before reaching a long rock cutting, where the path runs 6m above water level. You are now approaching the outskirts of Mullingar, whose twin-towered cathedral is visible ahead. The canal makes a wide loop around the northern side of the town; **Mullingar** lies in a hollow and even with the construction of high embankments, it was impossible to maintain summit level on a more direct route. Just before the main harbour, a small bridge spans a feeder channel from Lough Owel, which used to provide the canal's main water supply.

Mullingar's large harbour is divided in two by a road bridge. Divert left here to reach the town centre. For the train station, continue ahead along the greenway. Pass beneath a railway bridge and a road bridge, then turn left through a gap in the wall. The train station lies just 100m away on the right.

Section 3: Mullingar to Athlone – 40km

From Mullingar there is a choice of greenways. One option continues along the Royal Canal for a further 27km as far as Abbeyshrule in County Longford. This route leaves the waterway and switches to the Old Rail Trail, which follows a disused train line for 40km to Athlone.

Both routes begin along the same path, and are easily accessed from Mullingar train station. Simply cross the station car park, where you'll see a greenway information board on the opposite side of the road. Head up the ramp beside the board, then turn left onto the canal towpath. Follow this for 1.5km to the first road bridge. Just beyond the bridge the path forks; veer left here to join the Old Rail Trail.

The canal you have been following is now replaced by an old train track, overgrown in places by grass and flowers. The greenway remains flat and paved throughout, passing under numerous bridges and forming a quiet, tree-lined corridor across the Meath countryside. The line itself was built by Midland Great Western Railway, and once linked Dublin to Galway and Sligo. It opened in 1851 and finally closed in 1985.

The quiet, pastoral charm of the Royal Canal near Enfield, County Meath.

Boats and barges moored along the Royal Canal at Moyvalley, County Kildare.

The first major piece of railway infrastructure comes at **Castletown Station**, 11.5km from Mullingar. Here the trail is enclosed by two platforms, with the signal box, waiting room and former station (now a private house) all still intact. The station closed in 1963 but remains an evocative place. It's easy to imagine a brightly painted locomotive steaming through, trailing a line of brown passenger coaches behind it.

The path has been climbing almost imperceptibly for the last few kilometres, and reaches its high point soon after Castletown. Here you begin a gentle descent, past another old platform at Streamstown, to the next major station at **Moate**, some 16km away. Moate station is another charmingly preserved collection of railway buildings that spans both sides of the track.

Moate is also a good place to take a break. Follow the road left from the station for 350m to reach the town's main street, where you'll find a selection of shops and cafés. Alternatively you could continue along the greenway for another kilometre, where Dún na Sí Heritage Park lies just 300m off the path to the right. Attractions here include a children's playground, pet farm and café.

A final stretch of trail carries you into **Athlone**. This part of the line achieved worldwide fame when it was used as a location for the 1978 film *The Great Train Robbery*. This is where Sean Connery ran along the top of a moving steam train, sprawling flat to avoid upcoming bridges.

The greenway ends rather unceremoniously at a road junction, with onward progress barred by a red and white barrier. The town centre lies to the left here. To reach the modern train station, turn left onto the road, pass under a railway bridge, then turn sharp right at a large intersection. The station lies at the top of the hill on the right.

BALLYHOURA MTB TRAIL

Novices and experts alike will love the range of options at Ireland's biggest mountain bike centre.

 Great for

- Weaving around trees on fast, singletrack descents
- Visiting the venue several times and venturing further on each occasion

Conditions

- Dry ground

 Trip Details

- Distance: 6–51km (4–32 miles)
- Time: 40 minutes to 5 hours
- Ascent: 110–940m (360–3,085ft)
- Map: OSNI 1:50,000 sheet 73

Access

- Begin by heading to the village of Ardpatrick, located along the R512 in County Limerick. From here head south along the R512, then take the second right, following a brown sign for Ballyhoura Forest. The forest entrance is 700m later on the right; bring €5 in coins to operate the entrance barrier.
- Grid Ref: R 656 186
- GPS: 52.318356, -8.505757

Most of the loops at Ballyhoura follow singletrack trails through the forest.

Ballyhoura Forest boasts the most extensive network of mountain bike trails in Ireland, and promises an exhilarating day out whatever your ability. There's something here for everyone, with routes ranging from a beginner-friendly 6km route, to an epic journey of more than 50km that will challenge even the most experienced rider.

The trail system has been professionally designed, and is fully signed with colour-coded symbols. There are five loops in all, each exploring the hillsides just north and west of Seefin Mountain (528m). You'll pass through a mixture of broadleaf woodland and pine forest, with intermittent open sections allowing fine views across the surrounding countryside. Every loop includes long, twisting singletrack descents, sections of boardwalk, and climbs of varying lengths along wider forest roads.

Feeling Competitive?

As Ireland's premier mountain bike venue, Ballyhoura has hosted its fair share of competitions over the years. These range from national-level events to high-profile international contests, such as the European MTB Marathon Championships. Even if you're not a top competitor, there's nothing to stop you getting involved. The Irish Biking Blitz is a beginner-friendly mountain bike series spread across four Irish trail centres, including Ballyhoura. Entry options include a 'Baggy Shorts' category for novices, and youth events down to Under 6s. For more details, see www.bikingblitz.ie.

From a technical perspective, all the loops involve a similar degree of difficulty, falling somewhere between a blue (moderate) and red (difficult) grade on the British MTB trail grading system. You won't encounter any major hazards, just relatively small rock steps, cambers, boardwalk and long stretches weaving between the trees. The only real difference between each loop is the increasing amount of endurance required to cover the extra distance and ascent. The five trail options are:

- Green Greenwood Loop: 6km, 110m ascent
- Brown Mountrussell Loop: 17km, 260m ascent
- White Garrane Loop: 35km, 460m ascent
- Blue Streamhill Loop: 41km, 660m ascent
- Red Castlepook Loop: 51km, 940m ascent

Facilities at the trailhead are good, including map boards, toilets, changing rooms, showers and a bike wash. You'll also find **Trailriders** (tel: 087 2717 330; trailriders.ie), a small but well-stocked shop that hires bikes for €35 per day, and runs courses for beginners and intermediates looking to improve their skills.

In terms of equipment, a hardtail bike is sufficient for all the trails at Ballyhoura. Make sure to carry plenty of food and water if you're embarking on one of the longer loops.

Right: A copse of beech trees near the car park is particularly pretty in autumn.

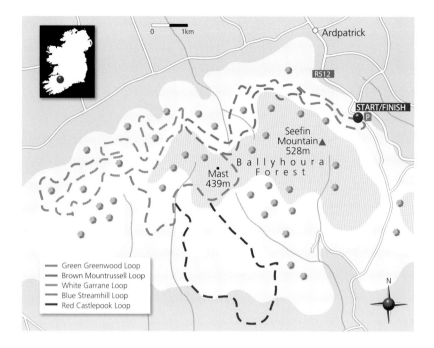

Green Greenwood Loop
Brown Mountrussell Loop
White Garrane Loop
Blue Streamhill Loop
Red Castlepook Loop

The Ride

The five trails at Ballyhoura are laid out in a cascading formation, with each loop leading onto the next. To reach the furthest loop, you first have to ride all the previous ones. Each circuit is signed in one direction only, and restricted solely to bikes.

From the parking area, the routes all start at an obvious wood-framed trailhead, located to the right of the amenity block. For a fun warm-up, try the 800m **Skills Loop** that veers right soon after the start. This sweeps through several cambered turns with more challenging technical options, then deposits you back at the car park.

When you're ready to embark on your main journey, follow the marker post decorated with the full rainbow of trail symbols. An initial section through attractive beech woodland brings you to a forest road, where the first climb begins. It's not long before the route returns to narrow **singletrack**, and begins to weave between the trunks of pine trees. As you progress along the route the forest changes character around you; wide-spaced, moss-cloaked boughs are replaced by thick plantations that restrict the light, then you emerge into beautiful, airy copses dominated by deciduous species.

The green loop turns left after 2.5km and begins to return to the car park – watch out for a tricky bend on wooden boardwalk on the way back. The remaining loops all continue onto another climb along forest road, followed by similar-style singletrack through the trees. Shortly before the brown loop branches left on its own return journey, there's an option to turn right on a marked **Technical Loop**. This adds 4km of free-flowing descent along cambered turns interspersed by a few small rock drops, and is a fun way to link into the white loop. If you have set your sights on just the brown loop, ignore this option, then turn left at a track junction a short distance later. The return part of the brown trail includes a long section of **elevated boardwalk** across a patch of clear-felled forestry.

The white loop includes some rougher forest roads and longer ascents, but spends more time out of the trees. The wider views make a pleasant change, but the open terrain is more exposed to wind and rain. There are also several options to shorten this trail if you prefer a route somewhere between the brown and white options. Look out for signs indicating a 'Shortcut Home' on marker posts 35, 36 and 39.

The green loop includes a tricky bend on wooden boardwalk on the way back to the finish.

If you have the energy to continue onto the blue and red trails, you'll find yourself exploring the more remote western and southern fringes of the forest. Expect longer, steeper climbs and rougher sections of singletrack. Only a small percentage of visitors to Ballyhoura ever complete the full red trail, and doing so is a major achievement. If this is your goal, be prepared for a full day's effort. Success is magnified by the satisfaction of completing the longest official mountain bike trail in the country.

CAVING

Prepare yourself for some unlikely positions as you crawl, squeeze and swim in any manner necessary to proceed. Pollnagolum, Fermanagh. (Robert Mulraney)

Ireland's Adventure Bucket List

TWO THINGS stand out when you enter the world of caving. First is the alien nature of the underground scenery. Hidden in this pitch-black world are rock and mineral formations of all shapes and sizes, from massive, intimidating caverns to tiny sculptures that shimmer delicately in your torchlight. Each one is natural and ancient, created over millennia by the imperceptible forces of erosion. Each one is humbling with its power and beauty.

The second most striking thing is the unlikely positions you're required to get into to explore this otherworld. If you've never scuttled like a crab across a blackened stream, with tons of rock bearing down above you, now's your chance. If you've never wriggled on your belly through a slimy, mud-caked tunnel or sunk chest-deep beneath an underground waterfall, here's your opportunity. It's like a cross between an army obstacle course and a child's dream playground, and you have to leave your dignity behind as you crawl, squeeze and swim in any manner necessary to proceed.

Yet the natural wonder of caving remains impossible to convey to those who haven't tried it.

While you should take all the time you want to admire cave formations, please adhere to the central rule of the sport. DO NOT TOUCH! These delicate sculptures take millennia to form, and can be broken with a single careless movement. Even gentle contact can harm them, as bacteria transferred from your hand can cause them to discolour. Proceed slowly, take nothing but photos and leave no trace of your visit.

The magical environment underground is like the enchantment of being underwater – it's so different from our normal, terrestrial existence that, until you've been there, you can never understand what you're missing.

The good news is that Ireland has some fabulous cave systems, spread all across the country. And while some are technical in nature, others are perfectly accessible to beginners. So unless you're a confirmed claustrophobe, there's no reason not to give the sport a try.

The massive chamber in Cradle Hole, Fermanagh. (Robert Mulraney)

Caves can be wet or dry, and are generally found in limestone rock. (Marble Arch Caves Geopark)

Know Your Cave Formations

The subterranean world is full of all sorts of weird and wonderful formations – or speleothems – that simply don't exist above ground. These form when weakly acidic rainwater seeps through limestone, then leaves a calcite mineral deposit as it drips away. More than 300 different structures have been identified and this quick guide will help you recognise some of the most common ones:

Flowstone

These sheet-like deposits of white calcite form where water flows down the walls or floor of a cave. They develop into rounded, bulbous masses as the deposit grows thicker. Mineral impurities may add colours, such as reddish patches caused by iron oxide.

Curtains or Draperies

These fluted calcite sheets hang downwards, often decorating the lower edge of overhanging flowstones. They look like an array of delicate organ pipes, and are amongst the most beautiful cave structures.

Stalactites

These are pointed pendants that hang from the cave ceiling, expanding imperceptibly with each mineral-laden water droplet. With an average growth rate of 0.13mm a year, they take 80 years to reach just 1cm long.

Stalagmites

As water drops from the tip of a stalactite, it deposits more calcite on the floor below, eventually resulting in these rounded pinnacles growing up beneath them.

Columns

Given enough time, stalactites and stalagmites can meet and fuse together into these solid pillars of calcium carbonate.

Straws

Baby stalactites in the making, these are fragile, hollow tubes around 5mm in diameter, which hang from the roof of the cave. Water drips through the middle of them; if the hole becomes plugged by debris, they develop into more familiar, cone-shaped stalactites.

The subterranean world is full of all sorts of fascinating formations, like these stalactites in Pollaraftra, Fermanagh. (Robert Mulraney)

Irish Caving at a Glance

Any region with plenty of limestone is likely to have caves lurking beneath the surface, and Ireland is well endowed in this regard. Though there are good caves all over the country, the most famous karst landscapes – and best-documented cave systems – lie in Counties Fermanagh, Cavan, Galway and Clare.

Irish caves vary greatly in character, and come in all shapes and sizes. The country's longest documented cave, Pollnagollum in County Clare, has 16km of passageways, while its deepest, Reyfad Pot, descends 193m below the surface. You will need specialist rope skills to explore vertical holes like this, but there are beginners' caves too, which are essentially horizontal tunnels you can walk right through. Some caves are dry while others are wet, with active rivers still flowing through them.

As in all parts of the world, Irish caving is weather dependent. Rainfall can rapidly alter the conditions underground, causing dangerous flash floods and blocking access passages. Many beginners' caves can flood after just a couple of hours of rain. Given the country's high precipitation levels, it is essential to check the forecast before you head out. Always be prepared to postpone or abort a trip if weather conditions change.

Essential Equipment

Caving is a mucky sport, so whatever you wear will get wet and dirty and have to withstand rock abrasion. The tighter the cave, the more abuse your clothes get. It's no surprise that caving gear tends to be practical rather than constructed from expensive materials. The most important pieces of kit are a helmet and head torch. The helmet protects you against knocks, while the torch should be powerful, have a good battery life and preferably be waterproof too.

The temperature of Irish caves averages around 9°C and the atmosphere is damp, so keeping warm is the main consideration. Combine warm, loose-fitting clothing, like thermal and fleece underlayers, with a protective oversuit. Old boiler suits are common as a top layer, though a tough fabric like cordura or PVC is best. Abrasion-resistant gardening gloves are often worn to protect your hands, while wellington boots are the most popular choice of footwear. If the cave is wet, swap the underlayers for a wetsuit and wear neoprene socks inside your wellies to keep your feet warm.

A dry bag is a handy way to carry essentials like a camera, food and drink. Someone in the group should also bring emergency supplies like spare torches and batteries, a first-aid kit and extra clothing. As you progress onto more technical caves, you'll also

Single Rope Technique (SRT) is used to explore more technical caves with deeper shafts. (Robert Mulraney)

need to add ropes, ladders and SRT equipment like harnesses, ascenders and foot loops.

Note that mobile phones don't work underground. Cave rescue, should you need it, is the responsibility of the police force in both the Republic and Northern Ireland.

Getting Started

Potholing, spelunking, speleology or simply caving, whatever term you use to describe the exploration of caves, there are various ways to get started. Many people experience their first underground environment when they take a guided tour around a show cave. There are some great examples around the country, including Marble Arch Caves in Fermanagh, Aillwee Cave in Clare and Crag Cave in Kerry. But while these caverns display many beautiful formations, they don't provide an accurate impression of the real sport of caving. For that you have to remove the lights, pathways and tour guide, and take a much more hands-on approach.

Like any adventure sport, novice cavers should only head out in the company of a more experienced person, who will ensure both the safety of the group and the protection of the cave environment. Never venture underground alone – a safe party contains a minimum of three people.

To try the sport properly, join a guided trip run by one of Ireland's three cave-orientated outdoor centres: **Corralea Activity Centre** (www.activityireland.com), **Petersburg OEC** (www.petersburg.ie) and **Burren OEC** (www.burrenoec.com). For longer-term involvement, nothing beats joining a caving club. There are several of these located around the country, many connected to different universities. For a full list of clubs, see the links page at: www.caving.ie

Extending Your Skills

Once you begin to explore more technical caves with deeper shafts, you'll need to become familiar with Single Rope Technique (SRT), which is a bit like rock climbing underground. While you can learn these skills from your peers, a formal training course is invaluable. The Speleological Union of Ireland runs an extensive training programme ranging from caving fundamentals, through individual caving skills, to leadership and instructor certifications. Courses are run throughout the year, and based at several locations around the country. See www.caving.ie for more details.

Finding Out More

Books: *Selected Caves of Britain and Ireland* by Des Marshall and Donald Rust is a practical guidebook detailing many of Ireland's main caves. The University of Bristol Speleological Society also publishes several regional guides, including *The Caves of County Clare and South Galway, and The Caves of Fermanagh and Cavan* by Kelly, Fogg, Jones & Burns.

Online: **www.caving.ie** is the official website of the Speleological Union of Ireland and offers a host of practical information about Irish caving. Northern Irish caving groups are governed by the British Caving Association – see **british-caving.org**.uk. It's also worth checking **www.cavesofireland.wordpress.com**, an inspirational blog site that contains many fabulous Irish caving photos. If this doesn't send you underground, nothing will!

Marble Arch Caves in Fermanagh are just one of several great show caves around the country. (Marble Arch Caves Geopark)

POLL A CHORRA, Owey Island

This 'lake beneath a lake' offers an easy introduction to caving, made all the more memorable by its atmospheric island location.

👍 Great for

- Discovering a two-tier lake: one at the surface, the other lurking below in pitch-blackness
- Admiring a host of spectacular coastal formations

☁ Conditions

- Calm or moderate seas for the ferry crossing

🗺 Trip Details

- Distance: 4km (2½ miles)
- Time: 2–2½ hours
- Ascent: 150m (500ft)
- Map: OSi 1:50,000 sheet 1

🏛 Access

- Owey Island is accessed via the R259 through the Rosses in north-west Donegal. Turn west from this road onto the L1463 opposite the Viking Hotel, following signs for Cruit Island (*An Chruit*). Cross the bridge to Cruit and continue all the way to the golf course at its northern tip. After crossing the fairway, and just 200m before the clubhouse, turn right onto a sandy track. This descends to a tiny harbour used by boats heading over to Owey.

    Passage to Owey is provided by a friendly and fascinating local man, Dan Gallagher (tel: 086 601 3893), using his small fishing boat. Contact him in advance to arrange a crossing, which is only possible in clement sea conditions. The trip costs €10 return, takes just ten minutes, and runs from May to August.

- Grid Ref: B 724 224
- GPS: 55.048196, -8.431919

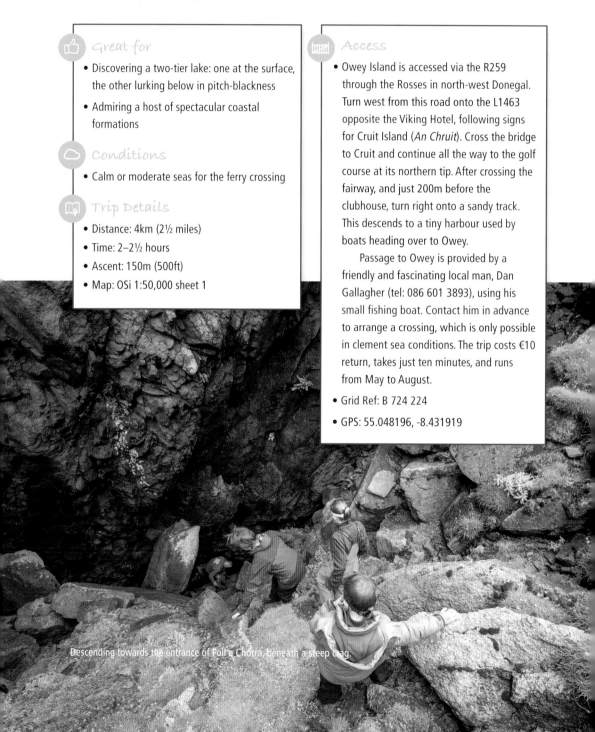

Descending towards the entrance of Poll a Chorra, beneath a steep crag.

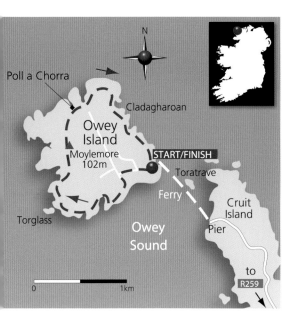

If you come to Owey Island looking for Poll a Chorra, you'll be following a well-established tradition. Yet within just 1.2 square kilometres, Owey boasts a whole range of dramatic natural formations, of which the cave is just one. The best option is to complete a circumnavigation of the whole island, visiting the cave as part of a longer walk.

The cave itself is quite literally a lake beneath a lake. On the surface, a small lough lies tucked into a rugged granite landscape. Pretty, but unremarkable. Yet at the northern tip of the lough, a sinkhole bores down between large boulders, disappearing into the inky depths. By scrambling down an underground gully you reach a large cavern holding a second freshwater pool, located directly beneath the first. Exploring this two-tier phenomenon is a remarkable and memorable experience, yet easy enough that you need no previous caving knowledge and even children can make the trip. Remember to bring helmets and good head torches for the trip underground.

Besides its landscape, the most impressionable thing about Owey is its history. The island was inhabited for 300 years, and by 1911, it had over 150 residents. The population soon began to dwindle, however, and the last people (including Dan the ferryman) left in the 1970s. Owey lay abandoned for several decades, but over the past 20 years its descendants have returned,

renovating many of the old cottages and living here during the summer months.

Owey still has no mains water or electricity. Today's inhabitants use the spring well, bottled gas and composting toilets. The islanders are remarkably welcoming and proud of their traditional lifestyles, and it's a genuine old-fashioned experience to stay here overnight. Either sample the unique atmosphere of **Owey Homestay** (www.oweyhomestay.com), or camp wild beside some stone enclosures just south of the harbour.

If you have a sea kayak, bring it. The trip from Cruit to Owey is just 800m long and the array of chasms, caves, arches and pinnacles you'll see on a circumnavigation of the island is simply breathtaking. There are over 120 graded rock climbs here too, including some of the hardest routes in Donegal.

The Trip

The boat to Owey deposits you in a narrow harbour inlet known as the Spink, in the south-eastern corner of the island. From here, follow the track inland towards the **village**, where the buildings include a working forge and former school and post office. Wandering up the main street (a dirt track) is like stepping back into history.

If you want to head directly to the cave, follow the track north-west for 800m until you see the lake. A much more satisfying option is to make a clockwise circumnavigation of the island. Cross the stream in the village and turn left to reach the island's southern shore. Turn right here and follow the coastline around

A Distillery Underground

Given the resourcefulness of islanders, it's no surprise that Owey's former inhabitants had a use for Poll a Chorra cave. After the Great Famine, it became a popular pastime to make *poitín*, a strong but illegal alcoholic drink. Even though gardaí rarely came to the island, the distilling equipment was hidden in the cave while not in use. Later, the islanders also began to make single malt whiskey, the water for both drinks coming from the stream that runs through the village.

the south-western corner, where you'll find some remarkable sea stacks and offshore pinnacles.

Now head north, climbing to the trig point that marks the 102m summit of **Moylemore**, the highest point on the island. The view includes the islands of Tory and Arranmore, as well as the conical profile of Errigal on the mainland. Descend north-east over scattered lumps of pink granite, heading towards the lake.

To locate **Poll a Chorra** cave, walk to the northern tip of the lough, then continue a few metres further towards the sea. The land here drops into a steep gully, which twists back on itself and disappears beneath a large crag. Keep to the right side of the crag and descend into a diagonal hole in the ground. The roof is fairly low near the entrance, then there's about 30m of scrambling over boulders before you reach the muddy cave floor. You are now at the end of a large cavern some 40m high. The floor is filled by a subterranean lake, which extends back into the twisting rock chasm for 150m.

Stay underground as long as you like before returning to the surface, where the world seems suddenly full of colour and life. The best return option is to follow the coast around the eastern side of the island, past the bay of **Cladagharoan**, which is decorated by more pinnacles and sea arches. The final big feature is a sheer sea chasm some 35m deep but just a few metres wide, separating Owey from a large rock outcrop. Continue south along the coast to return to the harbour where your trip began.

From top: You'll have to negotiate an underground scramble of 30m to reach the cave floor; Owey's upper lough. The underground lake lies directly below here; The cavern itself is some 40m high and 150m long.

WHITE FATHERS, Blacklion

A perfect introduction to real caving, this underground river canyon takes you past a series of stunning natural formations.

Great for

- Exploring three distinct sections of cave, each more dramatic than the last
- Wondering at your own sanity as you swim across a cold pool in pitch-blackness

Conditions

- Low water levels in the river

Trip Details

- Distance: 0.8km (½ mile)
- Time: 1½–2 hours
- Map: OSi 1:50,000 sheet 26

Access

- The cave is located beside the N16 Enniskillen–Sligo road, around 3km west of Blacklion. Turn south here onto the R206 to Glangevlin. Just 50m later, turn right onto a lane signed for White Fathers Cave. Park in a lay-by after 100m, in front of a second cave sign.
- Grid Ref: H 052 375
- GPS: 54.286397 -7.920898

Just inside the entrance to the second cave.

White Fathers Cave lies within the Marble Arch Caves UNESCO Global Geopark, one of the finest limestone regions in Ireland or Britain. It provides a great example of how a river forms a cave in a karst landscape. Inside is a host of beautiful formations sculpted by the calcite-rich water, including long swathes of curtain and countless stalactites both large and small. It's a perfect introduction to the subterranean splendour of caving, and you can't help but be impressed by the hidden drama you uncover.

The label White Fathers actually encompasses three distinct caves. The first is a short natural bridge just 20m in length. Then comes a second cave some 60m long, with the longest, prettiest 200m section reserved as a grand finale. The system is thought to have developed after the last ice age, and once would have formed a single tunnel before the intervening sections of roof collapsed. Today it acts as a roosting and hibernation site for a small population of Daubenton's bats.

Long bands of curtains and countless stalactites adorn the third cave.

The cave is horizontal and relatively spacious, so you can walk upright for most of the way. It is wet, though, and you'll be wading along a stream throughout. It is important to visit during a dry spell when water levels are low; at higher volumes a dangerous current runs through the cave and a sump forms at the end, meaning you can only escape by diving underwater. Even at low levels, when the water is generally between calf and thigh deep, the final section drops into a deep pool that you have no option but to swim across.

How far you should explore without professional guidance depends on your confidence, wild-swimming proficiency and previous caving experience. The challenge of completing a 40m cold-water swim in the dark is enough for most beginners to prefer the reassurance of a qualified guide. Alternatively, you could explore just the first two sections of cave under your own steam. In terms of equipment, the final swim also means a warm wetsuit and buoyancy aid are recommend in addition to all the normal caving gear.

Follow a footpath along the stream bank between the first and second of the caves.

Guided Excursions

Corralea Activity Centre (tel: 028 6638 6123; www. activityireland.com) organise guided trips through White Fathers from their base beside Upper Lough MacNean. They provide all the necessary equipment and charge £120 for two people, with larger groups at £45 per person. They can also introduce you to several other caves in the area; discuss the options with your guide.

Holy and Unholy Penance

This cave gets its name from a former monastery built nearby in 1953, then used as a novitiate by the White Fathers Missionary Congregation. After its closure in 1970, the centre was bought by the state and converted into an open prison now known as Loughan House.

The Cave

Begin by passing through a wooden gate beside the second White Fathers sign. The river lies immediately in front of you, with the entrance to the first cave on the left, and the second cave 50m downstream to the right.

Begin by assessing the water level to judge whether it is safe to proceed. There should be several rocks exposed above the water at the mouth of the first cave, with the water level calf deep or lower. If it's much higher than this you are advised to explore just the first two caves, or come back later during a drier spell.

The first cave, on the left, is a **natural bridge** that passes under the access lane. It's short enough that you can almost see both ends at once, but it still contains some interesting formations and makes a good introduction to the trip. After investigating it, return to your start point.

Top: Exiting the first cave, a natural bridge just 20m long.
Bottom: Holes in the limestone roof create natural skylights before the third cave.

Now follow a footpath along the right bank of the stream to reach the second cave. Two trailside panels offer background information, while a set of concrete steps and metal railing provide a viewing platform at the mouth of the second cavern. Descend the bank beside the steps to return to the water, then continue downstream into the **second cave**.

This is a relatively spacious tunnel, with the water no more than thigh deep. Inside you'll see a wider array of formations, with clusters of delicate straws hanging from the ceiling and bulbous flowstones protruding from the walls. Pick your way carefully along the river for 60m until daylight signals the end of the section. Along with a larger opening, there are several holes in the limestone roof around 1.5m in diameter, which create fascinating natural skylights draped with vines from the woodland above.

If you want to finish your trip here, exit the river via the left bank. Otherwise, continue ahead into the third cave. Here you'll be treated to the most **beautiful formations** of all, with long bands of curtains and stalactites of all shapes and sizes, including a massive one that hangs overhead rather threateningly as you pass along the river below.

Halfway along the cave the passage narrows perceptibly, and you'll find yourself twisting around rocky corners and negotiating small rapids. Progress remains straightforward, however, until the ground drops away and the water gathers in a deep pool. All limbs are now called into action as you swim across the final section, before emerging via **twin exit holes** at the end of the cave. The roof is low here, and this is where the passage becomes blocked at high water levels.

Once back in daylight, clamber up the edge of the sinkhole to flatter ground above. You have surfaced beside a high double fence surrounding the low-security detention centre of Loughan House. Turn left and follow the fence into woodland. Cross a makeshift stile over a wire fence, then pass through a metal gate. Now turn left across another fence to reach a grassy field, with the main road running along its opposite side. Cross a metal gate and the main road, then walk back along the access lane to the start.

BALLYMACLANCY CAVE, Cong

You can't help but be awestruck by the powerful atmosphere and beautiful formations of this remarkable underground journey.

Great for
- Descending small waterfalls in a narrow, subterranean chasm
- Being amazed by a stunning array of sparkling calcite formations

Conditions
- Avoid going out after heavy rain, when the cave can become flooded

Trip Details
- Distance: 1.5km (1 mile)
- Time: 2½–3 hours
- Map: OSi 1:50,000 sheet 38

Access – The Cave
- Ballymaclancy Cave is situated partway between Clonbur and Cong. From Clonbur, take the R345 Cong road, then take the third turn on the left. The cave is located at the back of a field, around 1.5km along this lane on the right.
- Grid Ref: M 113 549
- GPS: 53.536747, -9.338548

Access – Petersburg Outdoor Centre
- Begin by heading to the village of Clonbur, 6km west of Cong. From here, turn north-west onto the R300, following a brown sign for Petersburg. After 2km Petersburg is signed to the right, between two stone pillars. The outdoor centre is arranged around an old courtyard at the end of the road.
- Grid Ref: M 083 572
- GPS: 53.556796, -9.385035

Sitting in the cave entrance, which is about 1m high.

Ireland's Adventure Bucket List

The limestone landscape around Cong in County Mayo is riven by a host of different caves. Some are large chambers that are readily accessible, and have been visited by tourists for centuries. Others are more technical, and the preserve of experienced cavers. Ballymaclancy Cave, described here, strikes the perfect balance between challenge and accessibility. It's testing enough that novices need a guide, yet has few technical difficulties and is within the reach of most fit people.

It is also an immensely pretty cave, displaying a wide array of features typical of the karst underworld. You'll see stalactites, stalagmites and smaller straws, all formed by calcite-rich water dripping from the ceiling above. There are also several large flowstones and bands of beautiful white curtains.

The cave itself is 726m long, and up to 11m deep. Progress involves walking or crawling along an underground stream, so you will need a wetsuit to keep warm. While there's still a large number of formations in the cave, they are fragile and some have been damaged over the years by untrained visitors. To protect it from further damage, the landowner requests that inexperienced cavers explore it only in the company of a qualified guide from nearby Petersburg Outdoor Centre. See below for further details.

A Natural Treasure

As you make your way along Ballymaclancy Cave, you'll notice large sections of rock twinkling in your torchlight, apparently covered by gold and silver glitter. These sparkles are not precious metals, but colonies of yellow and white bacteria called actinomycetes. They attract beads of water, and appear to shimmer under light. Though they have no commercial value, somehow it's even more magical to consider that the glistening flecks are actually alive.

Guided Excursions

Petersburg Outdoor Education Centre (tel: 094 954 6483; www.petersburg.ie) have friendly and knowledgeable instructors who can guide you down the cave. Trips take half a day and all equipment is provided, at a cost of €100 for up to 4 people. Excursions run year round except during winter months, when bats use the cave for hibernation.

A particularly impressive calcite curtain ends in a fringe of white feathers.

False ceilings are twisted into fantastic shapes and encased with calcite deposits.

Ballymaclancy Cave is entered via an innocuous-looking stream.

The Cave

As with many caves, the entrance to Ballymaclancy is rather understated and you will need a guide just to find it. After parking along a narrow lane, you begin by hopping over a stone wall into a field. Just 100m later you reach an innocuous-looking stream. Even from right beside it, you'd never guess at the wonders that begin just a few metres away.

Enter the stream (which may flood your wellies straight away) and begin to head downstream. The route essentially follows this watercourse right through the cave and out the other side. The entrance is about 1m high, so you have to duck to get in. There are two possible routes at first: either keep right along the main stream, or pass through a second tunnel on the left. Both options necessitate crawling to avoid the low roof, then converge 15m later in a larger chamber about 6m high.

If you look carefully on the floor and walls of this chamber you'll spot fossils laid down some 300 million years ago when the rock was just sediment at the bottom of a shallow sea. On the right side of the cavern is the first of several impressive **flowstones**. This large white formation includes small gour pools at different heights, and looks like a series of ghostly paddy fields cascading down a miniature Asian hillside.

The stream has consolidated into a single channel now, and the roof is high enough to allow you to walk upright. The water is generally knee- to thigh-deep, and the passage often narrow enough that if you extend your arms you can touch both walls at once.

Around 60m from the start you come to a small **waterfall**. Just above this you'll notice several wooden planks on the floor. These date from the Victorian era, and were placed here to aid the progress of members of the Guinness family, who sometimes visited the cave from nearby Ashford Castle. The waterfall itself is a drop of about 1.2m into a waist-deep pool. This is the biggest obstacle of the route, though there are also several smaller drops to negotiate before you reach the exit.

Already you will have seen the walls glittering gold and silver with actinomycetes, and noticed several stalactites and stalagmites. Around 300m from the start you come to a place where a wide shelf opens out on the left, displaying another array of formations. A massive flowstone completes the scene on the right.

Some parties turn back soon after this, and retrace their steps to the start. If you continue please be careful, because the formations encroach ever more closely and can be damaged by the slightest touch. The channel becomes deeper too, and you sometimes find yourself wading chest-deep in water, with the rock just centimetres above your head. Any rock this low will be a **false ceiling**, however, with empty space above. These different levels indicate successive stream floors, before the water eroded deeper to form another streambed below. The false ceilings are twisted into fantastic shapes and encased with calcite deposits, and are really quite magical to see.

Another memorable formation along this section is a tall **calcite curtain**, which ends in a classic fringe of white feathers. The passage remains narrow here so contortions are required to pass it without touching.

You know you're approaching the end of the cave when a rope appears across the channel. This has been placed here to guide cave divers under a sump on the left. Duck under the rope so it's on your left side, then keep to the right to exit via a less technical route. Squeeze though a narrow tunnel then scramble up a muddy gully to emerge into woodland above. A brief walk across a field brings you back to the road. Turn right here and follow the tarmac back to your starting point.

HISTORY HUNTING

Napoleonic signal towers dating from 1805 can be found on coastal headlands around the country. Visit this one on Glen Head on a hike from Glencolmcille in Donegal.

IS HISTORY HUNTING an adventure activity? You might not find it advertised on the websites of any outdoor operators, but that fact is that visiting historic sites can be very adventurous in Ireland. The country has an unusually high number of antiquities scattered liberally across its landscape, yet many of the best ones are confined to such remote locations that you need to embark on something of an expedition to reach them.

In these wild places, isolated from modern life, the ruins are most redolent and the force of history can be felt most keenly. Here you can view history in the raw, often in solitude and far from obtrusive visitor centres, the site made all the more atmospheric for its wild surroundings. Standing alone on a windswept island or remote mountain summit, it's somehow easier to picture the reality of life for the people who constructed these monuments so long ago.

Even without looking for them, many outdoor activities take you past sites with a historic significance. You might pass Neolithic tombs, old promontory forts or ruined cottages, or some other landmark with story behind it. Simply by getting out into the Irish outdoors, you're often treated to an informal history lesson too, in the most enjoyable and interesting

The Perils of Preservation

Conserving historic monuments can be a contentious issue. In the Republic of Ireland, the Office of Public Works (OPW) is the state body charged with the maintenance and preservation of heritage sites, yet sometimes its actions have left it open to criticism. On Inishmurray there have been several bouts of sometimes undocumented 'restoration', including the dismantling and relocation of buildings vulnerable to coastal erosion. On Skellig Michael, archaeologist Michael Gibbons has noted the disappearance of St Michael's holy well, the loss of an altar from the main oratory and the removal of five sets of stairs from the monastery, and asked why there is no published record of what is 'imaginary, conjectural or original' at the site. Remote locations are subject to harsh forces of erosion, and high visitor numbers assert further pressure, but ultimately it's a question of what sort of preservation methods should be considered acceptable to safeguard the integrity of our heritage.

The deserted village beneath Slievemore on Achill Island was abandoned during famine times and is a poignant place for a walk.

way possible. Not every country has such a wealth of heritage on display, and it adds a unique dimension to the country's outdoor experiences.

Irish History at a Glance

There's precious little evidence of the hunter-gatherers who were Ireland's first human inhabitants. They arrived here sometime around 8000 BC, probably coming on boats from Britain. For several millennia the total population of Ireland is thought to have numbered only a few thousand, with people living in the forested lowlands and leaving only a few flint tools to mark their passing.

Farming began around 4000 BC, heralding the arrival of the Neolithic period. People now used stone axes to clear patches of forest, and established more complex, settled communities. Around this time the construction of large-scale monuments began, with tombs, dolmens and stone circles all built as places of religious and ceremonial importance.

For history hunters, these are the earliest remains you can expect to find. Amongst countless Neolithic monuments spread around the country, many are now relatively accessible beside modern roadsides. For a more primal experience, try hiking to the more remote mountain sites. The passage tomb at the summit of Slieve Gullion in County Armagh is a great example: after climbing to the massive cairn at the 576m summit, it's possible to duck beneath a stone lintel and enter the inner burial chamber. With 360-degree views encompassing the Mourne Mountains and Carlingford Lough, this is one experience that can't be replicated at lower elevations. A similar trip can be enjoyed by hiking to the 622m top of Seefin in County Wicklow, where the roof of the summit burial chamber has collapsed, allowing you to peer inside.

From top: Ireland has many pilgrim paths that reflect the country's religious history. This carved pillar dates from early Christian times and is visited on the Glencolmcille turas route; The remote outdoor altar at Maumeen, in Connemara's Maumturk Mountains, was used for worship during penal times. Today it's a fantastic place for a hike; The chapel at the summit of 764m Croagh Patrick is a place of Christian pilgrimage, but was significant for earlier pagans too. Start the ascent from the village of Murrisk.

Top: The 621m summit of Seefin, in the Wicklow Mountains, holds one of the highest Neolithic tombs in the country.
Bottom: The natural harbour of Portdoon on Inishturk was once used by Viking pirates as a base from which to launch raids.

The introduction of Christianity in the fifth century added a whole new set of antiquities to the landscape, in the form of old churches and monasteries. These are particularly relevant to wilderness history hunters, because the monks constructed long-lasting stone buildings that can still be seen, and purposefully located them in remote locations to encourage spiritual reflection and to escape persecution. There were once over 1,000 monasteries spread around the country, and the three sites included in this bucket list stem from the early Christian period. Pilgrim paths grew up around the most important sites, and still make fascinating journeys today. The steep ascent to the top of Croagh Patrick follows one such pilgrim path, and is a classic adventure into Irish religious history.

Not long after King Henry VIII dissolved the monasteries in the 1530s, penal laws were introduced to suppress Catholicism. Remote outdoor altars such as the one at Maumeen, in Connemara's Maumturk Mountains, date from this period. The persecution led right up to the Great Famine of 1845, whose ravages have left another lasting mark on the landscape. Deserted villages like the one beneath Slievemore on Achill Island are legacies from this period, and a walk through the ruins provides another poignant yet powerful outdoor experience.

Practicalities

As well as exploring the monuments themselves, a lot of the fun of visiting the country's more remote heritage sites lies in the journey necessary to reach them. For extreme places like Skellig Michael (page 207), a long and treacherous sea crossing means you have little choice but to climb aboard a motorboat. Other spots remain adventurous, yet are more accessible: Inishmurray (page 201) and Inichagoill (page 204) are within the reach of sea kayakers and inland canoeists.

In terms of preparation, you should plan for the activity rather than the destination. Sea kayaking to Inishmurray demands the same equipment, experience and groundwork as any other ocean paddle. The only real difference comes in the amount of time you're likely to spend exploring your destination. Extra food and clothing may be appropriate to let you examine the site at your leisure: the most rewarding history hunting is done slowly in a spirit of contemplation, not rushed because you're freezing cold.

The most satisfying trips of all are the ones where you can actually spend the night at your chosen location. How better to empathise with St Patrick spending 40 days and nights at the summit of Croagh Patrick than to bivouac there yourself? How better to imagine the harsh reality of life on an wild Atlantic outpost than to bring your tent and sample it first-hand?

It goes without saying that historic sites must be treated with the utmost respect, and no trace left of your passing. Yet given a suitably remote location and appropriately sensitive behaviour, there's nothing to stop you reliving history in the most enjoyable way of all.

INISHMURRAY

Inishmurray holds one of Europe's most celebrated medieval monasteries, yet exudes all the wild character of a remote Atlantic island.

 Great for

- Soaking up the atmosphere within the massive cashel walls
- Camping overnight amid an ambience of ancient spirituality

 Conditions

- Calm wind and sea for the boat trip

Sea kayaks pulled up at Clashymore Harbour, on Inishmurray's south-west shore.

Access

- Motorboats to Inishmurray leave from one of three mainland harbours – see Guided Excursions below. If you're sea kayaking across, the best departure point is Streedagh Point. Head along the N15 to Grange, then follow signs 3km west to Streedagh. Depending on the direction of the swell, launch either from Trawgar beach just west of the point, from the long Back Strand at the end of the road.
- Map: OSi 1:50,000 sheet 16
- Grid Ref: G 632 500
- GPS: 54.397518, -8.566970

Lying 6km off the north Sligo coast, Inishmurray is home to one of the best-preserved early monastic sites in Ireland. Measuring less than 1 square kilometre, this isolated outpost has been an unlikely centre of activity for millennia. It is thought the first settlers arrived during Neolithic times, with other artefacts dating from the Bronze Age. The early Christian period is what really stands out, thanks to the monastery established here by St Molaise in AD 520.

The monastic site remains remarkably intact, and includes a large cashel, three churches, several beehive cells, and the country's finest collection of early Christian engraved slabs outside Clonmacnoise. The low-lying setting may not be as spectacular as Skellig Michael (see page 207), but the archaeological remains are just as impressive and there's none of the tourist circus to contend with.

Inishmurray's last permanent residents relocated to the mainland in 1948, leaving the island to its wildlife. This includes seals, Irish hares, breeding colonies of arctic tern and storm petrel, and a winter gaggle of barnacle geese. The island is also home to a nationally important population of eider duck, a handsome black-and-white sea duck you're likely to see bobbing near the shore year-round.

There are several ways to access the island. People have been known to swim out, but the most popular options are either sea kayaking, or paying a local boatman to ferry you over. This is an exposed Atlantic coastline, however, so all crossings are highly weather dependent. Wild camping is great fun given

The early Christian churches and beehive huts on Inishmurray are reminiscent of those on Skellig Michael.

the atmospheric surrounds, and you'll find several possible tent sites at the back of Clashymore Harbour or beside the old schoolhouse.

The ideal time to visit is late May or early June, when much of the island is covered by a vast swathe of bluebells. For more details about the island's history, including a detailed map marking all the historic sites, see inishmurray.com.

Guided Excursions

You'll need some sea kayaking experience before paddling out to Inishmurray, but there are several operators who run guided trips. Try **West Coast Kayaking** (tel: 083 437 0893; westcoastkayaking.ie) or **Turf n Surf** (tel: 071 984 1091; www.turfnsurf.ie), who offer overnight excursions for €165 per person.

If you prefer the reassurance of a motorboat, passage is offered by two local skippers carrying up to 12 passengers each. The price generally comes in around €45 per person. Phone in advance to book your trip, then double-check sailing conditions the day before you travel. You should be allowed 2–3 hours to explore the island.

Sligo Boat Charters (tel: 086 891 3618; www.sligoboatcharters.com) depart from Rosses Point, and can include seal watching and light fishing if requested. **Inishmurray Island Tours** (tel: 087 254 0190; www.inishmurrayislandtrips.com) leave either from Mullaghmore Harbour, which is only accessible at low tide, or from Killybegs in County Donegal. The crossing takes between 50 minutes and 1¼ hours depending on your point of departure.

Spanish Treasure Ahoy

Inishmurray is not the only prominent site along this historic coastline. Streedagh – the departure point for sea kayakers – is also famed as the final resting place of three galleons from the Spanish Armada, which were shipwrecked here in 1588. In 2015, divers from the state's underwater archaeology unit removed four bronze cannons from these wrecks and transferred them to the National Museum. With numerous other treasures still to be salvaged, a local campaign has started to establish a permanent museum in the nearby village of Grange.

The Island

However you arrive at Inishmurray, you should pull up at **Clashymore Harbour**, a rocky bay on the island's south-west shore (grid ref: G 571 536). There's no jetty or slipway here, so motorboat passengers are deposited on a convenient boulder. Sea kayakers can land on the rocky beach at the back of the bay.

Modern tourists follow a long tradition by coming here; Inishmurray has been a place of pilgrimage since medieval times, with visitors following a turas trail of 11 stations around the island. To reach the main settlement, clamber up the boulders at the back of the beach, then turn right onto a grassy track. This track – known as 'the street' – leads along the southern shore and takes you past all the most important sites.

You can't miss the main **monastic enclosure**, which is located on the left after 300m. The site is protected by a large cashel, a circular stone wall some 4m thick, 5m high and 45m in diameter. Duck under the entrance lintel to emerge in an atmospheric world redolent of times long past. Inside are the remains of two churches, two beehive cells and a sweathouse. There's also a men's graveyard, two outdoor altars, and several carved stones, including two **cursing stones**. Medieval legend dictates that if you turn these stones clockwise you can bless someone, or anticlockwise to curse them. Take care that your curse is justified, for if not, it will revert back to you. Like many of the island's carved stones what you see here are replicas, the real

things having been removed to the schoolhouse for their own protection.

Outside the cashel on the seaward side is another church and graveyard. This is where women worshipped and were buried, because the cloistered ground inside was restricted to men. As you wander along the street towards the eastern tip of the island, you'll pass the ruined homes of the island's more recent inhabitants. The population of Inishmurray peaked during the 1880s, when 110 residents shared 15 houses. The final building in the row – the old schoolhouse – was refurbished by the OPW in the 1990s, and now acts as a conservation store for many of the unique cross slabs and other medieval artefacts found on the island.

The northern and eastern sides of Inishmurray are less constructed, but still contain various relics spanning the centuries. The ground underfoot is a mixture of rough grass and bog, but you're free to wander wherever you like to soak up the full atmosphere of the place.

If you travel by sea kayak, don't forget to circumnavigate the island before you leave. The shore is low-lying, with the exception of some 20m-high cliffs at its western end. Here'll you'll find **Pollnashantunny** (Hole of the Strong Wave), a narrow rock chasm that is well worth exploring before you head back to the mainland.

Inishmurray's monastic site is protected by a large cashel, a circular stone wall some 4m thick.

INCHAGOILL ISLAND

Lying at the heart of Lough Corrib in County Galway, Inchagoill is renowned for its ancient monastery, natural beauty and wilderness camping.

👍 Great for
- Wandering around fifth-century monastic ruins
- Camping and barbequing between woodland and shore

☁ Conditions
- Calm winds if you're travelling by small boat

🏛 Access
- Inchagoill lies in the middle of northern Lough Corrib. The two most established departure points on the mainland are Lisloughrey pier near Cong, and the quay at Oughterard. It is roughly 6km to the island from both places.
- Map: OSi 1:50,000 sheet 45, plus sheet 38 for the northern lough
- Grid Ref Lisloughrey pier: M 155 542; Oughterard pier: M 134 439
- GPS Lisloughrey pier: 53.531049, -9.275060; Oughterard pier: 53.438640, -9.304162

Inchagoill's Church of the Saints features a Romanesque doorway and dates from 1180.

At 176 square kilometres, Lough Corrib is the largest lake in the Republic of Ireland. Tradition holds that this watery expanse contains 365 islands, but the charts record many more – 1,327, to be precise. Of these, Inchagoill is the most famous, thanks to the early Christian monastery founded here by St Patrick.

Visiting Inchagoill is a fabulous way to combine an adventurous journey and wild seclusion with a first-hand history lesson. There are two main elements to the trip. One is exploring the island – and camping overnight if possible – and the other is getting there in the first place. In terms of getting there, the most exciting option is to take your own boat.

Canoes and kayaks can be launched from numerous points around Lough Corrib, offering plenty of alternatives in different wind directions. The shortest crossing is a 3km paddle from Inisdoorus causeway to the north-west. Other possibilities include a 6km trip from Inishmicatreer to the east. If you are paddling out, make sure to check the forecast carefully before launching; on a lake this size the waves can build into sizeable rollers given even a moderate wind to whip them up.

Guided Excursions

If you don't have your own boat, all is not lost. Local boatmen in Oughterard will carry you out for a fee – see www.oughterardtourism.com for details. Alternatively you can hop on board one of the summer ferries run by **Corrib Cruises** (tel: 087 2830 799; www.corribcruises.com). From June to September there are daily departures from Lisloughrey pier near Cong, with extra sailings from Oughterard during July and August. Adult tickets cost €20/€28 from each location, with children half price.

The Island

Most boats arrive on Inchagoill at the concrete jetty, which is tucked behind Burr Island on the north shore (grid ref: M 128 493). Beside the jetty you'll find a constructed fire pit with surrounding benches, and good grassy pitches for tents. This area can become busy during the summer, though. If you prefer peace and seclusion, head to the west or north-western shore of the island, where there are several more discrete camping spots amid the woodland.

Ireland's Oldest Roman Text

The Stone of Lugnad, in Inchagoill graveyard, is the island's most celebrated archaeological monument. The most remarkable feature is its inscription, which is carved in old Irish. Dating from the fifth century, it is believed to be Europe's second-oldest surviving text in the Roman alphabet; the only older example resides in the catacombs of Rome.

A map board near the **jetty** marks the island's 2.4km walking trail. Inchagoill is now owned and managed by the state, so you are free to wander where you like.

The Stone of Lugnad, in Inchagoill graveyard, holds Ireland's oldest Roman text.

Landing and camping are both possible at the jetty on Inchagoill's northern shore.

The main historic sites lie just 100m away at the back of the bay. The first building is a ruined stone cottage, home to the island's last inhabitant, Thomas Nevin. Inchagoill was purchased by the Guinness family in 1852, as part of the Ashford Castle estate. Thomas Nevin was installed as caretaker in 1931, and lived alone in this cottage for 17 years while tending the island.

The monastic site lies just behind the cottage, along a flagstone path. The first building is *Teampall na Naoimh*, or **Church of the Saints**. This dates from around 1180 and was built by Augustinian monks from Cong Abbey, which housed around 3,000 people at that time. The church's most distinctive feature is its Romanesque doorway, which is surrounded by carved heads depicting the ten saints of Lough Corrib.

Beyond the church is a small graveyard, where you'll find the **Stone of Lugnad**. Historians believe St Patrick and his nephew Lugnad came to Inchagoill in the fifth century, but Lugnad died during the construction of the adjacent St Patrick's Church. The stone marks Lugnad's grave, and is shaped like a boat rudder to reflect his role as St Patrick's navigator.

Beyond the monastery lie several more ruined cottages, home to six families who lived here prior to the 1900s. If you want to set off on the **loop walk** around the island, return to St Patrick's church and squeeze through the gap in the wall beside the building. The circuit weaves through beautiful woodland, swathed with bluebells and other wildflowers in the spring. On the way you pass several pebble or sand beaches, and various clearings with fire rings that act as alternative campsites. The only other structure is a stone folly on the west shore known as the Coffee House. This was built by the Guinness family in 1860, and comes complete with a stairway at the back to allow visitors to appreciate the view from the roof.

The walking trail finishes by depositing you back at the jetty where your journey began.

SKELLIG MICHAEL

Nothing can quite prepare you for a visit to this unique monastic site, which hovers atop a 180m cliff far out in the Atlantic.

Great for

- Climbing an ancient stone stairway to the teetering clifftop monastery
- Grabbing a quiet moment to imagine surviving on such a hostile outcrop

Conditions

- Calm sea and wind for the boat trip out

Access

- Skellig boats depart from several mainland ports, including Valentia, Derrynane, Ballinskelligs and Cahersiveen. The main departure point is the pier in Portmagee, which is located along the R565, near the western tip of the Iveragh Peninsula.
- Map: OSi 1:50,000 sheet 83
- Grid Ref: V 372 730
- GPS: 51.885982, -10.365753

The main monastic site contains beehive dwellings, oratories, crosses and a restored chapel.

Rising like a massive shark's tooth from the Atlantic Ocean, the remote and precipitous pyramid of Skellig Michael is more accurately described as a rock than an island. Like its twin, Little Skellig, this sharp pinnacle is the summit of a largely submerged mountain mighty enough to withstand the endless battering of the waves. Yet even more remarkable than its geology is the fact that people not only lived here, but endured on such an inhospitable outcrop for centuries.

The inhabitants of the 218m rock were monks, who settled in a monastery established by St Finian in the sixth century. The community survived 12km out in the ocean for an incredible 700 years before finally moving to the mainland. The remnants of their settlement is now considered one of the world's best-preserved early Christian outposts, and is designated as a UNESCO world heritage site.

The attractions of the islands don't end there. Both Skellig islands are nature reserves, and home to a plethora of nesting seabirds. Skellig Michael supports some of the world's largest breeding populations of storm petrel and manx shearwater, though most people's favourites are the comical puffins, which are remarkably unwary of visitors. Little Skellig meanwhile is stained permanent white by the guano of some 40,000 breeding gannets, which gather here in one of the largest colonies in the world. Try to visit before the end of July for the best seabird experience.

Though the location is certainly wild, trips to Skellig Michael are highly regulated and the large number of visitors means solitude is almost impossible to find.

Boats pause in front of Little Skellig to admire its massive gannet colony.

Though Skellig Michael had been popular with pilgrims and tourists for centuries, its fame skyrocketed after it was used as a location for two blockbuster *Star Wars* films. Filming took place in 2014 for *The Force Awakens*, and in 2015 and 2016 for *The Last Jedi*. The impact of the films has been mixed. On the positive side, many thousands of fans have journeyed to Kerry and increased the region's tourism revenue. On the other hand, the practicalities of filming and the pressure of more visitors have amplified the strain on an already fragile site.

The rock's popularity doesn't mean it is easy, and the outing should be considered like a short hillwalk. To reach the monastery you will have to climb 618 rough steps and negotiate some narrow rock ledges. Though there are some safety handrails low down, higher up the island is deliberately maintained as a wilderness site and there is nothing to stop you in case of a fall. There have been visitor fatalities in the past, so the trip is only recommended for fit people who don't suffer from vertigo. There are no facilities on the rock either, so bring all your own supplies, including good walking shoes, rainwear, sunscreen, food and drink. The only toilets are on the boats on the way out and back.

It is possible to sea kayak to Skellig Michael, but the journey involves a minimum round-trip distance of 30km, with no guarantee that conditions will favour landing once you arrive. It is considered one of the most committing sea kayak outings in the country, and best left to experts only. Kayakers are restricted to the same landing hours as motorboats, which they have to dodge to reach the jetty. Camping is strictly prohibited.

Guided Excursions

Access to Skellig Michael is regulated by the OPW, the state body charged with protecting the island. Boats are permitted to land only between mid May and the beginning of October. Just 15 local boatmen receive landing permits each year, and can carry 12

A long, stone stairway of rough-hewn slabs winds upwards for 140 vertical metres.

The island's puffins are so unwary you almost have to step over them as you walk.

people each. This means a maximum of 180 people can visit the rock daily.

There are always more people wanting to make the journey than can be accommodated, so the best advice is to book your passage far in advance. The small boats and exposed crossing means trips are often cancelled due to rough seas, so make sure to contact your skipper again the day before travelling to check weather conditions. If your trip is cancelled, you won't be offered a replacement date. The 45-minute journey can be bumpy; oilskins are often distributed to protect against the spray, while the seats behind the wheelhouse provide the most shelter.

Landing on Skellig Michael is only allowed between 10 a.m. and 4.30 p.m. Most boats leave the mainland between 9 and 10 a.m. and arrive back five hours later, giving 2½ hours on the island. For a full list of licensed boat operators and their contact numbers, go to **www.heritageireland.ie**, then navigate to Skellig Michael in the South-West section. The trip costs around €75 per person, which you pay in cash at the quayside. Many operators have restrictions on group sizes and don't carry children under 12.

If you can't get a place on a landing boat, consider an 'eco tour' instead. These trips circle both Skellig Michael and Little Skellig, letting you view the wildlife and monastery from water level. They are often run by the same people who operate the landing trips, but there are several departures daily, with places costing roughly half the price.

The Island

The boat journey to and from the Skelligs is half the fun of the trip. Bring warm, waterproof clothing and be prepared for a few splashes. Your first encounter is likely to be with Little Skellig, though landing here is prohibited. The sea and air come alive as gannets launch from their lofty nests and plunge arrow-like

into the water to hunt for fish. They dive at speeds of up to 100km/h and it's an impressive experience to sit at water level in the midst of their plummeting bombardment.

Just 2km later you pull up beneath the looming precipice of Skellig Michael. Boats land at a small concrete jetty in **Blind Man's Cove**, at the north-eastern tip of the island. Following a short safety briefing by an OPW guide, you should join the Lighthouse Road, a paved track that climbs gradually south along the coast.

After 400m public access is restricted, and you turn right to begin the ascent of the **South Steps**. This long, stone stairway winds upwards for 140 vertical metres, following a trail of rough-hewn slabs laid by the monks. Near the bottom of the path you must negotiate an awkward rock ledge, where accidents have occurred in the past. A chain is now in place for security, but there are few other safety railings as you climb higher. Particular care is needed in the wet, when the steps can be slippery underfoot.

At a height of 130m you reach **Christ's Saddle**, a grassy depression with the rock's two main peaks rising on either side. To the left lies the South Peak, where a series of rock terraces hold a hermitage and oratory. The access route is treacherous and is now out of bounds. Modern visitors must stick to the main pathway and make the final ascent to the monastery, which lies to the right beneath the North Peak.

The main **monastic site** is contained within the walls of a large cashel. Inside you will find a collection of beehive dwellings, oratories and crosses. There are also a monk's graveyard, two wells, and a recently restored medieval chapel dedicated to St Michael, patron saint of high places. The buildings were constructed so rain couldn't penetrate between the stones. Rainwater was carefully channelled instead into a large underground cistern, which provided the only source of fresh water on the island. It is the site's location that makes it so remarkable, teetering on the brink of such a high and unlikely outcrop. If you can, take a quiet moment to imagine the reality of actually surviving in such a place.

When you're ready, retrace your journey down the South Steps, then return to the jetty in time for the boat ride back.

FAMILY ADVENTURES

Summiting your first 800m mountain at the age of four is worth a celebration!

FAMILY ADVENTURES are becoming increasingly popular in Ireland, as more and more parents realise outdoor activities don't have to cease when they have children. In fact, bringing kids into the outdoors is far easier and more fun than you might imagine.

Watching a child discover the joys of the natural world rekindles your own sense of wonder. Every flower can be examined, every rock scrambled across. If the children are young the first few outings may involve guidance and encouragement, but before long their enthusiasm and competitive streak kicks in, and you'll soon find it hard to keep up.

By bringing children into the outdoors, you widen their horizons and open a whole new world to them. Studies have shown that children in the UK now spend less time outside than prison inmates, but outdoor adventures provide a counterbalance to their increasingly sedentary lifestyles. Trips into the wild are unbeatable educational experiences – there's no better way to appreciate natural processes than to witness them first hand. At the same time as learning about the environment, they are also developing all sorts of invaluable personal skills. It is no coincidence that most outdoor children have a great spirit of adventure, and are self-reliant, confident individuals.

If you head outdoors together, you'll find it also offers a unique opportunity for family bonding. This is quality time, when you share experiences and create memories that will be recounted for years. Whether it's shooting stars and marshmallows beside the campfire, or laughing about dad falling into the lake, these are precious moments that will stay with you forever.

You're never too young to start enjoying the outdoors!

Fear Conditioning in Children

Outdoor environments are full of physical challenges, but when should you encourage your children and when should you caution them? This is a question that may define their decision-making for the rest of their lives, according to paediatric psychologists. Fear conditioning begins when a parent tells their child to be careful in a playground, or to come down in case they hurt themselves. If parents are overprotective, this can lead to avoidance of the physical activities that are essential to developing confidence and new skills. Studies have also revealed a gender bias in how we respond to children: parents are four times more likely to tell a girl to be careful than a boy. This may help explain why men are more likely to pursue certain adventure activities than women. Rather than preaching avoidance, the best advice is to show your child how to pursue activities in a safe and balanced way, then act as a safety net while they find their feet. Enjoying the outdoors is all about being aware of the dangers, yet developing the skills to cope with them safely.

Ireland's Family Adventures at a Glance

By starting with short, easy trips, all the activities mentioned in this book can be completed by families. Whether you want to go cycling, walking, canoeing or swimming, there's a choice of suitably graded outings all around the country.

This bucket list includes five stand-out trips to get you going, but this is just the start of what's possible. Other specifically family-friendly outings in this book include The Sloc (see page 136), the Great Western Greenway (page 168), Poll a Chorra (page 186) and Great Saltee Island (page 87). By talking to other active parents in your area, selecting suitable outings from guidebooks, and paying for the odd guided trip, you'll find Ireland has a whole host of family-orientated adventures just waiting to be discovered.

Which Trip is Right for You?

Every child is different, and you need tailor your adventures to suit your children's individual needs. In the early days in particular, it is best to err on the side of caution when deciding what to take on. Far better to leave them asking for more than attempt too much and risk putting them off. With the right attitude, you'll be amazed what children can achieve. In 2015, Cian Quinn became the youngest person to climb the highest mountain in every county of Ireland. He tackled each peak with his father, and had summitted them all by the age of 12.

Children will love a wide range of outdoor experiences. Gentle horse rides are another fun activity for the whole family to try.

Remember to keep it fun: the ultimate aim of outdoor exploration is enjoyment.

It's quite feasible for children to begin climbing easy Irish mountains at the age of five. They're capable of sitting in a bike trailer or in the centre seat of a canoe well before that, and will love launching themselves into the sea as soon as they're competent swimmers. By the time they have a couple of years' experience of easier activities, you'll be able to bring them on more challenging outings. Some kids are capable of completing red mountain bike trails and Grade 1 scrambles by the age of seven. Appropriate activity depends on the child's previous experience, strength and confidence levels. Nobody understands their capabilities better than their own parents, so it's up to you to gauge what level of activity is suitable at any given time.

It's worth noting that once you bring children into the outdoors, you're accepting responsibility for their well-being as well as your own. Make sure your own skills are up to the task and that you are confident acting as guide and safety officer for people less experienced than yourself. If you want to try an activity but don't have the requisite experience to lead it, go out in the company of a professional operator familiar with running family trips. You'll all have a great time, and if you observe how the trip is organised and led, you should pick up countless tips that will help you plan independent outings in the future.

Practicalities

If you're used to exploring the outdoors as part of an adult group, there are several important differences to consider when heading out with children. Follow the six steps below to enjoy a successful family adventure.

1. Plan Ahead

Think carefully about the terrain you're likely to encounter and how your children will respond to it. If you're not sure if the trip is suitable for them, do it on your own first so you can assess how they might get on. Be extra-vigilant with navigational planning; this is not the time to get lost. Double-check the weather forecast too, and be more cautious about the conditions than normal. Adults may be able to push on when they're cold and wet, but children will struggle.

2. Pack Carefully

A big part of anticipating your child's needs comes down to what you pack. Warm and waterproof clothing is essential, but children are more liable to get wet and muddy, so a spare change of clothes and shoes may also be appropriate. Lots of snacks will help maintain energy levels, while a small plant or animal identification guide can turn a trip into a natural treasure hunt.

3. Encourage the Right Attitude

Outdoor activities can be taxing both physically and mentally, and it's up to you to promote a positive attitude that will help your children push on when things get tough. Be realistic about how difficult the trip is, and avoid telling them it's easy. Say it may sometimes feel hard, but it's a big achievement to reach the end; you'll stick together as a team and do it together. Most kids love a challenge, and if you can make them determined to prove how strong they are, they'll usually pull it off just to impress you.

4. Set a Few Ground Rules

The outdoors is a big and potentially dangerous place, so you'll need to promote a bit of discipline. Explain briefly what the hazards of the trip are and how you should behave to avoid them. You don't need to overstate the dangers and can allow an appropriate amount of independence, but this is an important first step in understanding how to behave responsibly in an outdoor environment.

5. Take Lots of Breaks

Children have incredible energy but may not have developed the long-distance stamina of adults. The trick to an enjoyable trip is to take lots of breaks and move at their pace, not yours. If a child says they're tired, use your judgement. You may want to encourage them on a bit further, or you may decide it's best to stop straight away. A three-minute break and small snack is generally all that's required before they're ready to rush off again.

6. Keep it Fun

Remember that the ultimate aim of exploring the outdoors is enjoyment. Most kids love discovering new places, but there are ways you can help keep it interesting. Fill them in on any interesting facts relevant to where you are. Point out flowers, birds and animals, or look for pretty shells. Set them tasks: collecting wood for a campfire, or exploring an area and reporting back what they've found. Teach them how to set up a tent and look at the stars together. Everything about outdoor living can be exciting, and it won't take them long to warm to its opportunities.

Take children to clubs and events where they can mix with people their own age.

LOUGH GILL – FAMILY CANOE

This short but scenic trip is a perfect introduction to inland canoeing, with an island picnic or wild camping recommended.

Great for

- Appreciating the scenic variety of a calm river and open lough
- Letting the children explore and rule their very own uninhabited island

Conditions

- Light winds

Trip Details

- Distance: 6km (4 miles)
- Time: 1½–2½ hours
- Map: OSi 1:50,000 sheet 25

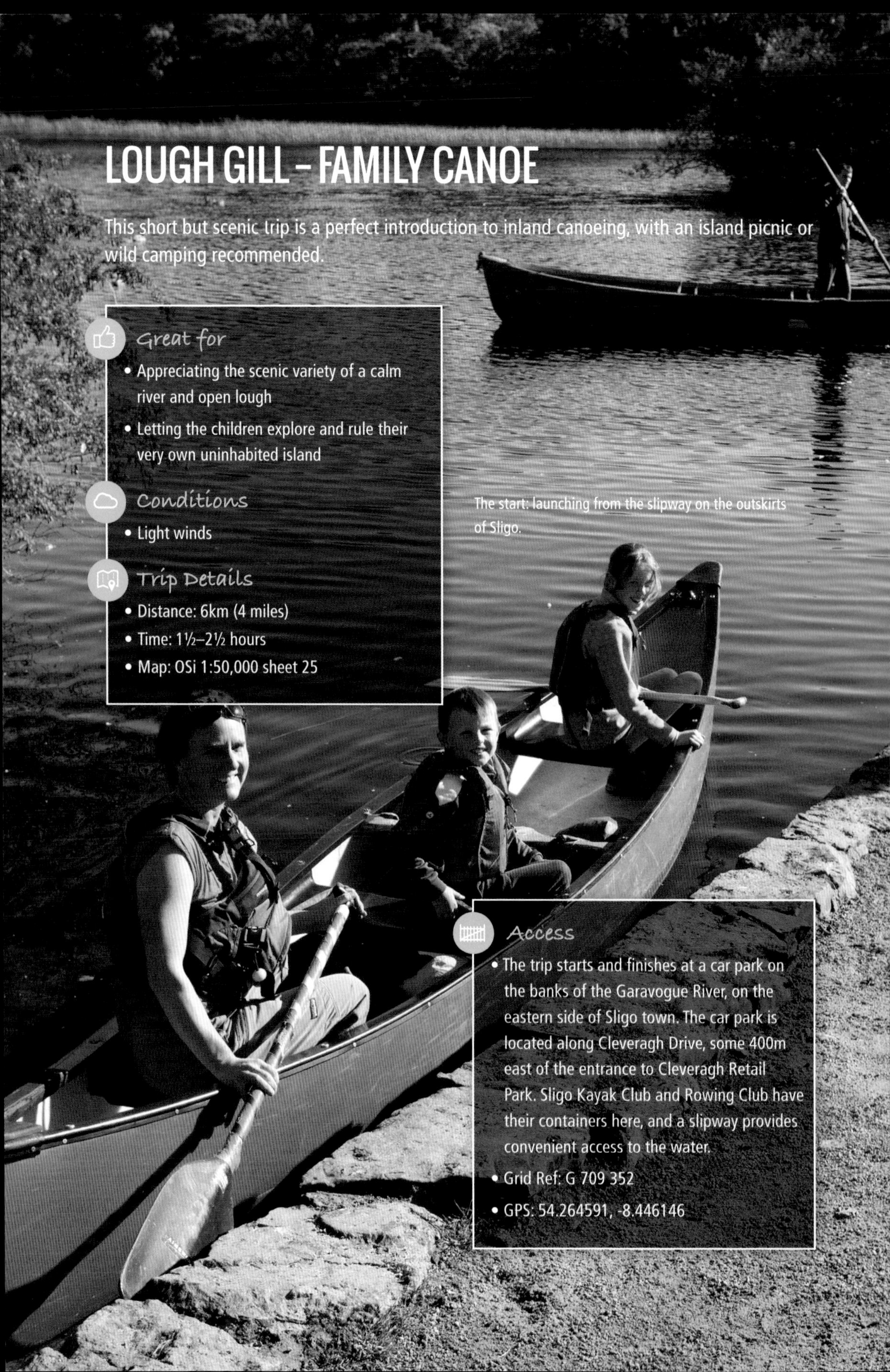

The start: launching from the slipway on the outskirts of Sligo.

Access

- The trip starts and finishes at a car park on the banks of the Garavogue River, on the eastern side of Sligo town. The car park is located along Cleveragh Drive, some 400m east of the entrance to Cleveragh Retail Park. Sligo Kayak Club and Rowing Club have their containers here, and a slipway provides convenient access to the water.
- Grid Ref: G 709 352
- GPS: 54.264591, -8.446146

Lough Gill – Family Canoe, County Sligo

There are many short trips on Irish inland waters that are perfect for family outings, and this excursion on Lough Gill, County Sligo, is just one example. It's a lovely paddle, with all the elements necessary to entertain people of all ages: scenic beauty, a variety of landscape from river to lough, an uninhabited island that's perfect for picnics, camping and exploration, and a secret reed-filled channel for intrepid canoeists to bushwack through. With plenty of scope for extension too, it charms both children and adults alike.

Lough Gill itself is about 8km long and 2km wide. It's a pretty lake, surrounded by hills and mountains, and with several woodland reserves lining its shores. Its microclimate attracts all sorts of wildlife, and it's a popular spot with birdwatchers.

The lake contains 16 small islands, including Cottage Island, the focal point of this trip. Spanning 14 acres, this is the lough's second largest island, and known to locals by its popular name, Beezie's Island. Beezie Gallagher was born here during the 1860s, and lived on the island for much of her life. She was Lough Gill's last permanent resident and a much-loved character; there are many colourful stories about her hospitality and her kindness to animals. Her ruined cottage still stands and can be explored by visitors, along with the remains of a nearby church.

Guided Excursions

If you don't have your own boat, there are several options for guided trips around Lough Gill. **Adventure Gently** (tel: 085 1821 547; www. adventuregentlyireland.com) offers both half-day and whole-day excursions in open canoes, while **Sligo Kayak Tours** (tel: 086 1999 015; sligokayaktours.com) run similar trips in kayaks.

The Paddle

There are several possible launch points around the shore of Lough Gill, but the start along the Garavogue River is the most scenic of them all. The slipway here is part of Doorly Park, with facilities including picnic benches and footpaths that run along the waterside. Launch between the ducks and swans at the slipway, then begin by heading right, along the **upper Garavogue**. You're paddling upstream, but the flow is generally so weak it won't hinder your progress.

A Literary Mystery

Many people are familiar with Lough Gill before they see it, thanks to the poem 'The Lake Isle of Inishfree', by W.B. Yeats. Yet Inishfree is one of the lake's least inspiring islands, an outcrop of rough shrubbery just one acre in size. Literary experts have suggested Yeats may have been using poetic licence with the title, and was actually describing one of the lough's other islands. Both Beezie's Island and Church Island have been proposed as the real subject of his affection, where he could enjoy his longed-for peace with 'lake water lapping with low sounds by the shore'. Given that Beezie herself was still in residence when it was written, Church Island seems the most likely candidate.

Reed beds border both banks of the river, with woodland rising beyond. After a few hundred metres you pass a couple of ruined cottages on the left, remnants of the Hazelwood Demesne. Roughly 1.5km from the start the river widens, and you'll see a number of old barges moored on the right. Move to the left bank here, and continue upstream to Bernard's Island.

This small, wooded island is separated from the east bank by a **reed-filled channel**. Canoes and kayaks can push right through the reeds, with children imaging all sorts of crocodiles lurking within.

The best camping spots lie at the eastern tip of Beezie's Island.

Reed beds and woodland border the first section along the upper Garavogue.

Continue past Nut Point, where the expanse of Lough Gill opens up ahead. Beezie's Island now lies just 500m to the south-east, a mixture of trees and low, grassy slopes. As you leave the Garavogue, take note of your surrounds so you'll recognise the entrance for your return journey.

After reaching **Beezie's Island**, it's nice to circumnavigate its shores. There are many possible landing spots, but the best camping lies at the eastern tip, so pull in here if you plan to stay overnight. You'll find several fire rings dotted around the island, but please heed the notices requesting that all litter is brought home. You'll find plenty to explore, including an old church hidden in the trees and the ruins of Beezie's cottage itself.

If you want to extend your trip, options include Church Island, 2km to the north-west, or the woodland trails of Slish Wood, just 250m to the south. Otherwise you can simply reverse your outward route along the Garavogue River, with the distinctive prow of Benbulbin beckoning you back.

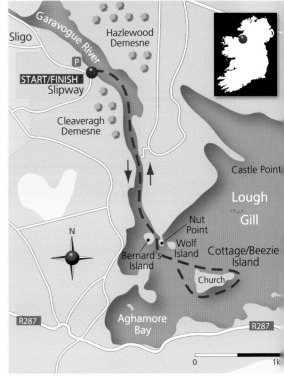

ERRIS HEAD – FAMILY COASTAL WALK

Kids will be as exhilarated as adults by this short but magnificent walk around the tip of a wild headland.

Great for

- Appreciating the mighty coastal scenery from the very tip of Erris Head
- Watching the kids run from post to post as navigators extraordinaire

Conditions

- Up to moderate winds and good visibility

Trip Details

- Distance: 5km (3 miles)
- Time: 1½–2 hours
- Ascent: 100m (330ft)
- Map: OSi 1:50,000 sheet 22

Access

- Start and finish at Danish Cellar, at the northern tip of the Belmullet Peninsula, County Mayo. From the roundabout in the centre of Belmullet town, head north along the R313. Roughly 600m later, continue straight ahead at a junction. Now follow signs for the 'Trailhead' and 'Ceann Iorrais', passing through several more junctions. Continue for 8km to the end of the road, where you'll find a car park and map board.
- Grid Ref: F 705 397
- GPS: 54.288640, -9.988761

Just 200m from the start there are already great views across Broadhaven Bay.

Enjoying the view south along the wild west coast of the Belmullet Peninsula.

Erris Head is a remote and exposed headland at the furthest reaches of Ireland's north-west coast. The scenery here is wild and spectacular, yet accessible too, thanks to a signed walking circuit that circumnavigates the tip of the peninsula. The endless scenic interest and short duration make it a perfect option for families, with children left asking for more.

The route passes near cliffs at the very end of the headland, so use your common sense here; hold the hands of any little ones, and don't venture too close to the edge. You'll need decent footwear too, because the terrain can be rough and wet underfoot. Choose between runners or wellies for the children, depending on the wetness of the ground.

The entire region around Erris Head has been designated a Special Area of Conservation. This is

Coastal Surveillance

Near the tip of Erris Head you visit an old lookout post dating from the Second World War. Part of a chain of 83 surveillance posts that stretched all around the Irish coastline, this was was manned continuously for five years. The logbook records frequent sightings of war ships and US aircraft heading towards Northern Ireland. Near the bunker you can just make out the word EIRE on the ground, designed to alert disorientated pilots to the fact they were crossing neutral Ireland.

designed to protect the alpine heath on top of the headland, as well as the cliffs at its fringes, where numerous species of seabird make their nests. If you can tear your eyes away from the filigreed coastline it's worth looking out for sea mammals too. Seals can often be seen swimming close to the shore, and numerous whale and dolphin sightings have been recorded.

The Walk

The route is signed throughout by purple arrows on black posts. Begin by crossing a metal stile beside the map board. This takes you into a grassy field, where sheep often graze. Turn right and follow the fence around the edge of the field. Already there are great views east across Broadhaven Bay to Benwee Head, with the jagged Stags of Broadhaven lying just offshore to the north.

The route follows a raised bank of earth and passes over two more stiles before emerging onto open moorland. Follow the peaty path straight ahead, crossing several small bridges and negotiating the occasional wet patch underfoot.

After a gentle climb you'll notice a line of marker posts coming across from the left; the route will return this way at the end of the circuit. Keep straight ahead for now, and climb across a promontory known as Gubastuckaun, or 'Beak of the Headland'.

The path soon becomes firmer underfoot, and dissipates altogether as you make the gentle descent towards the tip of Erris Head. The final waymarking post is set well back from the northern edge of the headland, but it's worth continuing (carefully!) to the edge of the cliff. Here, a sheer precipice drops some 40m into a narrow chasm, with the island of Illandavuck rearing steeply on the opposite side of the channel. This island was once attached to the mainland, but has been torn asunder by the mighty force of Atlantic swells.

The route turns sharp left at Erris Head and begins to climb south, heading toward a prominent watch tower on top of the hill ahead. This building is the ruins of a concrete lookout post dating from the Second World War. The added height only improves the view, with fabulous coastal scenery in every direction.

As you begin to descend south-west, look out on the right to see the word EIRE written on the ground in stones. The descent brings you to the edge of a deep coastal inlet known as Ooghwee, or 'Yellow Hole', where seals can often be seen. Turn left here and follow the chasm inland, then make a final short climb to the concrete trig pillar that marks the 82m summit of Erris Head. This is another impressive vantage point, with a 360-degree panorama that encompasses much of north-west Mayo.

The marker posts now head east across a narrow neck of land, and rejoin the outward route. Turn right at the trail junction, then retrace your initial steps back to the start.

Beside the 40m-high chasm at the northern tip of Erris Head.

DIAMOND HILL – FAMILY MOUNTAIN HIKE

The short, signed trail up this charismatic little peak gives great views across Connemara National Park.

Great for

- Mixing a high quality mountain ascent with playgrounds, café and visitor centre
- Benefiting from lots of scenic gain in exchange for relatively little pain

Conditions

- Dry rock and good visibility

Trip Details

- Distance: 7km (4½ miles)
- Time: 2½–3 hours
- Ascent: 420m (1,380ft)
- Maps: OSi 1:50,000 sheet 37, or Harvey Superwalker 1:30,000 *Connemara*

Access

- Start and finish at the large car park for Connemara National Park visitor centre. This lies a few hundred metres west of Letterfrack village, along the N59 Leenaun–Clifden road.
- Grid Ref: L 711 573
- GPS: 53.550547, -9.945578

Fine summit views from Diamond Hill allow you to appreciate the intricate Connemara coastline.

At 445m high, Diamond Hill is a fairly modest mountain, yet it packs as much character as many peaks twice the size. A far-flung satellite of the Twelve Bens range, it rises in isolation above the village of Letterfrack, its steep slopes narrowing to an impressive fin of quartzite some 500m long.

A signed pathway leads all the way to the top, where you're rewarded by fantastic views across the surrounding peaks and coastline. Its location within Connemara National Park makes it particularly family-friendly, with a visitor centre, café, picnic tables, grazing horses and children's playground all adding extra interest before and after the trip. The promise of an ice cream at the end is a sure-fire way to get the gang moving!

The trail is fully constructed across the lower slopes, but remains mountainous near the summit, where you may find yourself using your hands for assistance in some places. In wet weather care is needed here as the quartzite becomes slippery underfoot.

The Walk

From the car park, walk past an old admission kiosk and descend along a gravel path to the visitor centre, which is open from March to October. Either head inside to see the exhibits, or continue past the entrance and around the north side of the building. Pass a children's play area, then follow a wide gravel path north-east, heading away from the park buildings and climbing gently along the left side of a field.

An Equine Icon

Though a domestic rather than a wild animal, the largest mammal inhabiting this national park is the Connemara Pony. An iconic part of the Connemara countryside, several of these horses can be seen grazing in the fields around the visitor centre. These purebred individuals are direct descendants of a herd that was presented to the state by President Childers, the fourth president of Ireland.

The pyramid of Diamond Hill fills the scene ahead as you continue through a sprung gate and climb around a sharp corner. The trail now heads back south-east to a junction. Turn left here, following the signs for the Lower Diamond Hill Walk. The path begins to climb gently now, crossing sections of **wooden boardwalk** where the ground is wet underfoot. Soon you reach a junction marked by a huge boulder. Turn left here onto the Upper Diamond Hill Walk.

After a relatively flat section, the gradient increases as you approach the base of the summit slope. Turn left at another trail junction, which you will return to during your descent. Now climb a flight of steep, winding flagstone steps. Fine views below allow you to appreciate the broken and intricate nature of the Connemara coastline, the maze of islands, bays, inlets and loughs so intricately woven that the division between land and sea becomes blurred.

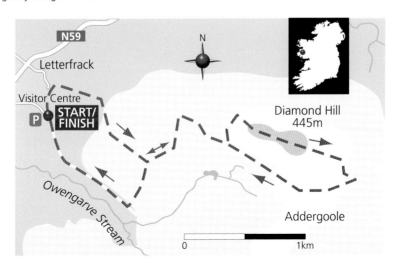

'A signed pathway leads all the way to the summit of Diamond Hill.'

The path skirts beneath a steep slope, then climbs diagonally through a cluster of quartzite outcrops. A short distance later it emerges onto the upper part of the **summit ridge**, where the gradient eases. A final, gentle climb brings you to the summit **cairn**, where you can enjoy sensational views across the Twelve Bens to the east. Below to the north-east is Kylemore Lough, with the Gothic turrets of Kylemore Abbey conspicuous on the lakeshore.

From the summit, continue to follow the Upper Diamond Hill loop. After an initially steep descent down the eastern flanks of the mountain, you can enjoy a largely flat return trip along a large terrace on its southern side. You may also get the chance to see the herd of **feral goats** that frequent this area. Continue around the western side of the mountain until you return to the upper loop junction passed on your outward journey. Turn left here and descend to the junction marked by the large boulder. Turn left again to complete the final part of the lower loop. Descend steeply to an old bog road in the Owengarve Valley, which brings you to a final junction. Turn right here to arrive back at the visitor centre and car park.

The Gothic turrets of Kylemore Abbey are conspicuous on the lakeshore below.

THE POLLOCK HOLES – FAMILY SNORKEL

The abundant sea life and calm waters of these large rock pools provide a perfect introduction to Irish snorkelling.

Great for

- Counting all the different species visible both above and below the water
- Smiling at children's exclamations as they discover a new marine creature

Conditions

- Low to mid tide and up to a moderate ocean swell

Access

- The Pollock Holes in County Clare are accessed from a large parking area on the southern shore of Kilkee's horseshoe bay. From the village centre, follow the coast road to the West End, then continue to the car park at the end of the road.
- Map: OSi 1:50,000 sheet 63
- Grid Ref: Q 874 602
- GPS: 52.681813, -9.663873

The Pollock Holes are popular with families during the summer months.

Perfect, low-tide conditions. The reef is covered by water at high tide. (Carsten Krieger)

If you're looking for a safe but natural marine park that showcases the full diversity of Irish sea life, it's hard to beat the Pollock Holes of Kilkee. Set amid the sandstone slabs of Duggerna Reef, four large pools and a maze of smaller ones play host to a multitude of aquatic species. Children spend hours here poking around with nets and buckets, but for the very best three-dimensional experience, encourage them to don a snorkel and mask and explore the underwater world as well. The natural shelter afforded by the reef makes it a safe haven for novices, and hundreds of local children enjoy their first glimpse of sub-aqua wildlife here each year.

The range of species both here and on neighbouring reefs is so rich that the shoreline is protected within a special area of conservation. Life thrives because the pools strike a perfect balance between regularly refreshed seawater and shelfter from the elements. With each high tide, the reefs are covered and the pools inundated by Atlantic flows. Yet at mid tide the pools re-emerge, replete with some

While the Tide Turns ...

The Pollock Holes aren't the only natural attraction in Kilkee, so if you have a few hours to wait while the tide turns, all is not lost. As well as the sandy beach at the back of the bay, more snorkelling and swimming options can be found between the pier and Byrne's Cove on the north side of the village. Two fine cliff walks also lead both west from the Pollock Holes and north around George's Head, leaving from the coastal car parks at either end of the village.

of the same creatures plus some new ones, ready for a whole new phase of exploration.

The pools' position within the tidal zone means you have to time your visit carefully. Access is possible both at low tide, and for two hours either side, so for around 4½ hours in each tidal cycle. Search online for 'Lahinch tide times' to view the daily cycle, then plan your trip accordingly. It's also worth bringing a pocket guide to the Irish seashore to help identify the different creatures you find.

The Snorkel

The Pollock Holes lie just beneath the car park and adjacent Diamond Rocks Café. If you can't see an obvious reef here, the tide is too high, and you'll need to come back later. Wait till the water has receded sufficiently that the swell is no longer flowing into the pools, and the rocky shelf surrounding them is free from waves. Even when westerly swells continue to crash onto the rocks nearby, the pools should remain calm and protected for the next few hours.

Once the tide is low enough, follow a well-trodden path down onto the rocks. The pools are spread over an area almost a quarter of a kilometre square, so you can wander from one pool to another, sampling the ecology of each as you go.

The **main pools** vary from around 20m to 50m in length, and from 1m to 2.5m deep. Entry is generally like a swimming pool – sit on the side and flop in – though there is one pool with a sufficiently high stack of rocks beside it to be a popular jumping venue. Make sure to launch feet first, however, because it's not particularly deep below.

Each pool has its own **marine ecosystem**, and snorkellers will see different species in each one. One of the main fish is the namesake pollock; intertidal zones like this serve as important nursery areas for juveniles, which head offshore to deeper waters as they mature. You may also see young wrasse, sand eels, shrimps, crabs, squat lobsters, jellyfish and endearing blennies, which seems to walk along the rock on their pectoral fins.

It's also worth exploring the smaller, shallower pools, where you will spot creatures like sea urchins, anemones, starfish and sea cucumbers. By the time you're finished, it's hard to disagree with the natural scientists who have labelled the reef a unique biological resource.

The larger pools offer a perfect place to introduce children to snorkelling.

The Pollock Holes – Family Snorkel, County Clare

WATERFORD GREENWAY – FAMILY CYCLE

The whole family will enjoy the mixture of scenery and history along this easy, off-road cycle path.

Great for

- Wondering at the construction of tall viaducts and coastal causeways
- Sending spooky echoes reverberating along the depths of Ballyvoyle Tunnel

Conditions

- No specific requirements, but fine weather will be appreciated

Trip Details

- Distance: 23km (14 miles)
- Time: 3–4 hours
- Maps: OSi 1:50,000 sheets 75 and 82

Access

- **To the start:** The section described here starts at Kilmacthomas Workhouse. Approach the area via the N25, then turn off for Kilmacthomas. The entrance to the workhouse lies 500m south of the dual carriageway; follow signs for the greenway to find the exact location.
- Grid Ref: S 406 056
- GPS: 52.202047, -7.406433

- **To the finish:** The greenway finishes in the centre of Dungarvan, at a crossroads on the eastern side of Devonshire Bridge. The best car park lies just north of the crossroads. Dungarvan itself is usually accessed via the N25 road.
- Grid Ref: X 264 934
- GPS: 52.092489, -7.616947

The greenway runs across the top of Kilmacthomas Viaduct, which stands almost 30m high.

The Waterford Greenway was launched in 2017, and is an excellent addition to the growing collection of purpose-built cycle paths around Ireland. It follows the route of an old train line, and still features many of the accoutrements of the railway, with several stations, viaducts, causeways and even a lengthy tunnel along the way. There are also lovely views across mountain and coastline, and plenty of modern facilities to make your journey easier.

The route is entirely off-road, and the surface flat and paved throughout, so progress is both safe and easy. There's no surprise it's a big hit with families, the youngest kids being towed in baby trailers while the older ones whizz past on their own wheels.

The entire greenway from Waterford city to Dungarvan is 46km long, so rather too lengthy for children, but frequent intermediate access points mean you can break it into shorter sections to suit your party. Here we describe the more interesting, western half of the route. At 23km this may still be too long for young families, so use your judgement to reduce it further if required. The most popular alternative start/finish point along this stretch is the car park at Durrow, just 10km before the finish at Dungarvan (Grid Ref: X 338 975; GPS: 52.129048, -7.5063394).

Bike hire is available from various outlets – try **Waterford Greenway Bike Hire** (tel: 051 295 955; www.waterfordgreenwaybikehire.com), **The Greenway Man** (tel: 086 835 1233; www.thegreenwayman.com), or **O'Mahony Cycles** (tel: 087 363 4344; abbeysiderentabike.com). Adult bikes cost around €20 per pay, with children half price. Some hire shops have several outlets along the route, so you can pick up a bike at one place and drop it at another. Others offer a free shuttle bus service to bring you back to your car at the end of the day.

Bus Eireann's Expressway service no. 40 also runs between Waterford, Kilmacthomas and Dungarvan at least four times daily, and may be useful in facilitating a linear journey.

The Ride

Kilmacthomas Workhouse, at the start of this route, is an old famine-era institution dating from 1850. The buildings once included a chapel, fever hospital and mortuary.

By the Sweat of Navvies

The Dungarvan–Waterford railway was officially opened in 1878. It was a remarkable feat of engineering across harsh terrain, and the most expensive line built in Ireland to that time. A small army of navvies used hand tools to construct two coastal causeways, a 400m tunnel and three tall viaducts spanning river valleys. All this within just the 23km section featured here. The product of their labour was not to last long, however; passenger trains ran along the track for just 89 years, and the line was closed altogether in 1990.

The greenway runs alongside the car park; turn left as you join the trail to head towards Dungarvan. After just 1km, elevated platforms on either side of the path herald your arrival at Kilmacthomas Station. A short distance later you cross **Kilmacthomas Viaduct**,

You emerge from Ballyvoyle Tunnel into a gorge-like cutting draped with ferns. (Luke Myers)

which has eight stone arches and stands almost 30m high. To really appreciate its elegant Victorian engineering, detour down a lane on the left just after the bridge, where you can view the viaduct from below.

The trail continues across verdant countryside for the next 10km, with a variety of wildflowers lining the route and good views to the Comeragh Mountains on the right. This brings you to Durrow Viaduct, another impressive, seven-arch bridge. Again it's best appreciated from below; turn right after crossing it and descend 300m to the banks of the River Tay to study it in more detail.

Back on the greenway, you may find the trail becoming busier after the Durrow car park. It's less than a kilometre now to the atmospheric **Ballyvoyle Tunnel**, where the path plunges right through a narrow 400m-long passage. Faint lights glow from regular alcoves, illuminating both the mineral formations within the recesses, and giving the tunnel an eerie feel. You emerge into a gorge-like cutting with ferns draped along the walls, and the whole section is quite unique.

The next landmark is Ballyvoyle Viaduct, which gives good views but is not of the same architectural calibre as the others, having been blown up by the IRA during the 1922 Civil War then rebuilt two years later. Soon after this, a small children's playground makes a popular spot for a break.

As you near the end of the Waterford Greenway there are fine coastal views across Clonlea Strand.

The greenway now rounds a corner and begins to head west, with the wide, sandy expanse of **Clonea Strand** visible on the left. Continue for a few kilometres to Clonea Road car park, where you have the option of detouring to the beach. To make this 3km out-and-back trip, turn left and follow the road to its end. This is not part of the greenway, but there's a cycle path along the pavement beside the road, and an ice-cream shop at the beach.

The official route continues straight ahead at Clonea Road, and soon crosses a 600m-long **causeway** over the Glendine estuary. This brings you into rather more urban surrounds on the outskirts of Dungarvan. Follow the path all the way to a crossroads beside the bridge in the town centre. The official greenway car park is located straight ahead on the opposite side of this junction, while some of the main bike hire shops lie along Sexton Street to the right. Also nearby you can find a range of cafés to celebrate the end of your journey.

OTHER ACTIVITIES

COASTEERING

The instinctive children's seaside adventure of scrambling over rocks and jumping from tidal ledges has become formalised in recent decades into the sport of coasteering. It draws from other sports such as wild swimming and deep-water soloing (a form of unroped rock climbing), and is now an established favourite of coastal activity providers around the world.

Ireland is blessed with an abundance of rugged coastline, and though some places are too dangerous or too flat for coasteering, there are plenty of Goldilocks sections, with small, well-defined cliffs, rocky inlets and hidden caves. Among the most popular locations are the Sloc on Antrim's Causeway Coast (see page 136), Old Head in County Mayo, Doolin in Clare and Menogahane in Kerry.

Coasteering at a Glance

At its most basic, coasteering involves swimming in calm waters, easy rock scrambling near the waterline, and low-level jumps. At the upper end it may involve swimming in rough water and breaking surf, tricky climbing at some height above the water, and intimidating jumps from 10m high.

Coasteering requires very little specialist equipment and no previous experience, and it's easy to adapt the degree of adventure and risk undertaken. Although it is naturally suited to the warmer temperatures of the Irish summer, you can head out throughout the year so long as the sea conditions are favourable and you are equipped with a warm enough wetsuit.

Getting Going – The Essentials

If you're trying coasteering with a commercial activity provider, you can expect to be given a wetsuit, buoyancy aid and helmet. You will probably need to provide your own footwear – old running shoes or wetsuit booties are ideal.

It is also easy to head out independently, though you will need to be properly equipped and familiar with the tidal and sea conditions of your chosen area. Professional group leaders often use ropes as a safeguard, but these can be dangerous in untrained hands; make sure you know how to use them properly before bringing them on your own trips.

The most basic safety rule is always to check for adequate water depth and hidden dangers before making a jump. If in doubt about an obstacle or the sea conditions, always err on the side of caution. Be careful in early summer not to disturb breeding seabirds, and never go coasteering alone.

Below: Confidence in open water swimming is a prerequisite. (Lukasz Warzecha)
Opposite: Cliff jumps are the most exhilarating part of coasteering. Start low and increase the height as you gain confidence. (Lukasz Warzecha)

HORSE RIDING

There's nothing quite like the exhilaration of cantering along a wild beach, the wind in your face and your horse's hooves pounding the sand below. Ireland's long, firm strands and extensive dune systems provide the perfect setting for coastal outings, yet there are horse riding opportunities all around the country too. From short hacks through rural countryside to longer treks across mountain and moorland, there's a huge variety of options to suit experts and novices alike.

Irish Horse Riding at a Glance

Irish riding generally follows the English style, with flat saddles and both hands holding the reins. There's a vast range of equestrian centres all around the country: the Republic has almost 170 stables approved by the Association of Irish Riding Establishments (AIRE), while Northern Ireland has another 20 affiliated to the British Horse Society. Make sure you ride at an approved establishment to ensure qualified instructors and high standards of safety and horse care.

Getting Going – The Essentials

No previous experience is necessary to go horse riding or pony trekking. When you're booking your ride, you'll be asked about your level of expertise. Be honest: you don't want to be allocated to a flighty horse you don't know how to handle. Most stables welcome beginners, with children as young as four able to sit on a quiet pony while they are led on a short hack. For novices, the experience of sitting so high on such a powerful beast is usually impressionable in itself.

Horses are easily spooked, so behave calmly and confidently around them, and wait for cues from your instructor before taking any action. Most stables provide helmets and boots, and you should wear close-fitting clothes that allow flexibility of movement in both arms and legs. If you haven't ridden for a while, build it up slowly. Nothing exercises your inner thighs quite like horse riding, and you'll soon discover the joys of throbbing 'cowboy legs' if you overdo it.

Finding Out More

Online: gohorseridinginireland.ie is the official website of AIRE. It includes a location map showing all approved riding stables in the Republic of Ireland. The horse riding section of www.outdoorni.com is the best place to find details of equestrian centres in Northern Ireland.

Experienced and novice riders alike can enjoy Ireland's fabulous horse riding opportunities. (Gardiner Mitchell)

KITESURFING

The joy of kite flying, harnessing the elemental energy of the wind, is a simple and ancient pleasure. Kitesurfing takes this concept and cranks up the power, employing massive, specialist kites capable of lifting an adult many metres into the air. Experienced kitesurfers maximise this force to achieve enormous hang time, staying airborne for several seconds while performing acrobatic manoeuvres.

The focus isn't solely on jumps; kitesurfers also ride ocean waves like traditional surfers, and make long-distance, open-water crossings. Although it takes years of practice to reach these skill levels, even relative novices can experience the thrill of skimming across the surface of the sea or a lake at substantial speeds.

Irish Kitesurfing at a Glance

Ireland has one of the finest wind resources of any country in the world, and with such a fractured and intricate coastline, there's always somewhere the wind is blowing cross-shore in the optimum manner.

In contrast to traditional wave surfing, the eastern seaboard has some excellent kitesurfing spots, with several operators offering lessons in the Dublin area. Yet the west is still best, with more options in different wind directions, waves if you want them and, of course, the incredible scenery of the Atlantic coast. Achill Island in Mayo and Castlegregory in Kerry are standout locations, but you will find great kitesurf schools spanning the west coast all the way from north Donegal to Wexford.

Getting Going – The Essentials

Kitesurfing has the potential to be extremely dangerous, not just for the riders, but also for those around them. It's imperative to get good-quality, professional instruction if you're just starting out. Most kitesurfing schools provide everything you need for a day of lessons, though it will probably take several sessions before you can progress to doing it independently.

Once you're ready to commit, buying your own equipment is likely to cost at least €1,000, though there is a good second-hand market. As with most sports, avoid kitesurfing alone, and always have someone providing safety backup on the shore.

Finding Out More

Online: iksa.ie is the official website of the Irish Kitesurfing Association. It includes a map showing the locations of all approved kitesurfing schools in Ireland, and offers valuable tips and safety guidance for beginners.

Top: Kitesurfers ride ocean waves and make open-water crossings, all powered by the wind.
Bottom: Aerial hang time – experienced kitesurfers can stay airborne for several seconds.

SAILING

The quintessential picture of Irish sailing has a backdrop of cliffs, mountains and headlands. Dolphins surf the bow wave and seabirds provide the only company as you anchor in the shelter of offshore islands. But whether you're launching a multi-day adventure along the south coast, furthering the revival of traditional Galway Hookers or entering a competitive event, you'll experience the same addictive thrill as the breeze fills the sail and your boat accelerates forward beneath you.

Irish Sailing at a Glance

Ireland has a wide variety of sailing venues, ranging from relatively sheltered lakes and harbours to open coastlines exposed to strong winds and big swells. Inland, sailing is particularly popular on Lough Derg, at the southern end of the Shannon, and on Lough Ree, Lough Corrib, Lough Erne and Lough Neagh. All these water bodies are home to sailing clubs, which organise instruction courses and offer boats for hire. There's also a string of sailing clubs that stretches right around the coastline.

Even sheltered locations are potentially dangerous environments, however, so it is important to get professional guidance from the outset.

Getting Going – The Essentials

If you're trying the sport through a club or sailing centre, all the equipment you need will be provided. Beginners normally learn on a small boat with a single sail and a minimum of lines. These manoeuvrable craft are perfect for sheltered waters and can be righted easily if they capsize.

Most sailing centres offer instruction ranging from 'taster' sessions just a couple of hours long up to week-long residential courses that teach you all the skills you need to sail on your own. If you join a club you're likely to have access to club boats, and there will probably be opportunities to help crew larger yachts under the instruction of experienced sailors. Crewing is an excellent way to learn while also enjoying a memorable sailing adventure.

Top: Feel the excitement as the breeze fills the sail and your boat accelerates through the water. (Neil Houghton)
Bottom: Learning to sail in Dún Laoghaire Harbour, Dublin. (Jason Baxter)

Finding Out More

Online: The Irish Sailing Association is the governing body for the sport in Ireland. Its website, **trysailing. ie**, gives the locations of sailing centres and clubs around the country. The Royal Yachting Association Northern Ireland governs the sport in the north, though you'll find most information in the sailing section of **outdoorni.com**. There's also a huge amount of news and information on the website **afloat.ie**.

235

SCUBA DIVING

If you've tried snorkelling and enjoyed the experience, scuba or sub-aqua diving could be something you'll love. The extra breathing apparatus means you can descend deeper and stay submerged much longer than snorkellers, and enjoy more intimate contact with sealife as a result. You'll be able to explore more of Ireland's submerged coastline, with modern drysuits meaning the cold water is no longer the deterrent it once was.

Irish Scuba Diving at a Glance

There are fantastic dive sites all around Ireland, ranging from simple shore dives in sheltered harbours, to spectacular outings to remote outcrops like the Skellig Islands or Stags of Broadhaven. There can be abundant fish life, octopus are not unusual, and you're almost bound to encounter inquisitive seals.

Local sub-aqua clubs form the backbone of Irish diving, with most clubs being active, well-equipped and welcoming to new members. You'll probably have access to club boats, and most clubs organise regular weekend trips, which are great social experiences too.

Getting Going – The Essentials

Of all the sports and activities featured in this book, scuba diving is probably the most technical. It certainly isn't a sport you can try alone. You'll need qualified instruction in a carefully supervised environment, and the country's diving clubs are the place to learn. Most clubs are affiliated to the Irish Underwater Council (CFT) while others – mainly in Northern Ireland – are affiliated to the British Sub-Aqua Club (BSAC). Clubs generally offer try-out sessions a couple of times a year in a local swimming pool, where you can sample the sport. You must then complete a beginners' course before being allowed to dive outside.

There are also commercial dive operators around the country, who run courses and programmes based around PADI qualifications. These companies offer discovery sessions for novices, which take you outside immediately and teach you the basics in shallow coves. Expect to pay around €140 for a whole-day experience, which should include two instructor-led dives. Any

Top: Diving has to be done with a support crew, which is usually provided by your local club. (Fennell Photography)
Bottom: Scuba divers can stay submerged for a long time, enjoying intimate contact with a wide diversity of aquatic life. (Fáilte Ireland)

experience gained through the PADI programme can then be transferred to the relevant CFT or BSAC level if you decide to join a club.

Finding Out More

Online: See **diving.ie** for information on clubs, qualifications and dive sites in the Republic of Ireland. **bsac.com** lists affiliated clubs in Northern Ireland.

SURFING

Ireland offers some of the best surfing in Europe. The north, west and south coasts boast scores of high-quality breaks, ranging from beginner-friendly beaches to world-class reefs. With a modern wetsuit, boots, gloves and hood, you can remain comfortable in the water for hours, even in the depths of winter. The majority of surf spots are in wild, remote locations, and there are many places where your group will be alone in the water, an increasing rarity in the world of surfing.

Irish Surfing at a Glance

The four dominant surf towns around Ireland are Portrush in County Antrim, Bundoran in Donegal, Lahinch in Clare and Tramore in Waterford. All have good surf schools and ideal beaches for learning, as well as a range of more challenging breaks nearby. These are not the only options – you will find a wide range of other breaks and schools all along the western seaboard.

Surfing is a physically demanding sport. Being a strong swimmer is a prerequisite, along with confidence in open water. As well as developing the strength and skills to paddle, duck-dive and pop-up, you'll have to become familiar with the workings of the sea. Set waves and rip currents are global phenomena, but each location reacts differently to swells of different sizes and directions. No wonder it can take many years before you're confidently riding the larger waves for which Ireland is famous.

Getting Going – The Essentials

Most people find their way into the sport through a surf school. These generally operate between Easter and early autumn, and provide all the necessary equipment, including a long, stable board designed to catch waves easily.

Having understood the basics, it's a question of getting out as often as possible to practise. Some people buy a body board and fins as an interim stage; these allow you to enjoy the same rush of speed as you hurtle down the face of the wave without having to worry about standing up. Other people join a local club to learn organically from other members.

Finding Out More

Online: irishsurfing.ie is the official website of the Irish Surfing Association. It includes a list of Irish surf clubs, and a map showing all approved surf schools around the country. **magicseaweed.com** is one of the best resources for finding out about popular breaks, and also provides surf forecasts.

Left: It takes years to get this good: tucking in for the barrel at a world-class break near Bundoran, Donegal.
Right: Start small and build bigger. First wave, age seven.

WHITEWATER KAYAKING

Whitewater kayaking shares many of the characteristics of inland canoeing, but ramps up the adrenaline by a factor of ten. Instead of being wary of rapids and waterfalls, these paddlers purposely seek them out. The challenge is to navigate stretches of wild, fast-flowing river, relying on solid skills to emerge safely from the bottom. Anticipation, exhilaration and euphoria are regular emotions, and there are few feelings as intense in adventure sport.

Irish Whitewater Kayaking at a Glance

About 150 stretches of whitewater are kayaked regularly around Ireland, ranging from largely placid rivers with occasional weirs to fast-flowing torrents offering several kilometres of non-stop rollercoaster ride. The standard river-grading system applies, with sections ranging from Grade 1 (flat water) to Grade 5 (extreme and continuous technical difficulties).

Contrary to expectations, waiting for rain is a big part of Irish kayaking. There are few dams here to regulate the flow of water, and most small rivers run off quickly. Watch out for high water and flood conditions, when difficulty levels increase dramatically. Natural hazards like fallen trees also increase at this time.

Getting Going – The Essentials

River kayaks are small boats, which can manoeuvre easily around obstacles and catch tight eddies mid-flow. You'll need to use a spray deck and know how to Eskimo roll – turn yourself upright again – in the event of a capsize.

As well as developing your strokes to the required level, there is a lot to learn about staying safe in a whitewater environment. The use of throw-bags and other rescue techniques should be thoroughly practised before hitting the big stuff, and it can take several years to become a reliable member of a whitewater crew. Most people join the sport through a local club, and complete formal training courses with qualified instructors to gain different levels of proficiency. From a whitewater perspective, Canoeing Ireland's Level 3 and Level 4 River Skills are the ones to aim for.

Finding Out More

Online: www.iww.ie is the home of Irish White Water, and has comprehensive descriptions of every whitewater river in Ireland.

The Canoeing Ireland website, **canoe.ie**, provides information on kayak clubs and whitewater races. **waterlevel.ie** provides real-time readings from hundreds of river gauges around the country.

Top: Boofing the Duff Falls in County Leitrim, one of 150 stretches of whitewater around Ireland. (Chris Roberts)
Bottom: Instead of being wary of rapids and waterfalls, whitewater kayakers purposely seek them out. (Chris Roberts)

WILD CAMPING

There's a sense of zen-like peace in whiling away a summer's evening in a beautiful wild-camping spot. The shadows lengthen, the sunset colours creep across the sky, then slowly fade to reveal the Milky Way beyond. The following morning you wake up, unzip the tent door and reveal a spectacular landscape that seems entirely your own. Add a bit of foraging, some outdoor cooking and exploring your surrounds, and you have a really relaxing experience that encapsulates the very essence of outdoor living.

Irish Wild Camping at a Glance

Ireland's best locations for wild camping tend to be on commonage, where property rights are shared amongst several landowners. Although you don't have a legal right to camp here, discreet and responsible camping is generally tolerated. In the west of Ireland, you'll find dozens of excellent coastal locations with spectacular sea views. Many islands offer similar opportunities, as do the hills and mountains, if you don't mind hiking in with your gear.

Inland, many of the country's wild areas are owned by state and semi-state bodies. Camping is permitted in most national parks. Permits are officially required for Coillte forestry. Private property and farmland are a different story. It's essential to obtain permission from landowners here, but in reality these are the least desirable places to pitch a tent anyway.

Getting Going – The Essentials

Quality equipment is vital to an enjoyable camping experience. Generations of Irish people have neglected this fact, spending one damp and miserable night in a cheap tent before vowing never to do it again. Don't scrimp on the quality of your gear, with smaller, lightweight products most suitable for wild camping. Waking up on a mountain summit is a unique experience, but you'll appreciate the weight savings of a bivvy bag over a large tent as you haul yourself up the slopes.

Wherever you decide to camp, please follow the principles of Leave no Trace (see www.leavenotraceireland.org/seven-principles). Pack out all your waste and leave the site as you found it. In some locations it may be appropriate to light a campfire, but use your discretion; be aware of fire-risk, use a pre-existing fire ring, and bring your own fuel with you.

Below: Campfires are great fun so long as the location is suitable.
Next page: Room with a view: many wild camping spots offer better views than five-star hotels.